THE CONDITION OF
THE CHRISTIAN PHILOSOPHER

THE CONDITION OF THE CHRISTIAN PHILOSOPHER

by
ROGER MEHL

Agrégé de philosophie,
Docteur en théologie,
Professor at the University of Strasbourg

Translated by
EVA KUSHNER, Ph.D.

JAMES CLARKE & CO. LIMITED
33 STORE STREET
LONDON, W.C.1

This translation first published 1963

© *James Clarke & Co., Ltd.*

1) Christianity - Philosophy

Printed in Great Britain by
The Camelot Press Ltd., London and Southampton

To the memory of my father

Adolphe Mehl

1879-1945

CONTENTS

Chapter I

THE PROBLEM

CO-OPERATION and *conflict* between Christianity and philosophy are both indisputable facts and ever contemporary events. While apparently Christian theology has never been able to dispense with the support of philosophical thought, analysis and expression, it has always harboured towards its strange ally a probably justifiable distrust. Not only the history of dogmatics, but also the history of the whole Christian Church and even the history of devotion bear at every page signs reminiscent of the succession of the philosophical systems; and, at every period where theology has endeavoured to achieve self-consciousness and become systematic, it has opened up the way for philosophical reflection. But, parallel to this, throughout the whole history of the Church a protest can be heard against any intrusion by philosophy which would indicate the existence of a confusion between the wisdom of God and the wisdom of man. The most systematized theological doctrines, those most pervaded by a philosophical attitude, have by no means been the least conscious of the necessity of such a protest. "Lest we lose ourselves in history, let us recall simply that the twelfth century, which witnessed the rise of logical studies, rang with the protests of many theologians against the use of the profane sciences," writes the thinker most familiar with the eventful history of this sometimes fruitful, sometimes unfortunate union.[1]

Actually, this collaboration as well as this conflict are inherent in the temporal conditions of the expansion of Christianity. Christianity could not have spread without encountering the wisdom of Greece, which, though it certainly does not represent the whole of philosophy nor all the possible forms of philosophical thought, nevertheless contains a demand for rational certainty immanent to any philosophical inquiry. When their encounter actually occurred, when the scholars adopted the new faith, the best minds in the Church appeared

[1] E. Gilson, *Christianity and Philosophy*, translated by Ralph MacDonald, C.S.B., Sheed and Ward, London, 1939, p. 3.

concerned. The early Church knew, as we do, that the new man, whose existence is consecrated by baptism, has not broken all links with his former self. Concealed in the new creature, this former self surreptitiously enters the Church. The anxiety, therefore, was legitimate, and it is found expressed with varying degrees of clarity in the writings of Clement of Alexandria, Origen, Lactantius, St. Jerome, St. Gregory of Nazianzus, Tertullian, Basil, St. Ambrose, and St. Augustine: how is it possible to accept ancient philosophy, or even the form of it, into the new faith? P. de Labriolle has shown[1] with great precision the resistance the scholars encountered in the Church which they were entering with all their pagan wisdom. In the caution with which the Church received these wise men, whom in other ways it felt honoured to count among its members, P. de Labriolle sees the proof that the Christian people would have been offended by philosophy under any form. Only a compromise could arise from this initial situation, and at the end of the fourth century a moderate doctrine was finally settled upon which left classical culture, and particularly philosophy, only as a preliminary method for the study of Christianity. Since then, Christian thought of all confessions has existed in this atmosphere of compromise. In heroic times, doubtless, it has tried to suppress this compromise, and the Reformation was marked, on the whole, by a rejection and a refusal of philosophy. But we know that after the Reformation, just as after the Pauline period, Christian theology again found itself face to face with an ever-demanding and ever-alluring philosophy and entered with it the path of compromise. Leaving aside the forms of the compromise in which the Christian faith was clearly misrepresented, let us consider only those in which at least it saved face. Then we shall be able to characterize the situation arising from the compromise in the penetrating terms used by Léon Brunschvicg: "The material of faith, defined by the authority of the Church, must fit into the moulds prepared for it by reason: hence a process of mutual adjustment between theology, which is *given* by revelation, and philosophy, also *given*, if not by Aristotle and Plotinus, at least since Aristotle and Plotinus."[2]

[1] P. de Labriolle, "Culture classique et christianisme", in *Revue de théologie et de philosophie*, Lausanne, 1917, No. 23, pp. 89-114.

[2] L. Brunschvicg, "L'expérience religieuse de Pascal", in *Revue de théologie et de philosophie*, Lausanne, 1924, p. 83.

Granted the method of compromise, numerous solutions are possible, and the conditions of the compromises can be improved upon by defining with more precision the respective spheres of Christianity and philosophy. The history of such compromises would assuredly prove interesting. Is it our purpose to write such a history?

Let us try to determine the ultimate outcome of this way of compromise. Why does one set out upon it, if it is not because one postulates that theology and the knowledge by faith which constitutes its basis lack something fundamental to become complete or reach man in his concrete reality; because one postulates some poverty in faith. In fact, when the philosophers entered the early Church, they did not wish to be identified with the mass of believers, whom they hastily qualified as "psychic". If E. de Faye's analyses of Clement of Alexandria are correct, the origin and the constant basis of every gnosticism is the presumption to carry the knowledge of God towards a certainty and a degree of intuition more perfect than those of faith, and to rediscover the direct and contemplative knowledge of Hellenic philosophy. It will, of course, be pointed out that the Middle Ages had a very different conception of the compromise, and that they only required philosophy to expose the tenets of the faith in rational terms, or else to justify them after they had been set down. Is it not clear, however, that this extreme reduction of the part played by philosophy is in itself a confession that the Word of God, which it is theology's mission to expound, is by itself incapable of forcing belief; that the Word of God is only believable under a philosophical cloak? As soon as one enters the way of compromise, one recognizes the right to existence of an autonomous philosophy. One recognizes that there exist in the scheme of salvation at least two possibilities: that represented by Christianity and that represented by the practice of philosophy. "One thinks and discourses in perfectly good faith but with a starting-point quite distinct from that of the Reformation; one no longer builds with the latter upon a supreme and irrevocable decision, but upon the sand of analysis, of comparison, and of the superior synthesis of *two* possibilities, of which the Christian faith represents only one—perhaps the one emphasized with more force and integrity, but still only one of two possibilities."[1] It is precisely

[1] K. Barth, "La Réforme: une suprême décision", in *Foi et Vie*, 1933, p. 812.

this idea of a partitioning of the spiritual life into autonomous spheres that most clearly clashes with the Evangelical faith. Possibly, at the moment when Christianity found itself in the presence of the philosophies (or, more accurately, the Church in the presence of the philosophers), a delimitation of the respective spheres was conceived. This would remain true even if it were shown (a demonstration which was made for many of the theological systems of the Middle Ages) that this partitioning was done, not empirically or at times politically, but with the desire to preserve a hierarchy. For we believe the very notion of hierarchy to be ambiguous, and that is why we cannot be satisfied without further examination with the formula, in other respects so attractive to a Christian consciousness, *"Philosophia ancilla theologiae"*. It is not enough, in our view, that philosophy be subordinated, or, as Gilson phrases it, "subalternated" to theology. For such "subalternation" can easily respect and leave intact the autonomous foundation of the subordinate discipline; it merely aims at determining the conditions under which philosophy is to be practised; it defines within what limits philosophical reflection can legitimately be exerted, what problems it has the right to approach; but it recognizes that philosophy has itself the power to examine and motivate the nature and meaning of its own basis. The philosophy of Descartes affords a fine example of such an ambiguous subalternation. His metaphysics does not presume to take the place of theology; it only claims to corroborate the truths of faith by way of a rational demonstration—*more geometrico*. It refuses to contradict theology and places certain essential truths of the faith beyond its own jurisdiction. With the uttermost sincerity, it is able to give theologians the assurance that they have nothing to fear from it because it submits to them. Descartes goes a step further when he ventures to show, by statements drawn from Holy Scripture, that his metaphysical enterprise is authorized by the Christian faith,[1] that God Himself wants man to know and glorify Him by making use of his reason. The hierarchy, therefore, is maintained, but the autonomy is none the less preserved. By separating radically that which stems from the natural light and that which comes from the supernatural light, and by postulating, furthermore, that it is possible to engage in metaphysical investigation

[1] Letter of Dedication and Preface to the *Meditations*.

without any reference to the data of revelation, Descartes proclaims the radical and inexpugnable autonomy of philosophy and of reason; and in the occurrence of any conflict between theology and philosophy, it is hard to see how this hierarchy could be maintained. Descartes postulates, with respect to the problems of the existence of God and of the immortality of the soul, a fundamental agreement between reason and revelation. But it is merely a postulate. What will happen when theology ventures to pass judgements upon the philosophical proofs of the existence of God? Has not Descartes asserted that they are more certain even than the demonstrations of mathematics?[1] What will happen on the day when faith claims to possess a greater certainty and theology declares (as it did with Pascal) these proofs powerless to encompass and mediate the living God, the God of Jesus Christ? There exists, then, a hierarchy which, while it respects the autonomy of the disciplines under its command, is yet incapable of ensuring the oneness of our certainty, and cannot avert conflicts within the spiritual life.

Without prejudging the possibility of subordinating philosophy to theology, we consider in principle that there cannot be a hierarchy between these two disciplines as long as the demand of the Christian faith is not recognized in its full seriousness. The Christian in his thinking must not allow, alongside the faith of the new man, and in varied degrees of harmony with his faith, the survival of beliefs, doctrines, and especially attitudes of thought which have a merely accidental and historical relationship to his faith. Faith lives in and on the promise of a total renewal of one's being. It is faith in a God who makes all things new and raises man from the dead. The spiritual attitude which is meant by philosophy will, therefore, be able to subsist in the believer only to the extent that the basis of this attitude and the foremost implications thereof will not be alien to the very essence of the Christian faith.

No philosophical attitude will be acceptable unless we are able to discover its Christian motivation. This means, in fact, that, confronted with any kind of philosophy or philosophical attitude, the Christian will have to ask himself what is the basis of such an attitude or such a philosophy; and in no case ought he to postulate as a self-sufficient fact the autonomous existence

[1] *Discourse on Method* (Part 4).

of philosophy. The theologian's very special function in this respect is to transform into problematics the certainty of philosophy; he will not admit *a priori* the existence of a philosophical truth, or a valid philosophical attitude, capable in an incidental manner of a more or less harmonious co-existence with the Christian doctrine. It is necessary first of all, according to Heinrich Barth's expression, that the foundation of philosophy should become "*fragewürdig*".[1]

In effect, it is not possible to claim Christian freedom as a basis for the autonomy of philosophy. The Christian freedom is a fact. But it only exists from the moment we accept the foundation upon which it and all other things rest. For no one could lay another foundation than that which has already been laid —namely, Jesus Christ—and no one could presume to build anything—not even a philosophy—upon any other foundation. Indeed, it should be clearly understood that philosophy's problem is not merely to maintain certain relationships with the Christian doctrine; otherwise, any philosophy which arose in the midst of a Christian civilization should be thought acceptable, as it would be most unlikely that such a philosophy should not bear the marks of Christianity. The ascertaining of Christian contributions to various philosophies is a secondary historical problem. No dogmatic or normative truth emerges from such a study. The real issue is that the basis of the philosophical attitude should not be foreign to the essence of the Christian faith. Now, "the Christian faith", as Cullmann[2] has shown recently, entails a very precise meaning. Let us simply recall that it is a faith centred upon Jesus Christ, who came in the flesh, who died and rose again for our salvation, whom God exalted in sovereignty by making Him Lord of all, till the coming of the Kingdom which it was His earthly mission to announce. The Christian faith considers that all other things are relative to this foundation and that nothing either in nature or in history is independent of Christ the Lord and Saviour. We must therefore resolve, strange as this assertion may appear at first, to accept only a philosophy related to this one foundation. It is not indispensable that this philosophy speak of Jesus Christ, nor that it insert His message in its content, nor even

[1] Heinrich Barth, "Der Christ in der Philosophischen Fakultät", *In Extremis*, 1935, No. 7/8, p. 188.

[2] O. Cullmann, "Les premières confessions de foi chrétienne", *Cahiers de la R.H.Ph.R.*, 1944.

that it culminate in Jesus Christ. The whole of nature was
created for Jesus Christ alone and in Him; nature's longing and
expectation are but for the salvation brought by Jesus Christ.
And yet nothing in nature speaks directly of Jesus Christ or
announces Him; nor does anything natural lead us towards
Him. Likewise, it will be admitted that art, and even more so
ethics, can have neither meaning nor basis but in Jesus Christ,
and yet never treat of Him directly or contain Him as the
subject-matter of their discipline. Honest action, resistance to
temptation, have no formal connection with Jesus Christ, since
it is possible for the unbeliever to act ethically; but the basis of
such action may be found in the Resurrection of Christ. To
renounce the autonomy of philosophy is, therefore, to search
for the fundamental relationship between philosophical meditation and the coming of Jesus Christ, His death, His resurrection, His ascension, and the Kingdom which, because of Him,
is at hand.

Such will be the spirit of our inquiry.

Should the reader find this attempt strange, let him reflect
upon the consequences which any other position would imply.
To maintain—for whatever reason—the autonomy of the
philosophical domain is to commit oneself to the theory that
there exist two distinct modes of knowledge, foreign and
irreducible to each other: faith and reason. Indeed, it is in
terms of this opposition that the opposition between philosophy
and theology has generally been defined. True enough, such
attempts have also been directed towards decreasing the distance which separates reason from faith; for faith can become
faith in what is reasonable, since it is understood that what is
reasonable can shock ordinary common sense; and reason is
not wholly unrelated to faith, since it implies in its roots, in the
very process by which it is constituted, an act of faith, either
towards itself or towards the rationality of the real. Here we
recognize one of the most hackneyed ideas in modern apologetics. It matters little that the two modes of knowledge should
thus be brought more or less close together; one fact remains:
the prior opposition of faith and reason implies that these two
realities have already been successfully subsumed under one
concept, integrated in the same category, or at least inscribed
in the same table of the general modes of cognition. This, we
feel, is precisely where the fundamental error which vitiates

the theory of knowledge, and more especially, the theory of religious knowledge, resides. It is necessary to renounce bringing together in one dichotomy these two realities: faith and reason.

For in effect, Christian dogmatics forbids us to regard faith as a *reality of a psychological order*. Faith does not simply come in to complete the natural man by conferring upon him a new meaning, by placing within his reach a novel instrument for acquiring knowledge. Grace adds nothing to nature; it is not a supplementary ornament of nature; grace restores and transforms nature. This assertion proves true at the psychological level; insufficient analysis and interpretation of religious experience tend to make us believe that divine grace endows us with a new mode of sensibility and that it is this novel way of feeling and vibrating which constitutes faith. And, indeed, the renewal of one's being does manifest itself psychologically. Yet these are only manifestations, sporadic or lasting, real or apparent, essential or accessory, of a decision which is not psychological, since it is not concerned with that diffusion of the subject in time which is our consciousness, but, on the contrary, with the insertion of the subject into being; since it is a metaphysical position, the very mode of being of man restored. Faith always lies beyond its psychological manifestations. Jesus can discern faith in attitudes and gestures which, from the psychological standpoint, are but superstitions. Let a woman approach Him in order to touch His cloak, and behold, Jesus declares: this woman has faith. It is obvious that no psychological analysis of her gesture can lead to such a conclusion. The existence of faith presupposes precisely that the reality of the subject, or better, of the creature, is not exhausted either in the psychological self which, according to the psychologists, is a fluid synthesis of states of consciousness, or in the "I" whose function is limited to being conscious of that self and will only turn to this psychological self. It is doubtless quite difficult to characterize in adequate philosophical language that subject which is really the bearer of faith; fatally, it will always be apprehended by means of psychological categories, or through some psychological experience, through some kind of *Cogito*. For this subject belongs neither to the order of substance nor to the order of accident. It is of the order of existence; by this, we mean that it is that subject whom God as Creator has called to existence; that it exists, therefore, as creature *before God*, having no existence apart from the fact that God creates and thinks him as creature, or apart from the fact that God, by His grace, restores him anew before Himself as creature, as *Imago Dei*. That is a subject no *Cogito* can apprehend, since any *Cogito*, whatever its nature, will always refer us to a *thinking* existent and not to an existent that is *thought of*, to the *act* of a subject and not to the *situation* of a subject that is conceived, created, restored, redeemed. Faith expresses the mode of being of that latter subject. It does so by means of quite varied symbols. That is why the analysis of neither the doctrines professed by a person nor that of his religious attitudes, nor of his effective feelings and experiences allows us to judge him in the matter of faith. All these factors constitute only more or less probable indices. Faith is a determination of the subject by God, a fact that Scripture endeavours to convey by presenting it as obedience: Matt. 28.19; John 13.34; Phil. 2.8; Rom. 1.5; Heb. 11.8. Far from being the exalting of some feeling or the defence of some idea, all our worship (provided it is worship grounded in faith) is primarily an act of obedience to God. Faith is adequately expressed in a confession, which is exactly contrary to a psychic act of self-determination. For confession really occurs only when the soul sees itself compelled to answer "Yes" to God's initiative.[1] If faith were merely one of the modes of our consciousness, it could not concern the whole of our life; at best it could, like any other psychic state, irradiate to a certain extent contiguous mental states. In such a case, however, the very notion of confession would lose its meaning; it would become a mere figure of speech, a hyperbolic expression. The peculiar nature of conversion is that in it the subject suddenly pervades being and faith substitutes itself for the autonomy of pride; the self-sufficient being has become a dependent one. This conversion, affecting as it does the subject's ontological situation, will doubtless be, in more or less adequate ways, translated into the diversity of psychic functions. Indeed, faith affects, penetrates, and transforms reason itself. It is in this sense that Scripture constantly refers to the "renewing of the mind" and of the knowledge faith imparts. Here is a decisive reason for not opposing reason to faith, as though they were two homogeneous entities of opposite sign. Moreover,

---

[1] Cf. H. Leenhardt, *La connaissance religieuse et la foi*.

B

opposing faith to reason amounts to an utterly false interpretation of faith, since reason is a psychological function; for opposition can only exist within the homogeneous. Merely to subordinate one discipline to another, one mode of knowledge to another, is to remain within the homogeneous. The hierarchy which subordinates reason to faith can still be equivocal because it locates both faith and reason in the field of psychological consciousness; and experience proves that reason thus subordinated can only consider faith as an incomprehensible and scandalous rival: reason cannot honestly understand why it should thus let itself be subjected. Fully conscious of its processes, proud of its authentic achievements, it can only rebel against the yoke and manifest its distrust against faith, which appears in no way to concern it. Pious thinking, often naïvely zealous, with its invectives against the rebellion of reason, has corroborated the current notion that between faith and reason there can be nothing but strife. The unfortunate thing is that philosophy has taken devout thinking at its word, and has thought it fitting to define its own final position in the following terms: "To believe or to verify, the alternative is inevitable. To portray unbelief as a negative state of mind is to play on the superficial meaning of words. In the philosopher's case, unbelief is as positive a virtue as bravery in the soldier's."[1] Thus, whether we presume to oppose faith and reason, and subordinate reason to faith on the strength of this opposition; or whether we refuse to do so, the result is the same: faith is misconstrued, and especially travestied in the eyes of the philosopher.

The consequence readily follows. "Man's reason receives, under the counter, so to speak, the right of standing face to face with Revelation, as a distinct entity, independent from Revelation."[2] The problem of philosophy and Christianity, faith and reason, has been totally falsified because theologians and non-theologians alike have agreed upon an erroneous definition of faith: a definition which, while it favours one of the psychological aspects through which faith is manifested, leaves out the non-psychological character of true faith. Henceforth, whether faith and reason are made to stand in opposition, or

---

[1] Léon Brunschvicg, *Le progrès de la conscience dans la philosophie occidentale*, L. II, p. 785.
[2] Heinrich Barth, *op. cit.*, p. 189.

whether an attempt is made to establish a hierarchy between them, they find themselves upon the same plane: both are means of cognition about whose respective advantages a discussion may be initiated. A landslide has thus taken place, which will reduce faith to being a mode of intuition. It is in this way that the problem has presented itself in the philosophies akin to Kant's, with perhaps a different terminology. It is no wonder, then, that the method of faith and the method of reason each found proponents. Man chooses between faith and reason as he would choose among the sharpest instruments or weapons.

This spiritual aberration reveals not only a profound error concerning the nature of faith, but yet another about the nature of reason. For in a Christian frame of reference it is possible and even necessary to speak of faith; it is understood that there is only one faith, that which looks to the God of Jesus Christ and which arises under the impulse of the Holy Spirit, as every confession of faith has emphasized: the Christian faith is faith in the triune God. It is the characteristic of man regenerated; and, though it undoubtedly may grow or decrease in intensity and vigour, it nevertheless remains identical in nature. Faith is by nature (or, more accurately speaking, by virtue of the object by which it is aroused and given life) foreign to becoming, lifted above the becoming of history. True, it has been possible to speak of the stages of faith; but this expression merely refers to the specific character of the Christian faith, with respect to the faith of Israel. From the Resurrection and Ascension of Christ till the day of His return and the coming of the Kingdom, there is only one possible faith. The theologian, there, is qualified to speak of *the* faith in the singular, not as an abstract and mysterious entity, but as a living, perfectly well-defined reality. Can the theologian, however, authorize the philosopher, in the dialogue which develops between them, to speak of reason in the same manner? It should be admitted that reason is customarily treated as being an absolute, an entity entirely independent of the process of becoming; in fact, one of philosophy's current assertions is that of the universality and immutability of reason. Such has been the universal belief elicited by this assertion, even in the eyes of the theologians, that the Catholic Church has sometimes found it difficult to admit that sin should in any way concern reason itself. Vain are the sociologists' attempts to retrace for us the history and the aetiology of reason; as a general rule, their endeavours tend towards an empiricism which in fact misunderstands reason. Reason, it must be admitted, has in itself many resources allowing it to be free from the impact of history and of becoming. Not only does it operate according to formal principles, which, in spite of the diversity of actual situations, and regardless of the degree of mental cleverness of those who use them, remain fairly constant, but in addition it appears always to follow an identical inspiration: whatever the actual occasion, it tends to make activity prevail over passivity, and spiritual freedom over routine and passion. Nevertheless, the philosopher must admit that reason can be reduced to a purely instrumental role, without losing any of its distinctive characteristics. It is possible to dissociate the rationality of structure from the rationality of inspiration.

A demonstration can be perfectly rational in its structure, devoid of any logical errors, free from the intrusion of any affective elements; yet the intention of this demonstration may not be a rational one: that is, its author's mind does not necessarily seek to attain, by means of the demonstration, the triumph of freedom over slavery, of activity over passivity. A political or economic system may have a thoroughly rational structure, while its inspiration may be drawn from motives as irrational as ambition or greed: that is, from emotional interests. Reason, moreover, avails itself of the universality and formalism of its own principles on the one hand, and, on the other hand, of the correlated multiplicity of its own applications, in order to lay aside any finality and to renounce any notion of totality. In this way it abandons the quest for the unity of truth for the sake of a purely formal unity which it represents in its own practice and methods. Thus, being a victim of its own methods and successes, reason becomes thoroughly attuned to the abstract; for, proceeding as it does by analysis, it remains content with abstract, partial truth. The more thorough the analysis, the more it results in simple elements, perfectly intelligible to the understanding, and the more self-assurance reason will gain; thus it will tend to assert that maximum rationality and maximum truth correspond to the greatest degree of simplicity and abstraction. In this way, mathematics will be considered as the domain of truth *par excellence*; any truth striving for recognition will have to be of a mathematical type. This gives rise to the tragic ambiguity of the abstract, of which occidental philosophy from Spinoza to Léon Brunschvicg offers us the spectacle. God Himself will be recognized by reason only inasmuch as He conforms to the norm of an abstract truth, and inasmuch as He acquiesces to being essentially a mathematician. God will be allowed to be the Creator in so far as creation coincides with calculation. *Dum Deus calculat, fit mundus.* The only permissible spirituality will be that exemplified by the mathematician in the progress of analysis; spiritual life will be the ability to abstract. Brunschvicg consistently thinks that mathematical experience is the very key to authentic religious experience.

These brief indications justify, from the philosophical point of view, the theologian's reluctance to consider reason as an immutable entity divorced from all history and becoming. In point of fact, a shift can occur in the activity of reason: it is unceasingly tempted to substitute the abstract for the concrete, the simplified truth of an ideal object for the truth and the fullness of existence. Reason even appears to be denied the knowledge of the mutilations to which it subjects the real. This is why the theologian, defying the apparent denial with which the constant progress of science seems to confront him, should have no scruples about inserting reason itself into the framework of history. He will not do so because he takes a malicious delight in writing the history of the empirical variations of reason. For it is impossible to draw any conclusion from these variations; their history testifies both to the aberrations of reason and to its magnificent achievements. But the theologian situates reason in a history which, even though it is still in the process of becoming, has already been written and accomplished in its entirety in the sense that its poles are definitely given. This true history alone gives meaning to empirical history and saves it from the nothingness of absurdity. By this we mean that history which is ever-present, ever-immanent to the destiny of any man, to the destiny of any nation, as well as to the whole duration of mankind, and which is marked by the moments of Creation, of the Fall, of Redemption, and of the coming of the Kingdom.

It is that history which has been described in the Biblical Revelation on the occasion of the empirical history of the people

22 THE CONDITION OF THE CHRISTIAN PHILOSOPHER

of Israel, of Jesus and of the Church. The entire empirical history of mankind is divided, subtended, and qualified by a certain number of aeons, the limitations of which are given by the above-mentioned events.[1] Even though reason were to remain identical with itself throughout empirical history or were even, according to the doctrine of progress, in a continuous process of perfecting itself, it would still be controlled by these aeons. There is a reason created by God, a reason that was affected by the Fall, a reason awaiting the renewing of the mind, and a glorified reason which will see God face to face. When the philosopher uses the word "reason", therefore, the theologian has the right to ask what reason he is speaking about: is it that which bears the mark of sin, that which knows itself to be sinful, or that which does not; or is it the reason which is already regenerated by Grace? Indeed, philosophy quite often presents itself as a kind of *theologia gloriae*. Spontaneously, and most of the time unconsciously, but sometimes also following the bias of pride, it rises to the level of a reason restored, perfectly adequate to its object, functioning with perfect purity, tolerating no intervention on the part of the deceitful powers of imagination and sensibility; realizing thus, in its very activity, the fullness of freedom, and conferring upon the reasoning subject the dignity of spirituality.[2] It is again, then, through an effort of abstraction that reason is lifted above the real scheme of the world, which is the scheme of the Fall. Its participation in time-bound conditions is denied though these conditions define man's existential situation. Medieval Christian thought, which was both philosophical and theological, avoided this error with remarkable lucidity. Yet it is well known that the theologians' attitudes on reason and philosophy were extremely varied. But, as Gilson[3] points out, the general opinion held in the twelfth and thirteenth centuries by St. Anselm or St. Bonaventure, who claim allegiance to St. Augustine, is the following: "They would certainly regard an exercise of pure reason as a possibility—after Plato and Aristotle, who could doubt it?—but they would view the matter not so much from the standpoint of the mere definition of

---

[1] Cf. J. Héring, *Le Royaume de Dieu et sa venue*, Chap. X, especially p. 186.

[2] It is to this kind of reason—a glorified reason—that logicians like Edmond Goblot feel compelled to appeal. Cf. E. Goblot, *Traité de logique*.

[3] E. Gilson, *The Spirit of Medieval Philosophy* (Gifford Lectures, 1931-2), translated by A. H. C. Downes, New York, Charles Scribner's Sons, 1940, p. 5.

reason as from that of the actual conditions of fact under which it has to work. Now, it is a fact that between ourselves and the Greeks the Christian Revelation has intervened and has profoundly modified the conditions under which reason has to work. Once you are in possession of that Revelation how can you possibly philosophize as though you had never heard of it?" Here is a crucial point: Christianity refers us to the concrete and actual history of the human mind. It refuses to use pure concepts, abstracted from this history. Reason is not *human reason* if it is not situated between the Fall and the Redemption. To accept the fact that reason has known and still knows the event of the Fall in all its gravity, to accept that the message of the Resurrection should be as valid for reason as for man as a whole, and that reason should therefore live, as does the whole man, in this state of tension between the Fall and the Redemption, such is the first demand which the theologian presents to the philosopher. Any philosopher who submits to this demand may from then on no longer speak of reason apart from its historical qualifications.

He will thus recognize that there exists no absolute rationality; or rather, that intelligibility can be neither defined nor exhaustively represented by that state of mind which at a certain moment of our spiritual history we call "rationality."

Because reason cannot be concretely envisaged apart from the judgement which qualifies and situates it in actual history, it cannot claim to determine an autonomous mode of knowledge. Precisely because it is the domain of reason, philosophy does not possess an autonomous foundation, and its legitimacy must be forever questioned anew. Gilson, in our view, has perfectly recognized the crucial problem upon which the Christian philosopher's condition depends, when he ruled that any such discussion must take place upon a certain plane which is "that of the conditions of fact under which the reason of Christians is to be exercised. There is no such thing as a Christian reason, but there may very well be a Christian exercise of reason" (*loc. cit.*, p. 12).

Because of these variations in the régime of reason, the attempt seems vain to *confront* philosophy, conceived as the domain of reason, and Christianity, conceived as the domain of faith, either in order to oppose them, to seek for a bond of subalternation, or even to determine their mutual relationships.

Pascal's doctrine of the diversity of *orders* should be opposed to the old, sometimes purely verbal scholastic doctrine of a hierarchy. To say that reason belongs to a different order from faith is not necessarily to confine philosophy within the limits of a compulsory autonomy. Justice is of another order than charity. Similarly, reason in its philosophical practice may receive from faith, and from theology, where faith expresses itself in a normative manner, a positive teaching and a new rule; from this rule philosophy will draw for its own existence a meaning which it would probably not have discovered by itself. Surely, if faith is indeed man's total obedience, and if as such it marks the beginning of man's total regeneration, there must exist a reason which, while remaining reason, i.e. human reason, and not a glorious and beatific vision of God, can participate in the life of faith and in the renewal of the mind promised to those who live in faith. Thus, our problem is to describe the reason and the philosopher consenting to life in faith.

Even now it is obvious that we are deliberately discarding from our preoccupations the traditional problem of a *Christian philosophy*. This problem is usually understood to consist in the question: Does there *in actual fact* exist a Christian philosophy, i.e. a philosophy in which *Christian elements* predominate? It consists, therefore, in subjecting a given system of philosophy to a critical and historical analysis in order to set aside those of its elements which are related to Christian dogmatics. In this research, most historians of philosophy are known to have reached extremely severe conclusions. Their point of view was well expressed by Gilson, who, summarizing a trend of thought which he does not adopt as his own, wrote: "Shreds of Greek thought, more or less clumsily patching up theology, that, we are told, is about all the Christian thinkers have left us. Sometimes they borrow from Plato, sometimes from Aristotle, that is to say when they are not engaged on something considerably worse, an impossible synthesis of Plato and Aristotle, an effort to reconcile the dead who never ceased to differ when alive— as John of Salisbury already remarked in the twelfth century. Never do we meet with a genuine impulse of thought which at one and the same time is thoroughly Christian and really creative; and it follows that Christianity has contributed nothing to the philosophic heritage of humanity."[1] It should be pointed out

[1] E. Gilson, *loc. cit.*, pp. 2-3.

that in this statement Gilson only sums up a current doctrine
which has become so classical that Max Scheler did not
hesitate to give it the following dogmatic formula: "Es gibt in
diesem Sinne und gab nie eine christliche Philosophie, sofern
man unter diesen Worten nicht, wie üblich, eine griechische
Philosophie, mit christlichen Ornamenten, sondern eine aus
der Würzel und dem Wesen des christlichen Grunderlebnisses
durch selbstdenkerische Betrachtung und Erforschung der
Welt entsprungenes Gedankensystem versteht".[1] It is not for
us to decide upon this question of fact; in order adequately to
weigh the terms in which this problem of a Christian
philosophy is set forth, we refer the reader to the memorable
discussion devoted to it by the Société française de Philosophie.[2]
But we understand fully the reasons of Christian dogmatics
which make it possible to question the existence of a Christian
philosophy. First of all, the concept of Christian elements is a
very ambiguous one; in order to make it legitimate, Christianity
would have to be reducible to a doctrine, that is to a consistent
whole systematically built upon a certain number of principles.
Christian dogmatics would have to constitute an organic
development from a certain number of postulates: a conception
easily admitted by Catholic theology, but which Protestant
theology emphatically rejects. For dogmatics itself, be it solely
from the standpoint of its *Formgeschichte*, cannot be strictly
assimilated to a doctrine constituted on the basis of principles
and intuitions. Dogmatics is the interpretation, or rather the
understanding of a revelation totally given from the first,
in which it is impossible to discern any elements. There are
certainly no objections to the use of such a notion of Christian
elements in an analytical or exegetical study for strictly
methodological purposes. Yet this is a conception without any
dogmatic significance. Let a doctrinal assertion, formally contained in the letter of Scripture, be detached from the perspective in which it was set within the whole of the Biblical Revelation, and it immediately loses its quality of Christian truth.
On the spiritual plane, secularization is nothing else but this

[1] "In this sense there is not and there never has been a Christian philosophy,
in so far as this phrase is understood to mean, not (as usually) a Greek philosophy
with Christian ornaments, but a system of thought arising from the roots and the
very being of fundamental Christian experience, through thoughtful contemplation and investigation of the world", (quotation translated by E. K.), M.
Scheler, *Krieg und Aufbau*, Leipzig, 1916, p. 411.
[2] E. Bréhier, "Y a-t-il une philosophie chrétienne?", *R.M.M.*, April-June, 1931.

arbitrarily produced break between a current Christian assertion and the whole of Revelation, which alone can shelter this assertion from ambiguity. To take a particularly clear example: is there a more authentically Christian affirmation than that of the infinite value of the human person? And yet, who would dare maintain that this is a Christian element which preserves its Christian significance in the midst of every system in which it is contained? Undoubtedly the early Church knew this danger of mistaking for Christian doctrines those doctrines in which elements would be found which had a certain affective echo in the Christian consciousness. The gift of discerning spirits which seems to have been so generously imparted to the early Church preserved it from this danger. The Apostle John is fully conscious of the risk involved for every Christian in accepting elements of Christian appearance. Therefore he advises viewing these elements in the light of the central and unique message of the Revelation as a touchstone for their appreciation: "Hereby know ye the Spirit of God: Every spirit that confesseth that Jesus Christ is come in the flesh is of God: and every spirit that confesseth not Jesus is not of God: and this is the spirit of the anti-christ, whereof ye have heard that it cometh; and now it is in the world already" (1 John, 4.2-4).

No element can be detached from Christianity for none has any meaning apart from Jesus Christ. Although we may find elements of Christian origin in this or that philosophy, the philosophy cannot be labelled Christian without a grave ambiguity. From the dogmatic standpoint, the concept of a Christian philosophy must be viewed with as much suspicion as that of Christian civilization.

For, like the latter, it implies not only that Christian elements can be detached from the Christian source, from the indivisible Revelation, and scattered throughout the world as a sort of Christian leaven, but furthermore, that through the presence of these germs or elements the world can be christianized, that there occurs a process in virtue of which Christianity can swarm over the world in the manner of the colonists who left their ancient cities, taking with them fragments of their native soil, in order to found new cities, replicas of the mother cities. Philosophy belongs to the form of the world, and doubtless expresses its most significant aspects; could not one, therefore, take a foothold in philosophy, christianize it, and thus have a grip upon all the forms of the world which yield to the prestige of philosophy? It must be recognized that Christians have very often given in to this seduction, which may be described as a political one. They forgot that the world cannot receive in its form foreign elements which make it Christian. The light came into the world "and the world knew him not. He came unto his own, and they that were his own received him not" (John 1.10-11). This dogmatic impossibility appears at the level of philosophical study as the impossibility to establish an acceptable link of continuity between Christian dogmatics and philosophical views. We fully agree with Léon Brunschvicg in denouncing these "disgraces of eclecticism".[1] One cannot over-emphasize the shocking repercussions on Christian dogmatics of those artificial constructions attempting to weld into one whole both rational reflections and revealed truths. Generally, these attempts consist in carrying philosophical reflection to an impasse and in showing afterwards how Christianity comes in to help philosophy save face and to crown majestically the philosophical edifice. With Brunschvicg, let us quote the typical example given by Malebranche: "Philosophers, my dear Aristus, are compelled to religion; for it alone can save them from the embarrassment in which they find themselves!" (*Entretiens sur la métaphysique et la religion*, IV, 17). The philosopher is disturbed in his reason by the various imperfections of the world. How can this problem of theodicy be rationally solved? It can only be done if faith makes us accept the existence of the first two persons in the Trinity: the Father who is Power, and the Son who is Wisdom. It will then be understood that had God acted solely in virtue of his power as the first person in the Trinity, He could have put an end by particular acts of will to the imperfections which scandalize us, even though they belong to the habitual concourse of the general laws. But God could not thus sacrifice the goodness of the end to the disorder of means. "God does not want His ways to dishonour Him" (*Entretiens*, IX). For God, *qua* the second person in the Trinity, is also wisdom. He will not interfere with the system of general laws. "It is not in God's power to deny

---

[1] This is said of the impossible synthesis between reason and religion that Brunschvicg sees throughout the whole history of philosophy. Cf. his book, *La raison et la religion.*

himself or to despise the laws wisdom prescribes Him" (*Traité de la nature et de la grâce*, I, IV, add.).

Because of the Son who is wisdom, God will therefore sacrifice part of His power, or at least of His intention to the demands of order which manifest themselves in the simplicity and generality of natural laws. It is easily seen why Malebranche's doctrine is dogmatically unacceptable: in order to regard Christian dogmatics as the linear extension of rational philosophy, Malebranche is led to introduce into the very concept of God a psychological dialectic. A psychology of God, worked out by means of concepts naturally borrowed from the psychology of man, such is the enormous blunder Malebranche arrives at, for having postulated that in the scheme of a Christian world faith and philosophy should be the continuation of each other. Any "Christian philosophy" runs similar risks. Either philosophy is merely the understanding of the Revelation, i.e. dogmatics, and then it abandons its concepts, its methods, its systems of reference; or else, it remains a human achievement, and then it can draw its *solutions* only from the light of nature. Of course, natural enlightenment may be subordinated to faith and brought into relationship with it; it still remains reason in its essential processes and cannot rationally adhere to mystery nor discover and exploit that which surpasses reason.

Philosophy, as well as theology, cannot but protest against this prejudice in favour of synthesis. For philosophy, as a body of doctrines, is not Christian; it is more or less rational; and at any rate it draws its validity from its rationality alone. This is what Gilson, a defender of a certain conception of Christian philosophy, is forced to recognize: "Some are considering philosophy in itself, in its formal essence as philosophy, abstraction being made from the conditions which rule either its constitution or intelligibility. In this sense, it is clear that a philosophy cannot be Christian, nor, for that matter Jewish or Mussulman, and that the idea of Christian philosophy has no more meaning than 'Christian physics' or 'Christian mathematics'."[1]

Having defined the spirit of our enterprise and the sense in which it appears to us different from the usual syntheses and the usual hierarchies, it remains for us to indicate how we intend to proceed in this undertaking. We shall seek to discover

---

[1] E. Gilson, *The Spirit of Medieval Philosophy*, p. 36.

not a philosophy of Christian structure, but a philosophy of Christian intention (and it is our belief that the problem would present itself in absolutely identical terms if it were a question of ethics). This means that we shall be more interested in the philosopher than in the philosophy; and that when we approach philosophy itself, it is the *work* rather than the *system* that we shall consider in it: we shall deal with the Christian's condition in so far as he engages in philosophical activity. For we can never regard the Christian otherwise than involved in the world; the philosophical involvement is but one particular aspect of this involvement in the world. Therefore, the problem of philosophy cannot be solved by a simple negation which would bar the Christian from access to philosophy. To see that this access is dangerous we have only to look at the numerous adulterations suffered by Christian dogmatics in its contacts with philosophy. But this danger could not inhibit him who has received, along with the assurance of salvation and forgiveness, the token of a glorious freedom. The philosophical activity cannot be denied the Christian any more than all other human activities. The crux of the question will therefore be to know what meaning his own work will have for the philosophizing Christian; in other words, the philosophizing Christian differs from all other philosophers in that he reserves for himself the right—and the freedom—to judge and test his own work by a criterion which is not philosophical, but dogmatic.

The condition of the Christian philosopher can be characterized from the start by the fact that he will not be content with verifying the rational validity of his work nor with testing its explanatory power in the face of facts; but that he will endeavour under any circumstances to grasp the manner in which the content itself of his philosophy can be *made intelligible* by the biblical Revelation. It can be seen how much this preoccupation differs from that which simply consists in establishing relationships between Christianity and philosophy: far more is at stake here than the relationship between container and contained. It is a question of knowing whether for a philosophy which is fully rational in other respects its reference to Christianity becomes a source of greater light or intelligibility: does the solution which I propose as a philosopher about the relation of time to eternity become enlightened by what

Revelation teaches me about the relationship between the Kingdom of God and the Church? Such is the question which at every moment weighs upon the activity of the Christian philosopher. And such is the sense in which the philosophizing Christian is subjected to the Word of God. To submit to the Word means to accept the judgement that God pronounces through it upon our lives and upon our writings.

But there is too great a tendency to interpret the word "judgement" solely in its sense of condemnation. In reality, to be under the judgement of God is to accept being placed beneath His light, to be enlightened by Him. When man as a moral being accepts to be placed under the divine judgement, this means that he accepts the condemnation introduced into the world by one man alone: the judgement of original sin, but by the same token, the observations made by the moral being and the rules which he sets for himself take on a new meaning. By becoming sin, our deficiencies and failures assume a clearer sense; we are tempted to say: a more positive sense; the ultimate weakness of our moral rules, as well as their indisputable disciplinary value are revealed to us when we understand that they both are manifestations of the Law. Thus with the philosophical work which the philosopher offers to the judgement of God: this does not mean that the work will be transfigured, miraculously erected as some intangible absolute; but that its rational successes, as well as its failures, will have meaning. Here it is impossible not to evoke the parable of the talents; those who had received them could do nothing but invest them and make them produce in normal and reasonable ways. Let us also point out that he who jealously kept his talent to shelter it from risks and responsibilities could also claim the support of reason, or at least of a certain kind of reason. Thus far we have moved amidst rational calculation; discussion may arise about the best procedure to follow, but reason remains the criterion. But suddenly the perspective is completely changed: judgement enters the picture. The acts of reason will be brought under a light which is not that of reason. It will appear that the various rational operations do not all have the same meaning, nor the same value. When a judgement of grace, reward or condemnation is pronounced, we understand that the various forms of dialectic in which reason is naturally involved have a hidden meaning that human reason cannot comprehend.

And thus, the question the philosophizing Christian must ask himself and answer is that of the relationship, or rather the mode of tension which exists between the truths encountered in the philosophical quest and the Truth witnessed to by Revelation.

One last ambiguity must be avoided here: to offer a philosophical work to the judgement of Revelation, so that this work will be not only condemned (which it will necessarily be, as any work of human wisdom), but also enlightened by Revelation, is not to re-establish surreptitiously a state of affairs which we have already rejected: a deductive continuity, a long chain of simple and facile reasons which would lead us from the Revelation to philosophy. The revealed cannot become a mere principle of intelligibility incorporated by the Christian into his own personal philosophy. For such is the pious temptation which ever theatens the Christian philosopher, and which Arnold Reymond has recently accepted on his own account: "The philosopher, if he is a Christian, will accept as true the fact of Revelation, because this fact constitutes in his eyes a source of rationality."[1] And Reymond incorporates this conception into his attempt at a universally valid explanation of man and the universe. He is, moreover, convinced that his attempted explanation has nothing to fear from the "widest possible information", just as a philosopher professing materialism[2] reckons that his views are further and further justified as science progresses. What to us appears impossible is precisely this incorporation of Revelation, *qua* a principle, into a philosophical system. No doubt, it is no longer a question of mere elements borrowed from Christianity. Rather, the whole of Revelation should itself become a principle of intelligibility within philosophy. This implies a recognition of the eminent dignity of Revelation and by the same token, Leibniz notwithstanding, an acknowledgement of the incapacity of reason fully to justify itself. Revelation is required to supply the philosopher's work with surplus legitimation; indeed, it is asked to validate reason. Revelation intervenes only to save philosophy from embarrassment. Yet, on the one hand, to annex Revelation to philosophy in this manner is to take away from it a

---

[1] We shall have to indicate the sense in which this assertion can be true.

[2] A. Reymond, "Philosophie et théologie dialectique", in *Revue de théologie et de philosophie*, Lausanne, 1935, p. 278.

measure of its judging power. To shed light means neither to justify nor to validate. It means to give significance, both with respect to the universe of the Fall and that of Redemption. The Revelation does not endorse rational deduction, but judges it, and in order to do so must definitely remain outside it. On the other hand, let us again recall the incomprehensible character of such a reduction of the revealed to principles. We thoroughly misunderstand the very character of Revelation as the personal presence of God in history when we attempt to express it in a principle. The pious attempt becomes impious; the Word must cease being flesh, though it is the second *person* in the Trinity, in order to become the verbal expression of an axiom. The revealed is never a formula, always an act; dogmatics is in no way the transforming of this act into principles, but, on the contrary, an effort to safeguard the specificity of the act against the effect of the formulas necessary for teaching it. Thus we know that philosophy is not to expect from dogmatics the elaboration of formulas susceptible of becoming principles of philosophical explanation. Such an operation would presuppose that, prior to it, Christianity was reduced to a philosophical system. And thus, to incorporate Christian principles simply means to carry out a philosophical endeavour of eclecticism and synthesis. This is why we greatly prefer to consider Revelation as a term which, while it remains outside any work of philosophy and cannot possibly be integrated in it, constitutes the judgement upon this work. Philosophy and Christianity cannot meet anywhere but in this judgement. And the entire condition of the Christian philosopher is to be attentive to this judgement. To examine the moments of this judgement, such will be the object of our inquiry.

Chapter II

THE CHRISTIAN CONCEPT OF TRUTH

We make an idol of truth. Truth, apart from charity is
not God, but His image and idol, which we must neither
love nor worship.

PASCAL; *Pensees*, 582

ANY philosopher who wishes to remain a Christian will
encounter Pascal's dilemma: the God of the scholars and
of the philosophers, or the God of Jesus Christ. Possibly this
dilemma is not, in the perspective of Christian dogmatics, an
ultimate contradiction. Also, the radical option forced on
Pascal may not be forced upon every philosopher. What is
certain, however, is that the experience of this dilemma is a
moment of every philosophy of Christian intention. For we
believe it is not by chance that the opposition between Christianity and philosophy, or the wisdom of God and the wisdom
of man, presents itself in the form of an opposition between the
knowledge of God in Jesus Christ and the rational knowledge of
God; nor is it by chance that the problem becomes most acute
and painful under this very form. Perhaps philosophy and
Christianity do not clash so much in their respective
assertions—though we do not wish to minimize this conflict—
as in the degree to which both claim to be activities oriented
toward the quest for truth, cognitive endeavours, approaches
to being. It is customary to consider that Christianity and the
various philosophies are divergent solutions of the same problem, and that, if the solutions become divergent in the end,
there is nevertheless a portion of the way common to all these
attempts. The very phrase "Christian philosophy" appears to
imply such a conception: philosophy can be Christian just as it
can be Platonic or Aristotelian.[1] Now, we believe that at this
particular point we touch the very root of the ambiguity: the

[1] Also, it is worth noting that the phrase, "Christian philosophy", did not always
have the precise and technical meaning we give it today, but in the writings of the
Church Fathers (and this use was retained by the Reormers) denoted Christianity
itself. Even the expression, "the philosophy of Christ", may be found, suggesting
immediately that Christianity is a branch of the eternal philosophy.

C

philosophies and Christianity do not really deal with the same problem; no doubt it is the same anxiety which drives men towards the philosophies or towards Christianity; but in each case the problem is not defined in the same terms, for in each case we find a different use of the notion of *truth*. If, then, the philosophies and Christianity, *qua* attempts at knowledge, have clashed, to the scandal of common sense which cannot admit of such a conflict among loyal efforts in the search for truth, it is because we are confronted here with two processes which differ, not so much in their psychological structure (faith holds no mystery for psychological analysis) as in the intention which animates them and the end towards which they are ordained: and this end is, in both cases, by unanimous accord called the Truth. The permanent conflict between the philosophies and Christianity attests that the notion of truth is by no means a universal one, and that, scandalous as this exigency may seem to reason, there does exist a Christian truth.

The Christian doctors themselves did not always fully realize that the problem is so grave and that it involves the very concept of Truth. For they would seek purely and simply to subordinate the God of the philosophers to the God of Jesus Christ; consequently, they postulate that the truth is homogeneous, and that divergent approaches to truth must finally be reconciled provided they are carried far enough. Accordingly, they are seen to attempt a synthesis of Christian truths and philosophical truths. And does not a superficial exegesis of Paul's discourse to the Areopagus appear to lend apostolic authority to such an undertaking? The Christian has no superiority over the philosophers other than that of being able to show them exactly the point of convergence at which truth appears in its luminous unity. "What, therefore, ye worship in ignorance, this I set forth unto you" (Acts 17.23). Does not the apostle insist upon this point, assuring the Greeks that the truth which he announces they already possess, having received it from the lips of one of their poets (Acts 17.28)? This scheme is to be found in the writings of practically all the doctors of the Church, since the day the Church first opened its doors to the philosophers: "Wherever a truth is pronounced, there Christianity is speaking", St. Justin was fond of repeating. Christianity can therefore assemble truths of all kinds, and integrate them all in the Truth. The relationship between the Christian

truth and the philosophical truths is conceived in the manner
of the relationships between the Old and the New Covenants:
as Christ does not abolish the law but fulfils it, as the law has a
place of its own in the scheme of Grace, so do the truths contained in the philosophical systems, as well as scientific truths,
find themselves fulfilled in Christianity. This parallel is obvious
in the works of many a doctor of the Church; it comes out
most clearly in the works of Clement of Alexandria who considers that philosophy, for the Greeks, was an educator:
"Philosophy would lead the Greeks to Christianity, as the Law
would lead the Hebrews."[1] "The Law for the Jews, philosophy
for the Greeks, until the advent of Christ."[2] The progressive
character of the concept of truth is clearly indicated: "Philosophy was given to the Greeks as a kind of testament for their use,
which was to serve as a stepping-stone towards philosophy
according to Christ."[3] All this seems natural to Clement, who
with the Stoics believes that there exists a universal reason,
immanent in all humanity: the φρόνησις,[4] which rivets men's
minds to the quest of the sole truth. Of course, the human mind
does not possess in itself power to attain the fullness of truth:
the Christian revelation will enlighten it, but finds it already
engaged upon the right path. Elementary though this position
may be, it has survived throughout the entire history of
religious thought. No fundamental difference exists between
Clement's theory and a conception of the relationships between
theology and philosophy such as the neo-scholastics find in St.
Thomas: "Theology remains in its proper place, that is to say
at the head of the hierarchy of the sciences; based on divine
Revelation, from which it receives its principles, it constitutes
a distinct science starting from faith and turning to reason only
to draw out the content of faith or to protect it from error.

"Philosophy, doubtless, is subordinate to theology, but, as
philosophy, it depends on nothing but its own proper method;
based on human reason, owing all its truth to the self-evidence
of its principles and the accuracy of its deductions, it reaches
an accord with faith spontaneously and without having to
deviate in any way from its own proper path. If it does so it is
simply because it is true, and because one truth cannot contradict another."[5] Resuming St. Ambrose's formula, which is

[1] I, *Stromateis*, 28.   [2] *Ibid.*, VI, 159.   [3] *Ibid.*, VI, 67.
[4] *Ibid.*, VI, 154-155   [5] E. Gilson, *The Spirit of Medieval Philosophy*, p. 6.

also that of St. Justin, St. Thomas was fond of saying: "Omne verum a quocumque dicatur, a Spiritu sancto est." Gilson follows the same doctrine when he states that Christianity implies every truth as the premise of a syllogism implies its conclusion: "If we decide to adopt this outlook on history we can still say with St. Paul that faith in Christ dispenses with philosophy and that revelation supersedes it; but supersedes it, nevertheless, only because it fulfils it. Hence a reversal of the problem as curious as inevitable. If all that was true in philosophy was but a presentiment and foreshadowing of Christianity, then the Christian, just because he is a Christian, is in possession of all that ever was or ever will be true in philosophy. In other words, and however strange it may seem, the most favourable rational position is no longer that of the rationalist, but that of the believer; and the most favourable philosophical position is not that of the philosopher, but that of the Christian."[1] Undoubtedly, the pre-eminence of Christianity and of Revelation is hereby entirely safeguarded: Christianity is the total truth. But how do we know that the elements of this total truth are scattered among the philosophies? How do we know that these elements are bound to converge in total truth? From the principle of the formal oneness of truth. Quite apart from Revelation, then, the concept is postulated of a formal truth, defined by oneness and harmony. We thus presume to define a notion of truth, at least in its form, without in any way resorting to Revelation. This truth, it is acknowledged, must contain Revelation, as well as those elements of truth which the philosophers were able to discover. Thus the whole truth appears as a sum of the various elements of truth: Christianity recapitulates the philosophies. Such a conception of truth certainly seems in agreement with the general trend of our thinking: whether we realize it or not, we constantly borrow from science its idea of truth. Now, though science has given up its attempts at setting up the entire and absolute truth, it retains the formal concept of such a truth: for it considers that all the detailed discoveries made in the various branches of scientific knowledge, and that progress in successive approximations' are all elements of this total truth. No doubt we cannot, here again, foresee the nature of the synthesis of these diverse elements, but it suffices to know that the particular truths will

[1] E. Gilson, *The Spirit of Medieval Philosophy* p. 28.

necessarily be co-ordinated within the total truth. It must be admitted that the scientist finds at every step and in the face of each new synthesis and of each new general discovery, a confirmation of the soundness of this conception. Truth is indeed total, in that it results from a totalization, an adding up of partial truths.

To accept this scientific conception of truth as a normative theory is necessarily to admit that the revealed knowledge—rational knowledge relationship is a relationship of one truth to another. But how can we then explain that a perfectly homogeneous truth should proceed from two sources as different from each other as reason and faith? It appears to us that the thinkers of the second, third, and fourth centuries who invented that most extraordinary myth of the participation of Greek wisdom in the revealed truth, appealing to the fact that Plato had been acquainted with the Mosaic writings, were submitting to a profound logic. Having received from Greece the idea that the truth must be one and homogeneous, and knowing that the total truth is to be found in Jesus Christ; yet unwilling to give up the truths they had learned at the school of the pagan philosophers, they could not but endeavour to integrate these elements of truth into the revealed truth. For the doctrine of the oneness of truth demands that all modes of knowledge be reduced to unity: thus the Christian doctors resorted without hesitation to the most bizarre theories in order to demonstrate that all truth proceeds from the Revelation; neither did they hesitate to declare exhausted the sources of rational knowledge. If Platonism contains any truth, it has borrowed it from Moses. Is it then astonishing that rationalism should not shrink from the inverse operation and proclaim that any truth necessarily arises from rational origins, and that if there is any truth on the side of Christianity, Christianity owes it to the presence of reason, hampered and enslaved, but still active. It is being taught almost without restriction that, if the Christian doctrine is still acceptable it is because in reality it lives upon the rational structure so patiently elaborated by Greek wisdom.[1] In Kant's dualism of the two reasons, and in the dichotomy of

---

[1] See A. Rivaud's book, *Les grands courants de la pensée antique*, written for popular consumption, but perhaps the more significant for that: ". . . The dogmas which constitute the backbone of our religions might never have been formulated had they (i.e. the Greeks) not prepared them" (p. 4). "In the formation of the new religion, Greek thought contributed by more than half" (p. 6).

transcendental knowledge and rational knowledge, Léon
Brunschvicg denounces a "baroque" survival which must at
all costs be eliminated, and which arises from the Christian
illusion of a truth the source of which is outside reason.[1]

Christianity, it must be recognized, appears to demand that
we renounce the formal notion of a unique truth, of which the
truths of faith and those of reason would merely be different
manifestations. At any rate, whoever wishes to maintain the
thesis of the unity of truth must deny the fact that different
truths coming from seemingly diverse sources can still in effect
be co-ordinated. Christian apologetics, in its controversies
against reason, has seldom refrained from this endeavour, and
well known are its numerous and often very popular attempts
to demonstrate that religion is not incompatible with science,
with philosophy, or with reason. But the demonstration stops
here, just at the moment when the compatibility is noticed and
nevertheless remains wavering. What still needs to be demonstrated is the fact that a necessary link exists between the truths
of Revelation and the truths of reason. It must be admitted
that such a demonstration has never been tendered. Would it
not be wise to recognize that there are different "orders" which
remain mutually impenetrable?

Let us attempt to point out how the Christian truth differs
from any rational truth.

Calvin encountered this problem while defining his position
with respect to humanism. He does not challenge the thought
that a considerable number of truths exists outside the limits
set by Revelation. He even specifies that these truths, foreign
as they may be to the biblical Revelation, must find their
supreme source and their warranty in God. "If we recognize
the Spirit of God as the sole fountain of truth, we shall not
despise truth, wherever it may appear, lest we insult the spirit
of God. For the gifts of the Spirit cannot be slighted without
casting contempt and infamy upon God Himself." It is impossible that a truth, of whatever order, should not proceed
from God. "We should deem nothing excellent or laudable
that we cannot recognize as coming from God."[2] That all
these truths find their unity in God is, however, an assertion
which has to be believed, hence an object of faith. But it could
not be demonstrated: for, at present, there are in fact two

[1] L. Brunschvicg, *La Raison et la Religion*, p. 167.   [2] Calvin, *Institutes*, I, ch. II.

"orders" of truths which we can juxtapose and view side by side, but cannot unite organically. There is Christian truth, which is contained in the biblical Revelation, and bears witness to the special grace that God bestows upon us in Jesus Christ; and there is secular truth which forms the content of wisdom and science of the natural man, and which bears witness to the grace that is common to all. By nature man is geared only to the latter kind of truth. Although his mind was perverted in the Fall (his appetite for truth "degenerates into vanity")[1] it is capable of reaching this truth. "None the less, when the human understanding undertakes a study, it does not labour so much in vain that it would in no way profit by it, especially *when it turns towards lower things*. Moreover, it is not so weak as not to get a taste of higher things, though it is lazy in seeking them; but it does not possess the same skill in the latter as in the former. For when it thinks itself raised above the present life, then precisely is it convicted of its own imbecility."[2] Yet, may we stop at a distinction as vague as this, opposing truths concerning things spiritual and truths concerning earthly things? Calvin himself regrets such a blurred distinction when dealing with the objects of the will.[3] In vain does he try to point out that earthly truths are those which do not concern the Kingdom of God. Theologically speaking, this distinction is difficult to maintain: can we really set forth truths, which in the face of the total demands of the Kingdom of God have no relationship to it? Is not the distinctive requirement of the Kingdom set forth in the Summary of the Law; does it not summon us to love the Lord our God with all our heart, with all our soul, and with all our mind?

Calvin establishes his distinction on the basis of a theory, currently admitted by scholastic realism, that our ideas are replicas of their objects, and that there exist as many orders of truths as there are orders of objects. From the radical distinction between the Kingdom of God and the kingdoms of this world, it follows that there must be two different orders of truths: heavenly truths and terrestrial truths. Yet, should we even admit the theory of knowledge implied in this thesis, we would still have to justify our right to give the name of truth to both these categories of knowledge. Even truths differing in their contents must be objectively united by their common

---

[1] *Ibid.*, Part I, ch. II.   [2] *Ibid.*   [3] *Ibid.*

relationship to that which causes them both to be true. Now this is the very problem which Calvin's theory leaves unsolved. Were it solved, the problem of the relation between theology and metaphysics would be solved also. But, because metaphysics has been concerned, much more than theology, with the unity of truth, it will always refuse to be confined to purely terrestrial occupations. It will obstinately insist upon grappling with all the last problems of man and upon taking a stand on all the matters which are also the theologian's concern; and thus we encounter again and again the anomaly which has characterized Western culture since rationalistic humanism split away from the Reformation: with all ultimate problems we are in the presence of one truth which is Christian and another which is rationalistic; and the two will not be identified. The chances are overwhelming that every time they reach a formal agreement it is at the cost of a gross ambiguity. Thus, it would be all too easy to show that the immortality of the soul has never been asserted in the same sense by Christian theology and by philosophy. Theology maintains that it is Christ and He alone who brought to light the immortality of the soul; this He does by means of His Resurrection through which He creates for us the new man. Apart from this Resurrection, the soul is not immortal; quite the contrary: having become carnal because of the Fall it cannot, by nature, participate in eternity. It has to be born anew; sown corruptible, it must rise again, incorruptible. It can acquire immortality only through the miracle achieved by Christ. Philosophy, on the contrary, has unceasingly sought to discover in the nature of the soul itself the reasons of its immortality. To become immortal, the soul must first of all be spiritual. This substantial spirituality is reached by means of analysis, critical reflection, and also by endeavours at purification or personal asceticism. It is in vain, then, that philosophy tries to lend its support to theology;[1] it can only disguise the cause it purports to defend. It is in vain too that theology, probably because of its lack of confidence in the power of the Word, seeks the support of the philosophers to constitute an apologetics for use by infidels, unbelievers, and semi-believers; such apologetics always attempt to present

---

[1] Cf. Descartes' letter to "Messrs. the Deans and Doctors of the Sacred Faculty of Theology in Paris", requesting that they extend their protection to the publication of his *Meditations*.

the truths of the faith under the guise of rational truths. The spiritual failure of apologetics (which can be accompanied by success as far as the creation of a Christian civilization is concerned) and its constantly renewed efforts must open our eyes to the conflict within the notion of truth, which cannot be resolved merely by dividing up objects of knowledge according to Calvin's distinction. In vain did philosophy, with the support of science, endeavour to purify its concept of truth and to define it under conditions excluding any anthropomorphism: the revealed truth of Christianity was left out of this concept; a philosophical spirituality arose in which Christian spirituality found no place and could not thrive. Léon Brunschvicg's recent book, *Religion and Reason*, derives its moving greatness from the fact that the author summons Christianity to resume the place it has abandoned within the philosophical spirituality. He rejoices in the signs of the rising ecumenical movement: for "Truth is unity".[1] We are convinced that Christian universalism will not coincide with philosophical universalism any more than did the special emphases of the various Christian denominations.

We are therefore thrown back upon the source of the conflict, which Calvinism, as well as the whole Reformation, had strongly emphasized without accounting for it.

Both philosophy and science see their own value in their constant effort to discover a truly universal truth, the universality of which is to be attested by its impersonality. It is quite true that "pure truth" is a truth of a mathematical type, and that real spirituality consists in creating in oneself a mathematician's soul. The Christian, however, especially if he is a theologian, feels a certain reticence in the face of this effort to suppress the subjective character of truth. Bossuet wrote to Huet about Descartes: "As for this author's other opinions, I let the indifferent ones such as those concerning physics and others of the same kind amuse me, I entertain myself with them in the course of conversation; but to be quite honest with you, I would deem it unworthy of a bishop's character seriously to take sides in such issues."[2] With greater finesse, and less contempt for profane truth, Pascal none the less writes: "I approve of not examining the opinion of Copernicus; but this . . . ! It

---

[1] *La Religion et la Raison*, p. 11.
[2] Letter of May 18, 1689, *Correspondence*, IV, p. 19.

concerns all our life to know whether the soul be mortal or immortal."[1]

Such an attitude seems authentically Christian. The Christian cannot abstain from a fundamental judgement of value, from an option both first and ultimate, whereby to a universal and impersonal truth he prefers one which brings him salvation. That the Christian cannot refuse to face this basic choice inevitably follows from his condition: he knows himself to be a sinner, wholly a sinner, unable to recognize any absolute truth or to perform any valid act until he is made free from this law of sin. As a direct result of his sinful condition, he must first of all seek the truth which will save him. No impersonal and universal truth can save him. This he can verify through experience. True, rationalism depicts for us a natural redemption, brought about by a system of universal truths. It explains that it is enough to be converted to these universal truths to be saved, that is, to proceed to a normal existence. But rationalism is compelled to deny, or what is even more serious, to forget the obstacle of sin which bars access to an allegedly normal existence. Rationalism always finds itself constrained to present as normal that which, in reality, is purely ideal. There is consequently a certain lie inherent in rationalism; or rather, metaphysical rationalism is the secularization of a heresy which from time to time threatens Christian theology itself: the temptation to erect itself as a *theologia gloriae*, divorced from the actual situation in which man lives. It is easily understood, then, why every rationalism has called forth the irony of some scepticism, the natural function of which is to stress the misery of the human condition. Though its lucidity which is great does not reveal to it the sinfulness of man that the Church confesses in faith, at least it recognizes in its wisdom that: "Man is neither angel nor beast." The conversion of the intellect to the universal truths of science, the indisputable purification that mathematical analysis imposes upon the mind by detaching it from the universe of discourse and of subjective synthesis (which in the last analysis is a universe of desire) do not extirpate from the human soul either its original pride or its revolt against God. The idol has assumed a different form: "We make an idol of the truth itself." From then on, salvation will be made out to consist in depersonalization;

---

[1] *Pensées*, III, 218, translation by W. F. Trotter, Everyman's, p. 62.

spirituality will be linked with the annihilation of the self, which in the last analysis will be identified with the annihilation of subjectivity. This type of thinking does not realize that the successive sacrifices which the scientific discipline demands of us do not exhaust our subjectivity. Quite arbitrarily, the notion is set up of a purified self which is a pure cognizing subject and which has none of the characteristics of the subject left; an impersonal subject, whose impersonality means eternity. As a consequence, the contemplation of truth would present no difficulties to such a subject; he would be exactly suited to it. For such a being, the problem of salvation and that of a saving truth no longer arise.

This attitude, exactly represented by the names of Spinoza and Brunschvicg, rests entirely upon an ambiguity, the same on which rest all the collusions between Christianity and spiritualism: the ambiguity of the objective and the true. We tend to make the objective coincide with the true and not to admit that anything can be true which is not objective. Indeed, it is quite right to say that in the search for truth and objectivity, the initial steps appear the same. The true is first of all recognizable by its independence from our will and desires. It cannot be arbitrarily constructed: it thrusts itself upon us, and all discussions centred upon truth are aimed at establishing its objectivity.

It will therefore be easily understood that in a mental regimen founded upon the primacy of science, truth and objectivity have been identified with factualness. Thus, fact becomes the measure and norm of truth; a law is true only as the expression of a fact. The experience of evidence is no longer anything but the primitive and brutal collision of the mind with the obstacle constituted by an object. It is not by mere chance that science has become phenomenalistic and that any dissolution of the "thing" results in a sort of scientific nominalism. We shall therefore model our conception of truth upon the "thing"; the abstractness of the mathematical relationship confers on scientific truth the rigidity of solid objects. It even surpasses objects in objectivity, because it is strictly univocal, whereas fact is univocal only at first experience, in a brutal contact. A more refined experience is bound to reveal that the object is susceptible of diverse interpretations, among which it cannot lead us to differentiate. A relation represents the very type of univocal determination; a multiplicity of relationships represents a possibility to dissolve the apparently equivocal character of objects. Objects are equivocal only when the determination of the conditions of their appearance has not been carried far enough. But the determination can be carried sufficiently far only inasmuch as the observer does not intervene in it. The paradox of scientific research is to require from the scientist an activity of self-effacement. Truth will be better attained in proportion to the scientist's ability to reduce his own ambitions and experience and to place himself under conditions which are an adulteration of man's real condition; each step forward will, moreover, show him that he is yet far from his goal. Microphysics will brand as subjective the attitude of the classical physicist who devises a physics on a human scale. Physical geometry itself will appear as the refuge of subjectivity, in so far as it is the expression of some preconceived, and therefore subjective, ideal of clarity and distinctness. At least the way is clearly indicated; the aim is to achieve a baring of the intellect which will make us escape even in defining objects from the utilitarian norms imposed upon us by perception. The essential spiritual progress of science has consisted in reviving the whole issue of the immediate proofs upon which the mind should first of all reflect in order to force us to discover a new immediacy, often completely unrelated to intuitive immediacy.[1] Thus we see disappearing from the very horizon of science objects which for centuries had been its favourites. Bachelard summons every scientist to submit his consciousness to a psychoanalysis which will reveal to him mysterious kinships between the world of objects as it appears to him and the secret designs of an unconscious which is even more subjective than clear consciousness. It is hardly necessary for our purposes to characterize any further this race toward objectivity. It suffices to ascertain it, and to ascertain that the confusion of the objective and the true corresponds to an indispensable moment of the dialectics of science. Indeed, the consequences of this appear clearly enough. The most important of these is probably the exclusion from science of any specifically human reality, because any human reality remains equivocal and acquires objectivity only in losing its essential meaning. Of course, sciences of man have

---

[1] Cf. G. Bachelard, *Le nouvel esprit scientifique*, and the example of the new scientific ethics given by the author under the title of *Psychanalyse du feu*.

arisen, but at the cost of what sacrifices and what a degree of abstraction! In reality they are much more concerned with *homo faber*, *homo oeconomicus*, *homo politicus*, etc., than with real man. Assuredly there is a science which, turned essentially towards the concrete, can never forget the reality of the human condition, and must endeavour to apprehend man in his integrity, in his intentions, in his hopes, and sometimes driven to the limit of his supernatural vocation. But, as R. Aron has reminded us, history, when it is worthy of interest, cannot pass itself off as an objective science.[1] Beyond the practical exclusion of man from the limits of objectivity, there is also the exclusion of values. The latter, moreover, commands the former. It is *qua* actualization of value that man eludes the jurisdiction of the objective sciences. The peculiarity of a value is to acquire the fullness of its meaning only from the moment when it becomes an object of our interest and is partaken of by the person who is interested in it; and when, to an extent which can vary *ad infinitum*, it is actualized by him. The peculiarity of a value is to lose its meaning and reality (since in it meaning and reality coincide) in the exact degree to which it is objectified and replaced by a system of objectively controllable determinations: a moral imperative is a value only in so far as our attention is not directed essentially towards its sociological explanation. A religious revelation only has religious value inasmuch as it does not become objectified into a religious phenomenon. The destruction of values is always carried out by means of some explanation of values; common sense is deluded in the process and abandons the values as soon as it is made to understand in what utterly contingent circumstances the values arose and how they were the absolutely necessary consequence of these absolutely contingent circumstances. In reality, it is because common sense forgets to maintain with respect to the contested values the attitude they demand that it becomes so easily convinced of their falsity. It forgets too easily that values cannot be grasped from every kind of spiritual situation. Yet, as soon as a satisfactory spiritual perspective is found—we shall refrain from defining it since it varies according to the values under consideration—the explanation or objectivization of values no longer appears perilous; we know that the operation is possible, but we also know that it does not reach the essence of the value,

[1] R. Aron, *Essai sur les limites de l'objectivité historique.*

but merely its historical, sociological or even biological conditioning. The true believer is not troubled when he learns that Moses is not the author of the Pentateuch or that the Mosaic theology is mythical, once he has discovered what God means to convey to him by these accounts; in the same way, he who has discovered what in a value has worth for him will understand that all attempts at the reduction or objectivization of values are of no avail.

In the last analysis, what has worth in a value is that which touches us in our concrete situation. It is the demand it presents us which is never objective in a value. The object itself never formulates any demand towards us. In relation to it, we are perfect subjects; we always have the initiative. It is therefore natural that at the end of the cognizing process we should also have the possibility of using the object—that is, of dominating it. True, we are here describing an absolutely ideal situation, one in which the object is only an object; in fact, it seldom happens that the object does not also carry some value. This occurs even in scientific experiments. But, as soon as this case arises, the object ceases to be neutral and passive with relation to an all-powerful subject. As soon as the scientist begins to question the conditions of his work, as soon as he allows his results to be judged and evaluated, he is compelled to confront his own ideas, theories, and convictions with the object. With relation to the system of knowledge that we build up about the object, the object *qua* touchstone for determining the solidity of the system is itself a value. We thus verify the fact that even in the extremely sketchy and sometimes simple experience of scientific knowledge value entails an exigency which we can only accept and in the face of which we are passive. All knowledge is not, therefore—despite the commonplace axiom—the relation of a subject to an object. It can also be the discovery by the subject of a demand which concerns him. Now, no demand can be felt by all subjects in uniform fashion. The demand—when it is received as such—gives rise to a mode of participation which is a function of our subjective situation. The vision of beauty arouses creative activity in some, simple enjoyment in others. In both cases knowledge is involved, yet the two are radically distinct, irremediably subjective; incapable of submitting to a common standard. The essential service that a science of values can render is to remind us that the concept of objective knowledge does not exhaust the whole concept of knowledge but is merely an impersonal mode of knowledge in which the subject is not involved as a whole.

The study of values reminds us hereby that a distinction must be maintained between the objective and the true; or better, between a knowledge of the object which concerns the subject only in so far as he himself consents to the characteristics of the object, and an existential knowledge, which deals with the "I" in its most irreducible and inalienable core.

It yet remains to define that which in the subject is irreducible and is thus involved in the fullest mode of knowledge found in philosophy: the knowledge of values. The term "subjectivity" is equivocal. It can denote that complex of biological and psychological peculiarities, hereditary and acquired, which in the world of living things makes them into distinct individualities. But it is quite obvious that this infra-personal—in some cases infra-conscious—subjectivity, wholly oriented towards grasping objects which stimulate psycho-biological tendencies, cannot engage in the knowledge of any transcendent object. It remains that subjectivity means no longer this complex of tendencies indifferent to any knowledge, but the peculiar vocation, whether recognized or supposed, whereby the subject asserts himself as a person in a world of persons. Obviously, the existence of such a subjectivity cannot be explained without the informing action of the values themselves. But subjectivity is strengthened as it seeks deeper insight into these values; and this deepening insight constitutes its essential act of knowledge. For the subject values have a vital, existential meaning; should they happen to disappear without being replaced by firmer values, the subject as such would be annihilated, as when the loss of a religious faith is accompanied by moral decadence.

The subject who knows the value is not the same, therefore, as the one who knows the object. The latter knows that it is not himself who is at stake, that his knowledge cannot modify him, or that it will only modify his theories, i.e. a reality which merely constitutes the periphery of his being. Hence the epithets of intellectual, impersonal, cold, by which we qualify the knowledge of objects. It may even be added that historically such knowledge only became possible from the day when the notion arose of an inanimate nature, ontologically foreign to the destiny of the subject; science could only be built upon the ruins of pantheism and pagan animism. On the contrary, the knowledge of values supposes, in order that the cognitive relationship may exist, that our own selves should be called into question—in the full sense of the word—by the very object of our knowledge. The Platonic doctrine of knowledge rightly supposes the existence of an ontological kinship between the soul and the world of ideas it is called upon to know; but we must add that a value constantly modifies the soul itself. Thus, the knowledge of values cannot have the serenity and the detachment which characterize objective knowledge. Only exceptionally do men fight for the sake of scientific truths; but they die for the sake of values. Here indeed we ourselves are at stake, and all our being too; for it is no longer merely a question of what we are at present; it is also a question of what we are called upon to become.

Such appears to be the opposition which, from the philosophical point of view, underlies the distinction of the objective and of the true. All objectivity is truth, but truth infinitely surpasses objectivity. Thus, from within philosophy itself there springs the demand for a truth which, to a certain extent, is already a saving truth, since it is capable of transforming and converting our being. The notion of conversion is by no means foreign to philosophy. But we are very far yet from the truth of which Christianity speaks. We have only attempted to break up the excessively narrow notion of objective truth and to understand how truth can appear as a demand, and as the demand for *a* salvation. The Christian idea of truth, while it extends this philosophical idea of truth, also explodes it. For in Christianity it is no longer a question of a knowledge of value, though this is implied, nor of indirect knowledge of the value by the mediation of a person, as liberalism and modernism have imagined. It is a question of a person who is value, and the supreme value: the knowledge of Jesus Christ. This identity of person and value, which remains scandalous even from the point of view of the philosophy of values, is the very centre of the biblical Revelation. Jesus said: "I am the way, the truth and the life." In the historically knowable person of Jesus we see absolutely realized the identification of value and being which so preoccupies philosophy and which stands in the way of a reconciliation between the philosophy of values and ontological philosophy. The philosophy of values understands perfectly that values can only continue to be such in so far as they remain open, "atmospheric", as LeSenne[1] terms them, and are founded upon a less partial and richer value. But, from one value to another value, one must at last reach a sovereign Value, that upon which all others are based and whose essence has sufficient fullness to provide grounds for a self-sufficient existence. Here a great temptation arises to call this sovereign value "God". But what right have we thus to pass from the value, which usually in our human experience transcends persons and gives them a basis, to the person himself and his being? How can we retrieve ontology? It is a fact that philosophy does effect this transition. But we must recognize that it is an arbitrary transition: value deals with persons; it is not itself personal. Christianity confronts us from the first with the Word made flesh, with the person who is the Truth, and, moreover, the only Truth; it confronts us with Salvation. "In none other is there salvation, for neither is there any other name under heaven, that is given among men, wherein we must be saved" (Acts 4.12). The demand in question, then, is addressed by a person to a person. We must apply to Biblical truth what Kierkegaard says about sin: "Fundamentally, sin does not belong to any branch of knowledge. It is the object of the sermon in which the Alone speaks to the Alone."[2] God assumes all values; He can be said to be at the same time the chief Good and the chief Truth, but He assumes them as a Person and confers on them a personal existence. In extreme cases values could become mere objectified abstractions; and they easily become so in systems of values and in legalistic religions. In God, in the demand of a God who is Himself a person, we understand the true meaning of value; we understand that they would soon cease to be demands were they not the will of the Living God. Theoretically as well as practically, the Christian cannot conceive of justice outside the will of a just God. There is a risk that the value of even the purest justice may become an idol, as can be seen in the lay philosophies, if the concept of justice ceases to be measured by God's will. That is why the reformed dogmatics, in contrast to Catholic dogmatics, have always opposed the substitution in the margin

---

[1] See *Obstacle et valeur*, Paris, 1932.

[2] Kierkegaard, *The Concept of Dread* (French translation, p. 24).

D

of the Revelation, though logically subordinated to it, of systems of natural ethics and natural law (and sometimes even
natural theologies), thus called because the values are linked
with an objective and constant nature and not directly bound
to the will of a personal God. The fundamental notion of
Protestant dogmatics, that of the Word of God, forbids us to
build up a system of truth which would not consist of the actual
words of the Living God.[1] What, for the Christian, makes any
eclecticism impossible and forces him to resist the temptations
of even the purest of idealisms is the fact that any syncretism
would compel him to displace the centre of gravity of the
contents of his faith and to measure the validity of his faith
by a system or hierarchy of values and ideals, whereas for
him, Jesus Christ, the Living Word of God, is the only norm
of truth.

The Christian finds it necessary to assert that there is no
absolute truth but in Jesus Christ. And the basis of this assertion
is that there is no salvation but in Jesus Christ. Jesus Christ is
thus the Truth which is our salvation. This truth presents us,
not merely with one demand among others, nor even with a
specially important demand, but the decisive demand, that
which confronts us with life and death, and which requires a
decision which is also total: the univocal decision of faith.
This helps us understand how particularly lucid the Apostle
Paul had to be in order thus to preserve the originality of the
Biblical message, and to continue, amidst alluring teachings,
some of which were doctrinally quite akin to Christianity, to
preach Jesus Christ only, the person of Jesus Christ crucified.

The Bible lays heavy emphasis upon the rigorously unique
character of this Truth which is at the same time a Person.
Jesus Christ is the only Son, come from the Father. There will
never appear, as in certain mythologies, such successive incar-
nations as would in the end blur and let recede into shadow
him who is the mere carrier of an abstract truth, so as to enable
an intelligent philosophy to make an exegetical interpretation
of the myths and to point out within the myth, at the mythical

---

[1] To illustrate this assertion, we refer the reader to the present-day efforts of
Catholic dogmatics to revive the notion of natural law (Cassian Weier, J. Maritain,
etc.) and the resistance and reticence of Protestant dogmatics (cf. Dr. W. A.
Visser 't Hooft, "Droit naturel ou droit divin", in *Correspondance*, January-February,
1943, pp. 81-92, and especially J. Ellul, "Fondement théologique du Droit",
Cahiers théologiques de l'Actualite protestante, 15-16).

hero's expense, the general and abstract truth. The coming of Jesus Christ occurs at as precise a point of history as of space. It will be of little avail to know the teachings of Jesus Christ, as the unbeliever can know them, to a certain extent; for these teachings only have meaning in the person of Jesus Christ Himself. The *logos* has meaning only if it is made flesh.[1] God Himself can only be known in Jesus Christ. God the eternal, the immutable, He who is outside time, in whom there is not the least shadow of change, demands to be apprehended in a history focused upon a decisive and unique date. Thus, in the Christian notion of truth, we find reconciled the two concepts which are always divided in objective knowledge and even in the knowledge of values: eternity and historicity. In the human order of truths, historicity always implies some measure of degradation and of contingency. In fact, we are always trying to transcend history; we recognize historical truth only when it assumes meaning for us living in a different period; in other words, we are forever endeavouring to perceive a universally valid truth behind contingent circumstances. The expressions, "truth" and "particularity", seem mutually exclusive; a rigorously specific truth, grounded in an exclusive point of time, does not appear valid to us. That is why we see science clinging by an incoercible movement to the timeless, which it obtains by means of repetition; and philosophy seeking under various forms an eternal present—an instant containing eternity. Often the religious life tries to constitute itself using these philosophical attempts as a starting-point; and the mystical life, prolonging philosophical wisdom, attempts to establish communion with God in an eternal present beyond the time which endures. Hence the astonishment of the human mind before the Bible's assertion that the fullness of eternal truth has in fact been manifested in the historical Jesus, who remains indissolubly bound up with the glorified Christ. The Apostles, in their preaching, were conscious of the singularity of their own message when they insisted that the Jesus crucified by the Jews was the same Jesus whom God raised from the dead. In a certain sense, Jesus Christ satisfies our craving for transcending time by reconciling in His own person eternity and

[1] W. Hermann (*Der Verkehr des Christen mit Gott*) has insisted very forcefully, though in a somewhat ambiguous manner, because he constantly uses the language of psychology and not that of dogmatics, upon the importance of the notion of the person of Jesus ("*das innere Leben Jesu*").

time. But in another sense He is to us an object of scandal, for even though He is the eternal Son of the Father, we can only recognize Him in the place of His incarnation, that is in the Biblical document. We would more willingly believe in Jesus Christ were He a mythical person, for it would then be easier for us to disengage the eternal from the temporal.

We prefer myth to history. That is why all pagan religions rest upon myths; and it is remarkable enough that modern hypercriticism, by increasingly relegating Jesus to the status of a mere myth, should often have thought that the eternal value of Christianity was not necessarily affected thereby, and that Christianity could remain the religion of the civilized West. Moreover, Christianity thus freed from its bond with historical truth appears far more robust to such hypercriticism. Myth confers upon Christianity a certain poetic quality which must find itself in harmony with the experience of eternal mankind.[1] This shows how difficult it is to accept the Christian notion of truth, even though it terminates the dissociation of the true from the historical.

Thus we find ourselves upon a plane of knowledge quite different from that of scientific and philosophical knowledge. This we can summarize by saying that thought is limited in its quest for eternity to move not merely within history, but within a very particular history; and to know the fullness of Truth in one Person only. All thinking must be made captive to the obedience of Christ. All knowledge is defined as a function of the truth it is called upon to know. The knowledge of revealed truth will thus be knowledge in Christ, whether it concerns the revelation made in the Old Testament (2 Cor. 3.14-16) or in the New. This knowledge, in its very obedience, is extremely free; for where the Lord's spirit is, there lies freedom. Therefore all will be made known accordingly, even the depths of God. We can assert that there exists a knowledge of mystery as such. Faith is always comprehension. At the same time, it is a kind of knowledge which can never turn into intuitive contemplation or dialectical gnosis. In the former case, knowledge would presume to reach revealed truth outside the historical place where the revelation was made; in the latter, it would presume to consider the revealed merely as an element making possible

---

[1] Such seems to us the significance, both metaphysical and epistemological, of critical works, such as Renan's, Couchoud's, etc.

a construction, as a datum which can be enriched by a synthetic and constructive effort of the mind. Such aberrations, often found in the history of heresies, prove how difficult it is to maintain the Christian notion of truth in its purity, and to model our mode of cognition on this truth.

The notion of truth is therefore a fragmentary one. In fact, there is no unity in truth; men can know truths without knowing God, who nevertheless is the Truth. This is a fact the neo-Thomistic theory forgets. If this fact is often passed over it is because it evidently contradicts our customary theories of knowledge. It seems surprising that man's mind should be able to move upon the plane of truth without encountering God. Every human judgement, when it reaches the truth, should be related to God, since God is the origin and the end of all things, the creator of all realities and all truths.[1] That this is not actually so is a paradox for which Christianity alone can account, by emphasizing man's special position—a position which affects his knowledge. If man lived in the time of creation, before the Fall, or in the time of restoration and glory, all truth would necessarily refer to God. But man is living and thinking between the two eras: he lives in the era of sin which is also that of grace; he is at the same time the old man and the new man, and knows truths which not only do not lead him to God but sometimes conceal Him; he also knows truths which reveal Him. He lives in a state of perpetual tension between these truths. The man that we are can conceive in the present neither the unity of creation nor that of the Kingdom. This strange situation causing man to be both rich and poor (2 Cor. 6.9-10) does not allow him to perceive the unity of creation otherwise than in faith, that is, as a promise. This concept, of which Cartesianism made such a rich use, remains difficult for the Christian to handle. The break in knowledge, reflecting that in the order of truth, also indicates the break which exists in creation because of sin.

The only thing which allows philosophy to believe in the homogeneity of truth is its customary ignorance of sin. The Christian ought to know that it is impossible to establish an ascending hierarchical order of truth from the objective truths of science to the revealed truths of the gospel through the intermediary of truth pertaining to value. The mind can at the

---

[1] See K. Barth, *Die kirchliche Dogmatik*, I, 1, p. 47.

utmost be compelled to pass from factual truths to value truths, from the objective to the existential; but from the existential in general to the existential manifested in Jesus Christ there can be no transition. Similarly, the Christian knows that it is not possible, as a certain idealism tinged with Christianity would often have it, to transpose the Christian truth upon the plane of philosophical truth, to say, for example, that God is the Supreme Value; this process, to which we are often forced by current language as well as by our desire to recover forcibly the unity of truth is, strictly speaking, the process of secularization. In it we pass from the concrete to the abstract, from the unique to the general, to use Kierkegaard's expressions. To thus subsume the concrete under the abstract always constitutes for us a chance better to possess reality. And conversely, it is in so far as the object of our knowledge remains rigorously unique that it eludes our grip. Always, secularization is accompanied by a process of objectification.[1] This process can be more, or less, completed. In the knowledge of values it is far from completion. The value continues to make demands upon us; it is beyond what we know of it. Yet the very possibility of systematizing values indicates that a process of objectifying has begun. This occurs within the realm of values; certain values have become our property to such an extent that we are capable of creating them—sometimes by the mere interplay of social conventions. Such are economic values, as well as some artistic values of a lower type (e.g. fashion). The realm of values is ambiguous. It oscillates between the concrete and the abstract, the existential and the objective, demand and utility.

If our analysis is correct, it may seem strange that the same word "truth" is applied to the different sectors of truth which we distinguished. Should we reserve the name of "truth" for Revelation alone, as preaching, even more than theology, has done? There is such a temptation. That objective relationships or values do not represent the fullness of truth does not imply that they are positively false: they are merely dangerous in so far as they make us stop and look on them as total truths. Thus, not a single word of contempt is found in Calvin's writings as regards human values. "If the Lord wishes that the iniquitous and the infidel should help us to understand physics, dialectics, and other disciplines, we must use them in those things, lest our

---

[1] N. Berdyaev, *Five Meditations upon Existence*.

negligence be punished, lest we despise the gifts of God wherever they are presented to us" (*Christian Institutes*, I, 2). Therefore we ought not to condemn search for these truths, even though at the point where they become systematized and pretend to be absolute, theology must intervene to rectify their meaning. By becoming objective truths become only partial; but, as in this process of objectification they keep their own evidence, as they are justifiable by the same logical criteria as the full truths of the Revelation, and as, furthermore, from the point of view of form, intelligibility exists in both, it is understandable that the title of truth applies to one as well as to the other. But we also have more serious reasons for maintaining, despite the break in the notion of truth that we have ascertained, the one-ness of truth. This oneness subsists for the believer as a promise. The present knowledge of God—knowledge by faith—is not the fullness of the knowledge of God. As long as the sinful man is not destroyed, there can be no question of seeing God face to face. The mystic contemplation is necessarily forbidden us. But by faith the Christian lives in the expectation of the renewal of all things—therefore also, the renewal of the mind. He knows that the era of faith itself is limited to the present aeon, that faith itself will pass away. It is with the clear consciousness of this special situation of the Christian that Protestant dog-matics refrains from any theory of intuitive knowledge and beatific vision. For the same reason, however, it maintains that any knowledge partakes of the eschatological expectation and hopes for its realization. This realization will manifest the one-ness of truth.

The state of the university symbolizes better than anything else the present state of our knowledge. The totalitarian con-ception of the university, prevalent in the Middle Ages, is destroyed; the faculties are no longer gathered under the authority of the faculty of theology, believed to recapitulate all the sciences. Theology has been compelled to admit itself incapable of systematizing all the sciences; it is even incapable of deciding whether specific doctrines, professed by specific sciences at a given moment of their evolution, are true or false. At best, it can warn against certain bold and generally un-scientific interpretations of a scientific theory. As early as in the Middle Ages it was found that theology could only intervene in the work of the other sciences at the cost of arbitrariness and by resorting to violence. This is tantamount to saying that, contrary to the Thomistic and Gilsonian postulates, the different sciences, and therefore the different truths, may not be coordinated into a single hierarchical system culminating in the revealed truth. We must go even further: it is impossible to grasp in a definitive and complete manner the meaning presented by the various objective truths with reference to revealed truth. Now and then a Christian is enabled to understand that the exercise of a certain scientific activity conforms to the vocation he has received from God, and that it is for him an integral part of the acceptable worship he owes God; that through this work he is working towards his own salvation, in the real sense of these words. But who can universalize this remark? Who can decide that such or such a form of culture or of science is indispensable to the exercise of faith? Who can presume that such or such a science is indispensable to the full completion of the knowledge of God? Alexandrian Christianity was able to do so, but precisely hereby it became suspect of heresy.

Undoubtedly, any activity the end of which is knowledge can be carried out to the glory of God. But this glorifying of God through human knowledge depends much more upon the spirit of our inquiry than upon the content of our science. Only with the greatest difficulty can theology establish a hierarchy of values between the various scientific disciplines; it can, at the most, and only to a certain extent, grant a privilege to the disciplines dealing with man and endeavouring to grasp the specific nature of man: namely, the philosophical anthropologies. For the eminent dignity of man in creation implies that he must make a reflective effort to determine his true place within the universe. Without claiming in any way that the scepticism manifested by certain theologians towards various secular disciplines, and especially towards the philosophical system, is entirely justified, one must recognize that this scepticism nevertheless reveals a fundamental truth: the impossibility of ordering human knowledge so as to subject it to the knowledge God gives in His Revelation. Between the word of man and the Word of God, between the truths and Truth, there subsists in the present scheme of the world a deep gap. This is why Cartesianism, which purely and simply juxtaposes natural reason and supernatural insight as two radically opposed modes of knowledge, though it recognizes both modes as gifts of God, appears spiritually less dangerous to us than neo-Thomism which, placing itself, so to speak, above the present time, effectuates or pretends to effectuate a progressive hierarchy of the orders of knowledge and of truths. It suffices us to know by faith that, in the order of things to come, all that is hidden will be revealed, that all things will take on their exact meaning, that all human activities will find their accomplishment, and that the truths we have reached will be unified. It is in this eschatological perspective that the problem of truth must be set.

But this position in no way implies that we should adopt the heteronomous position of a Descartes. To say that we do not perceive any common measure between the scientific and the philosophical truths and the Christian Revelation, between the truths which educate and mould personality and the Truth which saves it, does not mean that we deny any action of the revealed Truth upon human truths in the present. In the exact degree to which we shall take seriously the eschatological situation which is ours, and to which we shall endeavour to keep alive by faith this expectation of the accomplishment of all things, we cannot escape a confrontation between human truths and the revealed Truth. For the philosopher, the battle of faith consists precisely in this effort to offer his meditation and his truths to the light of the Revelation, while realizing that there can never be any harmonious continuity from his truth to that of Jesus Christ. The attitude of the Christian philosopher (and this is the whole thesis which we shall defend) consists in desiring to benefit from Revelation, without giving in to the temptation of setting up as a dogmatics the system which he is building, though this system, obedient as it is to Revelation, may have received from it considerable enrichment. The characteristic of any eschatological entity is to weigh upon the present with a demand which remains living and real in the present without completely fulfilling itself in it, i.e. while preserving its own nature as demand. In order that man's truths may preserve this right to the name of truth; in order that they should not become mere idols; in order that all truths should be prevented from being submerged in objectivity and enabled to keep existential meaning, they must be cut through by the ultimate demand contained in the Revelation. Lest, by a normal evolution, the earthly truths characterized by Calvin become contemptible in comparison with Divine Truth, he who deals with earthly truths must constantly feel upon his labour the weighty demand of the ultimate Truth, Jesus Christ; and this, even though we well know that no bridge can span the different orders of truth. The condition of the Christian philosopher can only be clearly defined if the entirely formal unity of the notion of truth has been previously disrupted and if the philosopher refuses of his own accord to enclose himself in a system of truths with regard to which revealed truth could present no demand. In so far as philosophy, breaking with the old tradition of philosophy constituting itself in the absolute and the eternal, consents to this refusal—and such is the philosopher's special act of faith—a fruitful dialogue can begin between philosophy and theology.

It remains to be ascertained whether, in the philosopher's work itself, there does not lie an intrinsic requirement radically opposed to our present formulation.

Chapter III

METAPHYSICAL EXPERIENCE AND CHRISTIAN
DOGMATICS

WE have discarded, as a matter of principle, the attempt to conceive between metaphysics and Christian dogmatics such a relationship as would suggest the wholeness of a pattern made up of metaphysical truths and revealed truths, without any discontinuity. Certainly, we have not rejected philosophy wherever objective truths are concerned, for it too presents us with existential truths in the form of values. But we did establish that the existentiality in question is not of the same type as that shown in the gospel. Our demonstration, however, is only valid on the basis of Revelation. In fact, philosophy all too often ignores the existence of any form of truth different from that which it studies, and when it does recognize such truth it claims to reach it by other means. We propose, therefore, to deal with the notion of philosophy as metaphysics, as the knowledge of being *qua* being. We must first of all describe the metaphysical experience in its essential structure, and consider what significance Christian dogmatics can attribute to this attempt. For the various metaphysical systems impart a positive teaching about God. Of course, we may suppose that this God is a value, or an entity, more than a person.[1] But the theologian must not stop at presumptions; he must examine the metaphysician's concrete processes and see what god it is that they lead to. For the theologian can never boast of possessing the fullest and the most complete idea of God, which would enable him *a priori* to brand as insufficient the ideas reached by systems other than his. Strictly speaking, he does not possess any idea of God. The essence of his function consists in reflecting upon the knowledge of God, in which God always keeps the initiative, both revealing and concealing Himself.

To what extent these philosophies speak of God, and to what

[1] There are, in fact, few personalistic ontologies, and few are the philosophers who have dealt with the problem of the personality of God—except in controversies with theologians.

extent the God of the philosopher is still an idol, can only be established *a posteriori*. True, it is difficult to discover the structure of metaphysical experience, because the different metaphysics are so varied. Ultimately, however, metaphysics can engage upon two paths only: that of describing human experience, and that of reasoning. For it can either search within immanency for transcendent elements actually inherent in it; or it can try to grasp a transcendent reality, starting from a rigorously immanent experience, by way of dialectical construction. In effect, we shall be led in the course of this inquiry to recognize that metaphysics actually has been capable of reaching the divine, that the supernatural does not constitute for it a forbidden domain, and that in a certain sense it can legitimately speak about God. We shall be led to recognize that there subsists for sinful humanity a grace common to all which, even outside the Biblical Revelation, allows men to know the existence of God, without, however, being able to find in this knowledge the elements of a genuine theology. We shall endeavour to show that the so-called natural theology pertains entirely to metaphysics and in no way to theology proper. It will thus be ascertained that, even though metaphysics and Christian dogmatics both deal with the subject of God, and in a certain sense the same God (as suggested by Rom. 1.20), yet metaphysics cannot serve as a prolegomena, a preliminary basis or a foundation for Christian dogmatics. That is a paradox that Christian thought itself has found it hard to assimilate.

One cannot evaluate soundly the structure of metaphysical experience until one makes a clean slate of certain idealistic prejudices in the name of which metaphysical experience is strictly limited to the domain of immanency: according to these, the subject of the experience can only discover himself and will never encounter an object in the proper sense of the term. The primacy granted to the *Cogito* in one of the most important philosophical traditions in the West, and the difficulties idealism has encountered in trying to pass from the *Cogito* to the *Cogitatum* have lead metaphysics and the theory of knowledge in a troublesome direction: it would seem that psychical monism becomes unavoidable, and from then on one can no longer think (to the great joy, perhaps, of some naïve theologians) in terms of discovering within human experience a transcendent reality, and of passing from religious aspirations and mystical experiences to the object at which they are aimed. Héring has justly summed up these difficulties where philosophy is in danger of secluding itself, in the following quotation from E. Schaeder's *Religion und Vernunft* (1917, p. 60): "Never will the psychological life lead to any conclusions qualified to in-influence decisions on any aspect of religious truth. This im-possibility is implied in the elementary fact that psychological research, though it may grasp the ultimate depths of the soul or the innermost springs of its activity, can never succeed in reaching beyond the confines of the soul. It will never attain the absolute, the divine. It is totally anthropocentric."[1] Those dogmaticians who, like Henri Bois, proposed to base their doctrine upon religious experience, have not failed to realize this difficulty which, in fact, has remained for them an insur-mountable one.[2] Given psychical monism, it would appear that the soul, in the multiplicity of movements by which it contracts and dilates, can only encounter itself, its own de-mands, aspirations, and limitations. Man, therefore, will meet with extraordinary difficulties in asserting the existence of an objective reality and in pronouncing himself upon a truth which is not innate.

But if, as it pursued the effort towards inwardness indicated by the *Cogito*, philosophy appeared impelled by an irresistible movement, we must recognize that it had in fact, as Husserl was to point out, misrepresented the essential meaning of the *Cogito*. By discovering the intentionality of consciousness, phenomenology was able to restore to the *Cogito* its full mean-ing. The deepest characteristic of consciousness is not, as classical analysis let us suppose, that it has an inside and an outside which lend balance to each other and sometimes come into conflict; its deepest characteristic is to be intentional, i.e. always directed towards a content different from it which, in a certain sense, transcends it. Consciousness would be nothing and could not even be defined without this orientation towards an object, this impulse away from itself and towards something outside itself. Undoubtedly, consciousness does manifest its radical subjectivity by the manner in which it is directed towards objects: intentionality is not of a uniform type, it is

[1] J. Héring, *Phénoménologie et philosophie religieuse*, p. 29.
[2] See the very curious text by Henri Bois (*La valeur de l'expérience religieuse*, pp. 41-42) referred to by J. Héring, *ibid.*, p. 128.

not the same in the case of judgement, hesitation, or desire. Always, however, consciousness implies the transcendent heterogeneity of the object towards which it is directed. "The word, intentionality, means nothing else but this fundamental and general peculiarity of consciousness to be conscious of something, to carry in itself *qua Cogito* its own *Cogitatum*."[1] Phenomenological analysis, or rather reduction, also makes conspicuous the existence of different subjects which aim at different types of objects; it is necessary to realize that phenomenology does not emphasize solely the fact that consciousness is directed towards an empirical object; it does not merely establish the correspondence between consciousness and physical reality, so difficult to reach in Cartesian idealism. On the psychological intentionality by virtue of which a subject turns towards objects, a transcendental intentionality is superimposed whereby a transcendental subject thinks "the World" in its totality and unity. Moreover, involved and incomplete as Husserl's thinking on this point may be, it makes us foresee the existence of a third form of intentionality called "constituent intentionality".

Above the transcendental "*I*" there is the " 'act' of a deeper '*I*' of a spectator who, without participating in the cognition of the world, witnesses the world present itself to the transcendental subject".[2] We can only note these perspectives here to make it clear that psychic monism must not be regarded as the fatal slope followed by philosophy as soon as it abandons naïve realism; but that philosophy has resources enabling it to re-establish over and against the subject, in correlation with the subject, and in a certain manner as an implication of the subject's activity, the presence of solid objects transcending subjectivity and constituting a real "Non-I". The object need not be constructed by the subject; it is a datum from the first. "A perception as well as a representation which would not be the perception or representation of *an object* (not immanent to the act itself); a cognition or a judgement which would not deal with *the fact* that A is B; a wish or blame deprived of any orientation towards an event, determined or not, would not only be incomplete but also devoid of meaning."[3]

[1] E. Husserl, *Meditations on Descartes* (French translation, p. 28).
[2] G. Berger, *Le Cogito dans la philosophie de Husserl*, pp. 47-48.
[3] J. Héring, *Phénoménoloige et philosophie religieuse*, p. 61.

The attempt to dilate human experience to the extent of discovering in it a transcendent reality which is also the object actually aimed at does not therefore appear as a contradictory undertaking. The dilemma into which psychologism and sociologism had for a long time presumed to shut philosophy is discarded. Berger makes this fact very clear when he writes: "The crucial problem of idealism: how to go beyond the individual consciousness, does not exist for phenomenology. One is never *confined* within consciousness and as though cut off from a mysterious transcendency, because the characteristic of consciousness is to be concerned with something outside itself. The first truth is not, therefore, *I think, therefore I am*, but *Ego-Cogito-Cogitatum*."[1] Because of this the theologian loses the right, seemingly conferred upon him by Kantian idealism, of simply discarding as non-receivable philosophy's pretension to speak the language of objectivity, ontology, and the absolute. The theologian is compelled to take seriously the ontological claims of philosophy and to qualify the supernatural alleged by philosophy in relation to Christian dogmatics. We say qualify, because one cannot limit oneself to the simple opposition of Pascal's *Memorial*: "The God of Abraham, the God of Isaac, the God of Jacob, not the God of the philosophers and of the scholars." It is important, therefore, to determine the real dimensions of metaphysical experience, in order to avoid arbitrarily restricting its scope, as certain theologians felt compelled to do in the name of a Kantian theory of knowledge[2] which, by doing away with intellectual intuition, necessarily lowers human experience to the point of identifying it with sense experience. Now the latter appears to us to be merely for the spiritual life of man, a sign to remind him that any solid knowledge proceeds from an immediacy, a contact or a shock encounter between the subject and the object. Thus, it does not only possess, e.g., utilitarian value; its irreducibility leads us to distrust anything that is artificially constructed or any discursive procedures leading to the creation of a universe of discourse. Thus, sense experience assumes an essentially symbolic value. But it in no way represents a measure of all the dimensions of human experience. The multiplicity of sensible experiences will immediately make us aware of an

---

[1] G. Berger, *ibid.*, pp. 136, 137.
[2] Cf. Karl Barth, *Word of God, Word of Man* (French translation, p. 180).

entirely new dimension: for their diversity could not be experienced were they judged to be equivalent. "To every sense datum there is attached a feeling, half retrospective and half prospective, which makes it appear solid or without consistency, profound or superficial, real or illusory."[1]

At every moment the given (that which is there), even in its sensible form, must be experienced as supplying our mind either with an opportune spring-board for its conquests, simply with the conditions of action, or, on the contrary, with an obstacle or with a limitation. Data would never really be data to our mind if they were not thus placed in an axiological perspective. It can be asserted that there are no such things as raw data. This is a truth that empiricism has found it hard to dissolve by means of a fallacious analysis. Thus, experience again and again offers itself to us as already affected by some *a priori* sign. This sign is not foreign to experience, for without it experience would not exist; it would lose all its flavour which is bound up with its degree of solidity, coherence, richness or fecundity. An experience, even a sensible experience, which could not be said to be more or less true, more or less useful, more or less disappointing, would ultimately tend to be confused with nothingness itself. The *a priori* and the absolute are thus implied even in the most rudimentary experience. Of course, these are not always discovered in experience; but their discovery in a clear and distinct form, or at the very least a foreboding of them, also represent degrees or dimensions of our experience. It is always by way of test or intuition that we shall be led to discern them. What we have just said about the *a priori* also applies to value. Doubtless the datum, in so far as it is limited and determined, offers itself to us at first as a negation of value, whence the current temptation to banish value from the realm of experience and to relegate it to the world of imagination; but could value thus be opposed to the datum if it were not suggested by it? Limitation only has meaning because it conceals the unlimited from us, while at the same time it gives us a presentiment of it. Value can only be known through the experience of a lack, an insufficiency or a defeat. The obstacle, which is, as LeSenne has rightly emphasized, the term antithetical to value, can only exist for him who is capable of experiencing the value which the obstacle prevents

[1] R. LeSenne, *Obstacle et valeur*, p. 13.

him from reaching. There can be, therefore, no experience of any obstacle which does not conceal in itself some experience—perhaps neglected, perhaps unexploited—but nevertheless real, of value. It is because the consciousness, disappointed, applies itself to the irreducible character of the obstacle that it is prone to leave unnoticed the objective experience of the value which it has just made, and made in a decisive manner. The poorest of orders still involves value, for even such an order, whether it concerns our ideas or things, could not constitute itself unless it were inscribed in a system of reference which in turn opens fan-wise into the realm of values. Arbitrary or determined as it may appear, the price-scale can justify itself, that is, manifest its own truth, only if it bears some relationship to the intentional attitudes of a consciousness aiming at values and endeavouring to use objects as the means of access to a life conformed to value; the price of bread is legitimate only if it enables every-one to live, i.e. to combine all the conditions indispensable to his spiritual growth. Every human attitude, every choice discloses an indefinite number of choices which condition one another. "When by each of our acts we acknowledge value, which ceaselessly invites us to thrust open the frontiers of our experience, we imply that human experience is but a narrowly limited section of universal experience; and that positivism is not justified in limiting the scope of any real experience to the postulates of perception and science."[1]

Let us again carefully note that our analysis is no longer moving in a universe of mere wish or mere sentimentality, in which the theologian would have the right of considering this dilated conception of experience as a subjective fancy and could oppose to it the objectivity of Revelation. In this expansion of its experience through being directed toward values, the consciousness obeys more than it creates; it obeys an appeal which transcends it. It is not free to move in a universe where everything is indifferent, orders and hierarchies arise at random, where one is not *compelled* to choose. In its inner distresses as well as its joys, it is necessarily referred to a conflict, or, on the contrary, to a happy concurrence of objective values. Here, the intentional analysis of consciousness really manifests its full solidity. Scheler has warned us with assurance:[2] though the

[1] R. LeSenne, *ibid.*, p. 221.
[2] Scheler, *Der Formalismus in der Ethik*, 2nd part, pp. 120, 122-123.

knowledge of values is unavoidably an emotional knowledge,
the structure of emotion remains quite different from that of
values. "Let us not confuse them with what is commonly called
a *feeling*. The latter, in so far as it is not completely foreign to
this realm, constitutes the subject's reaction in relation to a
perceived value. Thus, the joy which a beautiful picture
arouses in me presupposes an emotive perception of beauty.
This perception is ranked among acts which take cognizance of
a datum, i.e. among intentional cognitive acts (*Kenntnisnah-
men*), whereas the joy itself implies the soul's response to an
appeal that stems from the value (*Stellungsnahme*, resp.
Antwortreaktion). Once this distinction is made, it is easy to
see where axiological sentimentalism is right and where it is
wrong, if only it interpreted well its deep, but confused,
intuitions."[1]

This transcending, which occurs within experience itself
and does not require us to leave the realm of experience but
merely explores its extent, will perhaps be understood more
clearly if we reflect upon the discovery of a-temporal or eternal
reality.

The point of departure of this discovery has always been the
temporal, and therefore sensible, experience, to which Kant
had presumed to limit consciousness. For it is sufficient fully to
live the experience of time in order to realize that it drives us
out of time, or, at least, that it only subsists in the presence of an
eternity which negates it. The experience of time cannot be
merely the experience of a pure flowing away, a sliding, a continuous fusion of elements; it assumes this form in moments of
relaxation, or at times when consciousness, by a sort of magic,
endeavours to forget a form of temporal experience which is at
least as decisive: the experience of a discontinuity, or an
unceasing breaking-off of time. For we are not content to
experience the beautiful continuity of the past and to anticipate
a future which we endow in advance with the same continuity;
and rightly so, since in its turn it will become the past. In this
contemplative meditation we are interrupted by the advent of
the present. There comes a moment—and it is perhaps unique
—when the desired and anticipated object arises before us; it
is given to us, the instant of possession has arrived. The oscilla-
tion of consciousness between a past and a future of which it is

---

[1] J. Héring, *Phénoménologie et philosophie religieuse*, p. 95.

equally dispossessed comes to an end. Something (whatever its nature may be) has really *become* present for consciousness, and mingling with its present existence has become for it a subject or object for action, an occasion for appropriation; that is why we speak of the advent of the present. Any event is, by definition, present. But the event only draws its reality and distinguishes itself from the thing by the advent which brings it into being— that is, in the last analysis, through this inroad the present makes into our experience. Thus our experience of time is essentially that of the expectation of an event. Outside of this fundamental experience, our life would only be boredom and idleness. A time ever continuous would be empty time. The knowledge of the present consists essentially in a break, along with the irruption into the normal flow of our experience, of a completely new reality offering itself to our possession. More-over, this reality is necessarily heterogeneous with respect to the former content of our life; and, although it is not without relationship to our past, and can even be considered from a utilitarian point of view as an outgrowth of our past, or as its fruit, it cannot in a strict sense be considered as its effect. The past does not beget the present; from the non-actual, the actual cannot arise. On the contrary, it is the past which appears as a storehouse of the present; the continuity of time is mysteriously created from these ruptures, from these successive advents of the present; the past is the oblivion of what was radically new, radically other in the present, of this opening of experience which occurred at the moment when a reality became existen-tially present for the consciousness. To apply causation and determinism to events (we do not say to objects which, by definition, are outside of time) is to disregard both the funda-mental nature of the present in which the event alone is given, and the ontological priority of the present over the past. Hence the first conclusion: our experience of time is not one of con-tinuity or homogeneousness, but an experience which, thanks to the present, constantly opens itself towards the *wholly other*, the indeterminate, the novel.

This present indeed appears, moreover, to have characteris-tics which make it a non-temporal reality, precisely because it is the contrary of a flowing away. When we say that the present is an instant, that it is the meeting-point of the dying past and the future about to be born, do we not renounce defining it in terms of duration? Does it not contain an invitation to define it in terms of eternity? How could we think of eternity otherwise than through the combined notions of the fullness of possession and the fullness of certainty? Now, the present does offer us this double possibility: the possibility of possessing both our-selves and the objects, whence results the possibility of action, and on the other hand the possibility of certainty, as witnessed to by any doctrine of intuition: truth can only be known intuitively, i.e. in the instant. There occurs, then, in the present, a kind of contamination between time and eternity; time, which in its flowing appears as depossession, ageing, and which, as such, has always been characterized either as non-being (in the philosophies of Antiquity) or as a falling away from eternity (neo-Platonism, Plotinism), or at least as a dis-persion of being, finds itself, in the present, contaminated by eternity. It cannot be said that time thus leads to eternity, but at any rate it opens itself to it, it lets itself be penetrated by it. The desire, manifested by many philosophies, to cling to the present alone shows a very legitimate concern for eternity.[1] In our view, Cartesian philosophy has proved incapable of defining and maintaining a distinction between the temporal present and the eternal present; and such a confusion was indeed unavoidable. It is so in effect because of the contamination between time and eternity which occurs in the instant. Of course, we must not forget that the present is also contaminated by duration. No sooner has it revealed to us the flavour of eternal possession and perfect joy than already it fades away, leaving with us, however, the promise that it will be born again. It is precisely these disappearances and rebirths of the present which remind us that we have not yet left the temporal order, that in our experience eternity is prefigured or suggested, but can never be actually given. In other words, our experience can open up—that is, see its dimensions expand—without losing for this reason its limited character. The presence of the eternal within the temporal is thus an equivocal, contaminated, debat-able presence. Even the mystical ecstasy cannot claim to orient itself upon a metaphysical experience. In a certain sense, however, independently from its religious significance, the ecstasy at Ostia is a metaphysical experience:[2] it clearly bears witness to the indefinitely extensible character of human

---

[1] Cf. Jean Guitton, *Justification du temps*.   [2] St. Augustine, *Confessions*, X, 23.

experience, and permits every hope; and yet, in so far as we expect from it a definitive annihilation of our limitations, it clearly fails. The old scholastic principle, *finitum non est capax infinito*, only holds true to the extent that the word *capax* is taken in its most rigorous sense; but it does not account for human experience and its ability both to receive the infinite and reject it. It seems to us that when Barth writes, "Man may want certain things, yet not the Spirit",[1] he takes too easily for granted the Kantian—it might even be added, the positivistic —conception of human experience. St. Augustine appears to have infinitely better grasped the mysterious rhythm of human experience when, in his analysis of time, he discovers in it an alternation of extension and attention; if time left to itself is mere extension, and for this reason unseizable, and if it is not susceptible of any measurement, it is through attention that we grasp it again, that we measure it, and settle ourselves in the present. Man is ever ready to scatter himself in a becoming devoid of any meaning; capable also of concentrating within this process of becoming, in order to grasp again that which the becoming had appeared to negate. No doubt, our analysis in the preceding chapter warns us that the discovery of values does not *ipso facto* constitute a discovery of God, and thus that human experience cannot hope to avail itself too easily of the knowledge of God. It must be recognized, however, that even though God is neither exclusively nor essentially value, He is value among other things; value is implicit in Him, and God animates values.[2] In so far as values are not monopolized by us, in so far as we do not rigidly mould them after the patterns of those situations which were for us the occasion of their discovery, values can only refer us to a fuller, richer, less exclusive value, to a power which unifies values without sacrificing any of them in any way, which transforms into harmony and participation the discrepancies we cannot fail to experience in the universe of values. For it is precisely the assurance that such a power exists which gives us confidence in values and allows us to love

---

[1] *Word of God, Word of Man* (French translation, p. 180).

[2] "Wherever thought is capable of discussing with itself the reasons for belief in the existence of God, we find the assertion of an absolute truth to whose standard all particular beliefs must be referred. Such an assertion more or less confusedly implies the affirmation of God," J. Lagneau writes (*De l'existence de Dieu*). In slightly different terms, this is always the path followed by idealistic philosophy, and by the philosophy of values: God appears as the necessary condition for the hierarchy of truths and the edifice of values.

them as such. No experience of values can be sustained, or can avoid being solidified into the mere possession of sacred objects and taboos, if values are not brought together in a hierarchical harmony culminating in an ever-present infinity, in an ever-active presence: in short, in God Himself. Moreover, it is important to realize that God is not only, in such a case, as one would be tempted to believe, the chief value, i.e. the value crowning all others; in reality, there is in these particular values an abstraction and an imperfection which would prove deadly for them, were they oriented only towards a value which would remain abstract; for the system of values would then be identified with the system of ideas.

Values can only keep their originality inasmuch as they are capable of being actualized by a being. For values of an inferior type, it is enough to be open to an eventual actualization. But the chief value must be actualized by a being who will not sacrifice it in any way; otherwise this sovereign value would appear either as a chimera or as a mere requirement of logic. There exists, therefore, an actual bond between axiology and ontology, although this bond is not always indicated with precision, and the characteristics of value appear at first to exclude a transition towards being, for this transition risks being a sort of solidification of the value into a system of determinations. But this danger must not make us oblivious of the fact that no experience of value is possible unless we visualize the ultimate reason for the actuality of the value. Now, just as particular values can only be actualized by persons, the chief value can only be actualized by a person, who in the very act of actualization sacrifices nothing of the value.

In the last analysis, the expansion of our experience does not consist in discovering God in it, besides or among other objects of experience. For in our experience, expanded though it may be, in so far as it is determined, nothing presents itself that resembles God or value. But every moment of experience owes its significance to the value implicit in it, and values themselves owe their reality to the being who assumes and actualizes them and summons us to seek him, seizing the opportunity of the values he suggests to us. The experience of values leads us, not to postulate the existence of a God as a first principle, but to posit what LeSenne calls a "theandric relationship", a relationship whose unity is the very token of the seriousness of our knowledge of God (though we can never grasp God in His absoluteness, as classical ontology naïvely wishes it): "Without God, the I could have neither nature, nor existence, nor vocation. If God is reduced to the Absolute and all power of apprehending Him is denied the self, the self without truth or value is left to itself, given up to the contingency of phenomena; it is not and nothing is for it; for in the affirmation of any being, faith in a real principle is implied, a principle which not only possesses unity but is inherent in the positiveness of that which we grasp. If we counter the blow by denying the self, the absolute can no longer be called God, for our existence no longer verifies its creation. It is no longer either powerful or good."[1]

What the expansion of our experience allows us to do, therefore, is not so much to verify the Absolute as such, but to experience the truth of a theandric relationship upon which our own being depends. When the theoreticians of religious knowledge are compelled, in order to account for this knowledge, to presuppose the existence of an ontological bond subsisting between God and man in spite of the vicissitudes of human history and of the separation caused by sin,[2] they are, in fact, dealing with this theandric relationship which is implied in any experience of value. Yet the language of ontology can be very misleading here. The existence of a theandric relationship in no way presupposes that some part of man or of the human soul—let it be called reason, for the sake of clarity—has been spared in the Fall; that original sin ceases to be the sin of the whole human being. What makes us prefer the expression, "theandric relationship", to the expression, "ontological bond" is precisely that the latter presupposes the survival, in man, of an ontologically pure island, of an unalterable substance capable of an adequate knowledge of God. On the contrary, the experience of knowledge which we have described is no other than the effort accomplished by a subject who knows himself to be limited, to perceive, not some datum in his own experience, but something implied in experience and which can only be apprehended as an implication. It is therefore by no means necessary, in the hypothesis we are envisaging, that the subject forget his condition as a sinful creature and claim the ability to achieve direct

[1] R. LeSenne, *Obstacle et valeur*, p. 224.
[2] H. Leenhardt, *Connaissance religieuse et foi*.

cognition of God. When we maintain that philosophical experience can have metaphysical scope and can reach a certain knowledge of the true God, we do not go beyond the assertion of Scripture: "The true God has left witness of Himself in the world (Acts 14.13-17) where he does not fail to signify His presence through His work. It is due to a divine motion that men gropingly seek God (Acts 17.27). In certain ways, the invisible perfections of God are accessible to them (Rom 1.20). Even His will is obscurely made known to man in his conscience (Rom. 2.15)."[1] Heresy only begins the moment it is asserted that this knowledge of God (which we refuse to call natural, since it is not the knowledge of a natural object) is sufficient, and consequently saving, knowledge. We must feel all that is obscure and even impure in this knowledge. Pascal has warned us not to be deceived about the value of such knowledge: in it, man proves to be both capable of God and unworthy of Him: "It is then true that everything teaches man his condition, but he must understand this well. For it is not true that all reveals God, and it is not true that all conceals God. But it is at the same time true that He hides Himself from those who tempt Him, and that He reveals Himself to those who seek Him, because men are both unworthy and capable of God; unworthy by their corruption, capable by their original nature."[2]

By forcing us to discover that any cognition and any axiology imply a theandric relationship, philosophy dilates our experience. It opens our experience towards God, but this God is only "the wholly other". From the present, man knows only a reality quite different from his own, a reality which appears to him as the negation of his own limitations. This reality he can only describe by adding a negative prefix to his own qualities. The important factor in the theandric relationship remains undefined. This is, moreover, necessary, lest the experience of values become closed, lest it solidify into a conceptual system. But this undefined factor is only apprehended in its opposition to man; in a certain way it is a function of man. It is not independent of the theandric relationship of which man constitutes the first term. That is why the recognition of God as the "wholly other" is not, from the Christian point of view, a real knowledge

---

[1] F.-J. Leenhardt, *La foi évangélique*, p. 21.

[2] *Pensées*, Section VIII, No. 557 (translation by W. F. Trotter, Everyman's), p. 154.

of God. No doubt, the Bible stresses time and time again the otherness of God; but this otherness stems from the domination and the judgement that God exerts upon man and the nations; whereas the otherness to which we are here led is conceived and postulated on the basis of man and allows a certain continuity to subsist between the reality of man and the undefined reality of God: a continuity which is positively experienced in the theandric relationship. A Christian dogmatics which would claim to be content with defining God as the wholly other would be naïve, ready to be contaminated and absorbed by a philosophy of values or of the expansion of human experience.

An exact evaluation, however, of the meaning of this knowledge of God will only be possible when we examine the second manner in which philosophy has endeavoured to reach God. This second manner is that of dialectical construction. Through an effort of reasoning, the intellect attempts to determine the notion of God as possible, and then to demonstrate its necessity. The goal is to render the demonstration of the existence of God as certain as the demonstrations of mathematics. Descartes[1] even adds that this demonstration can be more certain yet than those of mathematics, meaning that the demonstration, as it deals with only a small number of elements, is not accompanied by any dispersion of the mind, and no longer carries with itself the risk of error involved in mathematical deduction, because of the intervention of memory. The real proofs of the existence of God, then, will be those excluding any contingency; they will never be inductive; the cosmological proofs, appealing as they do to the principle of causation, are notoriously insufficient because the cause-effect relationship they establish between the Creator and creation does not possess undebatable necessity. It is, therefore, in thought itself, in the conditions of its exercise, that we must endeavour to find the true proof of the existence of God. It is not by mere chance that in Descartes's philosophy the proofs follow the *Cogito*, whereas ontologically they are prior to it, and that the *Cogito* only assumes its full meaning in the light of the existence of God; it was first of all necessary that the ground upon which the demonstration is to be carried out be solidly established. And this ground is that of thought conceived as the locus of necessity. Philosophers have emphasized with the utmost firmness the bond which unites

---

[1] *Discourse on Method*, 2nd part.

the *Cogito* to the existence of God; nay, even those whose foremost concern it was to avoid limiting themselves to the plane
of pure logic, and to conceive a kind of necessity more spiritual
than logical: "The real moral proof is a proof resulting from
the reflection of thought upon itself in its effort to comprehend
itself, the necessities it obeys when attempting to demonstrate
the existence of God, and the obstacles which it is unable to
overcome in this demonstration. The problem is to find God, in
thought itself, in the very impossibility to prove His existence
apart from thought; but let this impossibility be viewed together
with the moral obligation for thought to assert something more
than that the necessity of which it can understand. This proof
which we are seeking is both a moral and a metaphysical one;
by this, I mean the proof whereby thought rises absolutely
above all nature, even its own, and finds the supernatural in the
very impossibility of remaining content with affirming nature."[1]
No doubt, this reflective method carries us farther than
Descartes had envisaged:[2] we are no longer upon the plane of
mathematical demonstration or that of syllogistic demonstration. Here, the rational connection reaches a new depth; the
necessity at stake is one which is not only logically proved, but
which also appears to us as ethically and metaphysically legitimate, since it saves the very existence of thought and guarantees the jurisdiction of spirit over nature. In other words, the
existence of God must be conceived of as bringing about the
synthesis of necessary being and the being that ought to be.
God cannot be pure necessity, for then He would be confused
with some monstrous fate. As Lagneau emphasizes, we cannot
think of establishing the being of God—that is, His necessity.
"What thought requires in order to declare itself satisfied is an
absolute necessity; but this idea of an absolute necessity is
contradictory, for an absolute necessity would be a necessity de-
pending upon nothing, and consequently would subsist independently from thought and would therefore impose itself upon
thought and annihilate it; thought cannot, therefore, seek a
necessity which would not depend upon anything."[3]

We still must find its justifying reason. Here the rational
explanation is supported by a spiritual justification. It is all
the more interesting to find that here too mind starts from its
own existence, from the *Cogito* through which it has perceived

---

[1] J. Lagneau, *De l'existence de Dieu*, p. 44.   [2] *Ibid.*, pp. 44-51.   [3] *Ibid.*, p. 49.

its own spiritual nature. This finding is not without importance: it warns us that the dialectical effort by which philosophy endeavours to ascertain the existence of God is an attempt similar in nature to that which we have examined under the name of "expansion of human experience"; it is but the extension of this attempt. But it has the particular characteristic of objectifying the discovery of God by submitting it to rational verification; of being supported by logic in spite of being translogical; and therefore of not being content with suggesting to man experiences to be made, deepened, or signified. It sets out to convince man, even if he be unwilling. In short, this attempt intends to prove, whereas the discovery of the undefined limits of our experience had no other aim than to arouse in us the indefinitely encouraged hope of a personal test of the supernatural and the absolute. It is precisely this intention which leads the philosophical dialectic of God no longer to regard God merely as "the wholly other", but to define Him with precision, to give some definiteness to the concept of God, and to determine, through an operation not unrelated to the proof itself, the main attributes of God. We have passed from a philosophy of values to a philosophy of objectivity. The atheist is aimed at directly; he must be confronted with the logically necessary fact of the existence of God, so that he can escape only at the cost of an inconsistency. He is summoned to be reasonable and for this purpose to recognize the existence of God.'[1]

However—and here the non-mathematical character of the whole operation appears—in order to administer a proof of the existence of God, it is not enough to start from objective knowledge, constituting a sort of premise for the demonstration; there is no question of founding the reasoning upon a universally valid and previously admitted proposition. On the contrary, it is necessary, whether we are dealing with the ontological proof or with the proof by the idea of perfection, that the mind should first of all discover in itself, at the cost of an intellectual self-abstraction which can be difficult, the starting-point of this reasoning. This point of departure is not, in fact, an idea which

[1] Let us point out, to ward off any ambiguity, that what we are describing here is the demonstration of the existence of God in pure form, objective philosophy at its limit. A thought such as Lagneau's, to which we have alluded, should find its place between the philosophy of values proper and objective philosophy; whereas classical rationalism, in a philosophy such as that of Leibniz, even more so than in Descartes's philosophy, goes to the very end of objective philosophy: God is demonstrated, not only in His existence, but in the *possibility* of His existence.

can be made perfectly objective; whether we deal with the idea of the infinite, that of the perfect or even that of being, their extension as well as their comprehension cannot be defined with perfect rigour; for, as Descartes well perceived, though he did not derive from it the obvious consequences, we are in the presence of an intelligible which is not at the same time comprehensible. Language itself is often incapable of supplying the concept with anything beyond a negative expression, which sometimes leads one to suppose that the notion of the infinite has no real content and merely represents for the mind a hazardous transition towards its own limitations. That is why the positivity of the idea of infinite, or of being, conceived as the fullness of being and not as bare and indeterminate existence, is at first contested by the mind anxious to discover to what sort of experience such an idea can correspond in the intellectual, or even spiritual and moral order. From this, a confusion often results between the infinite and the indefinite, which only represents a provisional infinite that will re-enter the limits of the finite as soon as we find the instrument or the point of view enabling us to measure and determine it. Some inner controversy is always required in order that the peculiar reality of the infinite may be grasped. It seems to us, precisely, that the mind will always contest this reality until it has found its landmarks in all the dimensions of its experience.

Descartes wisely warns us that innate ideas may very well be in us without our noticing them, for lack of attention. But this reason is not sufficient; it is not so much attention that must be accused, but its orientation, or possibly the *intention* of the attentive consciousness. Until attention has become both critical and reflective, and as long as it concentrates upon data and the logical conditions of their existence rather than upon data and the actual implications of their intelligibility, it runs the risk of never becoming aware of this notion of being or perfection. In short, we find ourselves in the presence of a value rather than an idea. Although the system of ideas can only be maintained through the values upon which it opens, and although in spite of its systematic character it is by no means closed, it is a fact that attentiveness to ideas and attentiveness to values represent two opposite orientations of consciousness. The idea of the infinite is not to be found in the form of an idea actually capable of immediate application; yet the mind must realize that every one of its operations and every one of its evaluations has no meaning apart from the reality of the perfect and the infinite and finds its sole effective justification therein. Any act whereby we aim at producing an improvement, any thought in which we make a value judgement, i.e. by which we insert a being or an object into a hierarchy, are condemned to sinking into inanity or verbosity unless the mind keeps within sight the foundation of all progress as well as of all hierarchies: namely, the infinite or the perfect. For a hierarchy cannot be suspended in a vacuum, unless it is merely the result of a social convention; it must communicate with all the hierarchies and must gradually lead to the infinite. The most humble value is devoid of meaning unless a relationship can be traced from it through the scale of values up to the most exalted one. Thus, the infinite and the perfect are immanent in all acts of thought; to think is to judge, but to judge is to perceive a determination within the infinite and the perfect, and to grasp less and less dimly the participation of this determination in the infinite. It could even be said that the progress of thought consists essentially in establishing with clarity the mode of participation of a determination in the infinite. That is why any system of thought is crowned by judgements of value or judgements affirming being in the full sense of the word. Any determination is thus carved out in the infinite. The infinite can, therefore, only pre-exist it. But the meaning of this pre-existence must be agreed upon; it is not a matter of purely logical pre-existence; the infinite is not a condition prior to the determination, and with which thought could cease to be concerned when setting the determination; the infinite is an actual implication of the determination. Whereas we can fully think of an object independently from the logical conditions of its existence (which occurs every time we think of the physical world without thinking of the principle of conservation of mass), we cannot think of it in a concrete manner if we abstract it from its actual signification, which is supplied to us by its actual implications: I should not really be thinking of the value of a thing if I did not subordinate it to other values. To grasp that the same dialectic is required for the discovery of the idea of *being*, it suffices to remark that being also is value. It is not ready-made reality, but gradually comes to light as phenomena and appearances vanish. It is that of which phenomena partake when they acquire solidity. It is of practical importance to us to be able to appraise the degree of solidity of the phenomena upon which we act or which regulate our action: that is why the idea of being must constantly be present in our minds and immanent in our actions. The internal logic of scepticism drives it to suspend all judgements and leads it to renunciation in the order of thought as well as in the order of action. Why? Because the sceptic, due to an insufficient analysis of his own experience, does not perceive in it the actual implications of being. This, on the contrary, shows that the idea of being is involved in every moment of our spiritual life. In the last analysis, we can see that the demonstration of the existence of God can only be effected on the basis of concepts the reality of which must first of all be discovered and tested by an expansion of our experience. The demonstration of the existence of God is therefore not objective in the mathematician's sense. By the same token we are also in a position to assert that the paths upon which philosophy engages in order to become metaphysics have real unity.

Once these ideas of infinite, perfect and being are discovered, and their objectivity tested, the demonstration proper can begin. That is when it assumes the character of a deduction founded solely upon logical necessity. No longer is anything required of the mind save the refusal of contradiction. It is in no way our design to examine the mechanisms of these proofs. Suffice it to say, although certain forms of deduction appear, as in Descartes's proof by the idea of perfection, to imply over and above the deduction proper a theory of the nature of the idea (the distinction between objective reality, formal reality, the eminent reality of the idea, the relationship of causation between these various realities), the mechanism of the proof is independent from this technical apparatus and can subsist under different apparatuses. The proof by the idea of perfection is no less rigorous in the *Discourse on Method* than in the *Meditations*; yet it is infinitely more simple in the former. One cannot detect in the demonstration any logical error, any contradiction, any *petitio principii*. Those who contradict Descartes usually make their criticisms bear, not upon the rational connection itself, but upon the spiritual necessity which leads to the determining of the point of departure of the idea of perfection or the idea of being. But we believe we have already replied to these critics by showing that indeed these notions do not impose themselves in the same way as the notions of determinism, but presuppose a deeper examination of the dimensions of our experience or of its actual implications. We feel strongly that the rigorous character of these proofs should be admitted, and that one should not hasten to proclaim upon this point the infirmity of reason, reputed incapable of committing anything but paralogisms as soon as it leaves the limits of sense experience. Kantianism, in its secret desire to substitute belief for reason, has doubtlessly taken the easy way out.

To appreciate sensibly the real scope of the proofs of the existence of God, it is rather to Pascal that we should turn. He does not contest their character as proofs, the rigour of their logical sequences; but he denounces their inability to convince and their incapacity, brought out by the facts, to convert men to God. It appears that in connection with the proofs of the existence of God we see verified in experience that which Paul declared about the pagans, to whom the invisible perfections of God were revealed in creation, who knew God in His majesty, but were incapable of serving and worshipping Him as God. "Powerless proofs", says Pascal in a striking combination of words. We must first of all grasp the inability of reasoning to beget certainty. We are deceived by the mental process which we believe we observe in mathematics; we imagine that in the process of reasoning certainty grows and follows the same ascending progression as the reasoning itself. In reality, this is only possible because the certainty pre-exists in the reasoning. We know in advance that the technique we follow in reasoning is perfectly adequate to the realities with which we deal, that it has a hold upon them, and that, unless our attention slackens, it inexorably leads us towards the expected result. There exists a mathematical certainty which is prior to the operations which manifest it; it is no doubt that certainty which gripped Descartes upon the famous night when he saw, as in an illumination, the universality of the mathematical method. Every operation is but an opportunity of verifying the soundness of our certainty—a kind of witness we bear to our own certainty. As to the certainty that we acquire with respect to a given truth which we have just established by means of demonstration, it would not subsist for a single moment without that fundamental certainty which is of an intuitive order: the discovery of the fruitfulness of the mathematical approach. As to reasoning, it does not bear upon ideas themselves, upon the objects of intuition. It is the locus of the intellect, and, as Hauter emphasizes, the intellect never establishes contacts between ideas and the self but only between ideas; it is indifferent to ideas as such; if the logical sequence is clearly established, the intellect is fully satisfied. Now certainty consists, less in the relationships between ideas, than in their relationship to the self. Certainty arises when an idea becomes isolated and is taken out of the sequence in which it is found in order to be brought into a determining relation with the self. The absoluteness of an idea lies in this isolation, by virtue of which it presents itself to consciousness, as a single datum. Consequently, no reasoning will ever lead to a certainty; the process of elaboration of a certainty takes place on a different plane. A certainty, then, will never deserve the title of objective; it is subjective because it consists in a specific relationship established between the idea and the self, a relationship which cancels out or tends to cancel out any distance between the self and the idea. Of course, this subjectivity must not be confused with arbitrariness.[1]

Thus, it is not technical perfection of the demonstration that we must seek in the proof of God's existence. Technical perfection certainly allows us to account for our certainty, and it is indispensable in view of the social dialectic which builds itself up around the proofs of God; yet it does not provide the grounds for certainty. On the contrary, one is almost tempted to say that it is a sign, an attestation of certainty. In the order of certainty—and this is our most decisive inheritance from Cartesianism—nothing can replace the compelling clarity of intuition; it is in the intuitive contact with truth, when by a kind of grace the mind finds itself in the presence of the true, that certainty can arise. That is why it has been remarked that the proofs of the existence of God will only have compelling power upon those minds in which the certainty of God already exists; this would also explain the fact that, in spite of their convincing character, the proofs do not convince. Thus, their character as "powerless proofs" becomes confirmed. It may be objected that, though the demonstration in its own right be incapable of producing certainty (in the sense in which producing

---

[1] Ch. Hauter, unpublished course in dogmatics, given at the University of Strasbourg.

is causing to be born, calling into existence), it can nevertheless enclose the mind in a system of necessities so strongly
connected that this state of compulsion will correspond for all
practical purposes to a certainty: I have no absolute certainty
with regard to the existence of a given historical person who
has no meaning for my life; yet the historian builds up for my
benefit an edifice of proofs which prevent me from doubting.
In the absence of real certainty, cannot the proofs of God's
existence at least keep me from doubting? There is no doubt
that because of their very perfection they constitute for our
reason a permanent source of anxiety; no longer can reason
behave as if these proofs were null and void, or as though they
were refuted or refutable. Although they may not convince us,
they make it inexcusable for us to decide to live, in spite of
them, in indifference and atheism. They take away from any
serious atheist the good conscience with which scientific
materialism, for instance, vainly attempts to endow him.
"There is sufficient clearness to enlighten the elect, and sufficient obscurity to humble them. There is sufficient obscurity
to blind the reprobate, and sufficient clearness to condemn
them and make them inexcusable."[1] Such is the ambiguous
light which streams from the proofs of the existence of God;
the believer admires the fact that in them reason can express
something of his faith; the unbeliever becomes exasperated in
the face of reason's inability to condemn or confirm the attitude
he has chosen.

But we must go further: what is the worth of the mind's
intention in its attempt to establish the proofs? What does it
mean: to wish to prove God? Clearly, this consists essentially
in establishing, and, in a sense, in determining the *existence* of
God. Now it is this notion of existence which is not satisfactory
when it is a question of God. First of all, let us notice the
essentially poor character of the notion of existence. No doubt,
an existence is in some manner a victory of being, a regression
of non-being. That is why the judgement of existence is a first
judgement; but it is also, in every sense of the word, an elementary judgement. Of course, we suspect that existence in itself
conceals a promise of development, of fullness. But our expectation may be disappointed; it is possible that we are in the
presence of a bare existence, whose boundaries with unreality

---

[1] Pascal, *Pensées*, VIII, 577, translation by W. F. Trotter, p. 160.

F

and non-being are difficult to detect. Thus, when confronted with the existence of a man of infinitesimal human value, I say, in a well understandable paradox, "This man does not exist". Existence alone is not sufficient to qualify a being.

Wishing to emphasize Elpenor's insignificance, Homer is content with telling us that he died—that is, that he has existed. Thus, we feel free to use the verb, to exist, with respect to any kind of reality; we know that we are not going too far, that we are not compromising ourselves. Thus we say of a stone that it exists, of a man that he exists, of God that He exists. Can we seriously speak of the same kind of being? Are we not artificially maintaining a kind of ambiguity with regard to these various modes of existence, being unwilling to distinguish among them? And yet, God cannot possibly exist in the manner of a stone. In reality, thought endeavours to preserve underneath these utterly heterogeneous manners of existing a purely formal unity. Here we catch a glimpse of the deep arbitrariness which often characterizes human knowledge; it identifies that which does not admit of identification. It is really impossible to consider abstractly the existence of God; for one is immediately led to situate God among other existences, to make Him an object among other objects. Is not the great sin of the spirit, as Berdyaev has so often emphasized, the will to objectify? Any existence must be situated either in time or in eternity. But God cannot exist *in* time nor even, as it is naïvely believed, *in* eternity, for then there would be an eternity which could exist by itself apart from God. God does not live in eternity; He is the Eternal. Because we consider God as an existence and ultimately as an object, we attribute properties to Him, and among these properties we place first and foremost eternity— for to exist is, in the final analysis, to possess (and therefore to be capable of receiving) a certain number of properties. But Christian dogmatics reminds us that eternity is infinitely more than a property of God, more than a determination of His existence: it is His very essence; God coincides perfectly with it. In Him we discover the whole of eternity. God is unto Himself His own time or His own eternity. Hence the appropriateness of St. Augustine's statement: "*Non enim aliud anni Dei et ipse Deus, sed anni Dei aeternitas Dei est.*" What so profoundly separates Christian dogmatics from metaphysics is that the latter sets out first of all to grant an existence which it subsequently determines by adding attributes to it, while dogmatics knows that God's existence cannot receive determinations which are posterior to it. His is not, to begin with, an indeterminate existence, a formal existence, which could subsequently be enriched by being inserted into time or eternity; it is, from the first, an existence of a thoroughly unique type, it is *a priori* the existence of God. What we fear in the mind's attempt to establish the proofs of God is this metaphysical intention which consists in first granting an existence and afterwards in enriching it by way of conceptual analysis. The God of the Biblical Revelation is not, first and foremost, an existence; He is not at first nor essentially shown us as an existence. It is the object which is given to us in this manner. True, when we speak of knowledge it is difficult for us not to set up man as the sole subject and think that all he knows is necessarily an object.[1] That philosophy should begin with the problem of the existence of God is a revealing sign of its manner of proceeding; it means that it considers God, whether it wishes to or not, as an object. It is precisely against this spiritual attitude that the whole protest of "Biblical philosophy" is directed. Has not the entire spiritual and intellectual, theoretical and practical effort of the Reformation been to ascend against the stream of both scholarly and popular philosophy and to save the subjectivity, that is the primacy, of God? The characteristic of the object is first of all to exist, and by this very existence to oppose itself to us, i.e. to our subjectivity, as an obstacle, but also to offer our subjectivity a matter upon which to exert its power.

To try and know God as a simple existence—that is, as an object—will lead us to all the idolatries. One only knows God as such if He is for one, not an existence (it is remarkable to find that this problem vanishes completely in the believer's life) but a *presence*. The essential problem of Christian dogmatics is that of the presence of God. That is exactly what the reformers felt when they abandoned the problem which had not ceased to preoccupy the rationalist theologians of the Middle Ages: that of the existence of God. In so doing, these theologians acted as if God did not reveal Himself, as if the essential idea on which all religious knowledge is grounded were not that of the presence of God, that is, the *act of God making Himself*

---

[1] "Classical psychology has set up man as a subject and all that is not man becomes an object", writes H. Leenhardt (*Connaissance religieuse et foi*, p. 81).

existent for man. "One of the main consequences of this error is the attempt to prove or to refute philosophically the existence of God, as though God were a thing or an idea always to be reached, *because never absent*, and presenting itself in an immediate manner to the eye or to the mind.

"If the *Divine presence* possesses such importance, then it is impossible to define apart from it the basis, the starting-point or the nature of religious knowledge. As to *Christian theology*, one of its main tasks, if not the main one, will therefore consist in saying what, in this religion, is the particularity of the divine presence."[1]

The quest for the existence of God does not place us in a truly and fully religious atmosphere. To seek, essentially, to prove the existence of God is perhaps to make oneself incapable of finding God as such; for existence is not a quality essential to God's mode of being. In fact, existence can be the quality of someone absent.[2] The absent may have a full and whole existence; he nevertheless remains absent. Now, God in our life is first of all a *presence*. Scripture unceasingly reminds us that He is the ever-present One, He who, when encountering man, always speaks in the present, and always says to him: today. God is nothing if He is not, first of all, God-with-us, Emmanuel. It is surprising that remarks of such simplicity escaped the attention of the rationalistic theology of the Middle Ages. It is surprising, further, that rationalistic theology should have so much energy in demonstrating a property which is not necessary for characterizing God. Epicure's atheism was in no way founded upon a demonstration of the inexistence of the gods; the gods exist, but they live in inter-world spaces which they cannot leave; they cannot become presences-for-us. This justification of atheism is remarkable because it is effective. In order to propagate atheism, it is necessary to destroy God in that which constitutes Him essentially: His presence. The true propagators of atheism are not the scholars who strive on the intellectual plane, by means of dialectical argumentation or historical criticism to bring to light the inexistence of God, or

---

[1] Ch. Hauter, "La présence divine comme probleme de la dogmatique protestante", in *R.H.Ph.R.*, May-October, 1936, No. 3-5, p. 321.

[2] Gabriel Marcel writes in the same sense: "When I determine another person as 'him', I treat him as being essentially absent; it is his absence which allows me to objectivize him, to reason about him as about a given nature or essence. But there is a presence which remains the model of an absence. I can behave towards someone as though he were absent" (*Du Refus à l'Invocation*, p. 48).

even the impossibility of His existence; they are those who give rise in the heart of the faithful to the doubt: is your God really interested in you? Is He really present? That is indeed the argument used by all those who wished to turn Israel away from Jehovah; and inversely, the role of the prophets—this is perfectly perceptible, for instance, in Deutero-Isaiah—consisted essentially in showing Israel, through its history, the particularity of the Divine presence. The formula so frequently used at the beginning of prophecies and revelations, "Hear, O Israel, I am the Lord thy God", is not only a ritual phrase; it is the testimony of a living presence, of a God who both makes Himself present to us and brings us into His presence, who compels man to stop before Him, in a formidable confrontation, sometimes in a struggle, in a hand-to-hand fight which is the most striking expression of this encounter. Also, is not the meaning of the Incarnation, as well as that of the Eucharist and of the doctrine of the Holy Spirit to announce God's presence in the world, God's presence in history, and His eternal contemporaneity in relation to all men? The "God to Whom the heart is sensitive" is no other than the present God. That is why the Christian doctrine of the Incarnation differs so fundamentally in its meaning from many myths of incarnation with which the history of religions abundantly supplies us. Whereas the main concern of these myths is to show us some supernatural alchemy, some mingling of substances (for example, spirit and matter),[1] Christianity, which is as alien as possible to any kind of belief in magic, makes use of infinitely less gross notions, as it speaks to us only of God's real presence in the world.

The problem is not to try and explain the activity of God by means of concepts more or less borrowed from human processes: neither the doctrine of the Incarnation nor that of the Eucharist has such an intent. The point is only to bring man face to face with a God who was and who is actually present for us. As John's Gospel reminds us, He came "unto His own". The whole history of the Revelation is only a description of the world and of the particularity of God's presence in the world. The different eras which constitute that history represent different aspects of the presence of God. When we say that the

---

[1] Incidentally, the Catholic doctrine of the two natures lends itself to such an interpretation.

time which elapses between Pentecost and the Parousia is the time of the Holy Spirit, we mean that it is a period in which God attests His presence in the Church and in the world by means of the inner witness of the Holy Spirit. Thus, the idea of God's presence is indeed the only idea in which Christianity is interested.

From a philosophical point of view, moreover, we can attempt to grasp the reason for this: God, especially the God of the Biblical Revelation, is a person. Certainly, it is impossible for us to define or to understand the personality of God. But we can at least catch a glimpse of its meaning by analogy with the human person. A human person is a being who is able freely to become a presence for another, and who just as freely is capable of refusing himself. In any case, he possesses existence— but it is not in pure existence that the person manifests himself. This existence either eludes him, or he remains indifferent. Under normal circumstances, I am indifferent to the pure fact of my existence, but I keep a watchful eye upon my presence and the mode of my presence. I know that therein lies a truly inalienable wealth which constitutes my self in my deepest subjectivity. No one can compel my presence. No doubt, social authorities can assign me a time and place, require hours of attendance of me; but neither they nor I have any illusions as to the real nature of such a presence. Both they and I know very well that even though I may be compelled to be in attendance at a given place and time, I shall always be able to remove my presence. To be present is to be able to withdraw oneself. In spite of the material, psychological, and moral means at his disposal, the judge cannot force to presence the mind of an accused who has decided not to participate really in the trial and to consider the outcome of the trial as indifferent. The great conflict between the person and society, which to various degrees always harbours totalitarian designs, has its source precisely in the fact that society has a foreboding and a fear of this mysterious power every person possesses to take himself away, to refuse himself, to escape by the artifice of language, of disimulation, of day-dreaming, of distraction. Presence is indeed the mode of being of a person.

Presence can also be considered as the manner in which the person integrates himself into time; it is not without reason that the term "presence" conceals a temporal significance. To be present, for someone, is to enter with him into a relationship which defies the passing of time. For to be present is to refuse one's participation in this flowing away of time which, in the same manner as spatial separation, separates consciousnesses and gives them up to what is most particular and corruptible in their respective subjectivities. In order to signal my presence to someone, I must stop with him and rivet my eyes with him upon some value of eternal worth—I must cleave to the eternal which, because it is always offered, is always present. The act of being or rather of becoming present presupposes, therefore, an effort of freeing oneself from determinism, which drives us through the indefiniteness of duration, and from the resulting dislocation of personality. That is why the communion between persons who accept to be present to each other conveys a most vivid feeling of eternity; should death come, the communion thus established will not be destroyed.

Presence is therefore synonymous with freedom; where personal presence draws aside, blind and anonymous determinism immediately takes over. Many social and economic laws, though reputed unalterable and natural, are but signs of the absence of persons; similarly, when self-consciousness becomes less active, the person tends to vanish, giving way to an individuality governed by set reflexes and patterns of behaviour. There is no presence save that of a person. For the sign of the Person is the ability to give, or to refuse himself—therein lies the constitutive nucleus of personal freedom. Thus, we cannot contemplate demonstrating a presence. A presence does, or does not, impart itself and when it does, any demonstration becomes pointless. The presence of an *I* gives itself in perfect self-evidence. Of course, this self-evidence is not always obtained in an immediate way; it may be that the other person's *ego* intends merely to feign presence. Yet even so, he cannot screen himself away completely. But there will have to be a whole series of tests to verify whether his presence is without reserve, until, as occurs in the case of friendship and love, certainty becomes complete. It is necessary to understand well this basic difference between testing (precisely by means of proofs and verifications), and claiming to command a demonstration. In testing, he who tests only has to discover the attitude required of him in order that he may see and that truth may become for him an occasion of self-evidence and certainty; the point is that I should convert myself to the object in order that I may see it in its true light.

On the contrary, in demonstrating the problem is to obtain, and even to create, a new truth; demonstration bases itself upon simpler truths, then combines them according to pre-established rules. By opposing these two mental processes it will be immediately understood that the latter cannot be suitable when a presence is at stake; the demonstrating process can be carried out without my being actually involved in it. At the most, a certain degree of attention is required of me, but this degree may vary *ad infinitum*; at the limit it may be practically nil, as can be seen in certain mathematical operations, and as Leibniz thought at the time when he was engaged in trying to make real Lulle's dream: the thinking machine. And even though our attention were wholly required, as in certain new and complex reasonings extending to a great number of propositions, let us not think that attention *ipso facto* involves the presence of the subject as such. As I lend my attention to an object, I devote to it something of myself, but at the same time I withdraw myself. Only certain supreme forms of attention, among which Malebranche reckoned prayer, presuppose the total involvement and presence of the subject. But, in order to know the presence of another person, I must myself be present; I must offer myself to this presence which reveals itself to me. Those are right who say that there is no love but that is shared; love cannot exist without this subtle dialectic, which it is probably impossible to reconstitute afterwards, of the gift and the offer, of the anguished quest and the fervent response. There can be no other way of reaching another person so that two beings may become persons for each other and emerge from the anonymousness of the crowd, and so that in human relationships the "me" and the "he" may become superseded by the "I" and the "thou."[1]

The relationship between persons supplies us only with an analogy of the God-man relationship. Yet, we can conceive of no other ambition than to meet God personally. This is, in the last analysis, the reason which forbids us to seek in the proofs of God's existence a sufficient basis for our relationship with God. One cannot sacrifice the notions of God's presence and of

---

[1] The reader will find in the work of Martin Buber, *I and Thou*, a slightly dramatized yet correct explanation of this dialectic of the personal presence.

the personal character of God without immediately relapsing into the static ontology of the Greeks. There, God is thought of as being; He is, He exists; He is devoid of all mystery by virtue of His very motionlessness. On the contrary, the Biblical Revelation presents God to us as a presence and a person, which means that it shows Him to us in His mobility, in His freedom, with the successive acts which are the manifestation of His total autonomy; it signifies to us that God is in no way bound by the static laws of His creation.

Thus, the atheist is right when, though he cannot rid himself of the proofs, he refuses to declare himself satisfied by them. He is right when he demands to be brought face to face with the living God, and of the God who for him could be a person, that is, an indubitable presence. In the same sense, Gabriel Marcel writes, "I have always thought that the attributes of God such as they are defined by rational theology: simplicity, unalterability, etc. . . . only assume any value for us when we succeed in recognizing in them the characteristics of a 'Thou' we cannot treat as a 'he' without distorting its nature, without reducing it to our human and miserable measurements."[1] Let us acknowledge that, if reasoning could yield God to us, God would then precisely cease to be a Person. It is therefore the duty of Philosophy itself to understand that God *must* reveal Himself, that we *must* meet this God who reveals Himself to us in order that certainty may arise. Even in contemporary idealistic philosophy we may find, so to say, presentiments of this truth. At least, such is the feeling conveyed, for instance, by the religious philosophy of Lachelier, as it is expounded by Devivaise: "The order of the proofs corresponds . . . to a progress and an enrichment of the concept of God— with the ontological argument leading to a still very abstract Being, then the cosmological proof ushering us into the world of mechanism, the proof by finality into the fuller reality of life and spontaneity, and that by eternal truths and perfection making us penetrate into the realm of the spirit, while the moral proof, delving deeply as it does into the idea of freedom, prepares us to receive that which is beyond philosophy itself."[2]

In effect, it is impossible for philosophy to encounter freedom

[1] Gabriel Marcel, *Du refus à l'invocation*, p. 53.

[2] C. Devivaise, "La philosophie religieuse de Jules Lachelier", in *Revue des sciences philosophiques et théologiques*, t. XXVII, 1939, p. 439 (*re* the unpublished course of lectures on Theodicy given by Lachelier at the École Normale).

in its concreteness without being led thereby to the discovery of personality and without turning away from the abstract notion of a God limited to existence, without having a presentiment of the notion of a personal God who gives Himself to us as a presence, that is, who reveals Himself. As soon as this necessity of a revelation is perceived, we recognize that philosophical dialectic has achieved its constructive work: we are ready "to receive that which is beyond philosophy itself". Thus it would seem that philosophical dialectic—especially that of the proof of the existence of God—can pave the way for Christian dogmatics and constitutes a kind of negative apologetics which gives us a very vivid feeling of philosophy's inability to make us reach certainty with regard to God, and also refers us to a necessary revelation of God. This brings us back to the often-defended doctrine showing philosophy as the antechamber, and an indispensable antechamber to Christian dogmatics.[1] Following this trend of thought, could we say that reflecting critically upon the proofs of the existence of God leads us to doubt our ability to know Him by our own means and to question our certainty, and reveals to the unbeliever the desperate character of his existence? This could hardly be denied. Neither St. Anselm nor Descartes appear to have harboured such a purely negative intention—a Kierkegaardian one, we might say—in constructing their metaphysics. Nevertheless, the proofs, rigorous though they may seem, we must along with Pascal confess powerless. Shall we then conclude that his negative philosophical preparation is of interest either for dogmatics or towards the advent of faith? By recognizing, as philosophy can certainly do, that we have no chance of knowing God unless He reveals Himself to us as a personal presence, do we already commit ourselves to regarding this hypothetical necessity as also and primarily a reality and an actual reality; and do we say that in fact and historically, in the web of human destiny, God has revealed Himself? Are we already prepared to receive

---

[1] A trace at least of this conception may be found in the theology propounded by Brunner (*Natur und Gnade*, pp. 43 and 44). What remains in us of the *imago Dei*, the formal aspect of this image—namely, our quality as reasonable, intelligent, responsible and comprehending subjects (*Wortmächtigkeit und Verantwortlichkeit*) should create in us a kind of predisposition to receive the word of God. To cultivate this predisposition would be one of the tasks of the *theologia naturalis*. But the latter is never conceived as independent from Christological theology. In our view, it only has a pedagogical significance. Barth appears to us to have attributed to his doctrine a rigidity and a systematic character it does not possess.

the Revelation of God at the time and place where God has become for us a presence—Emmanuel?

Indeed, asking these questions suffices to make us realize that we have as yet made no headway towards God. It may be that we shall stop at this point with our despair and our power- less proofs. Or it may be that in spite of this failure we shall keep within us our thirst for God, and that God will remain for us a perpetual torment. It may even be presumed that the philosophy of the proofs of God's existence and the critical reflection that grafts itself upon it will maintain in our hearts a religious anxiety. While recognizing that God is a person, that a person can only reveal himself to us, we may not also acknowledge that we ourselves as sinful creatures are incapable of causing this encounter with God. For after this discovery, prisoners that we are of the analogy between the human person and the person of God, we may be led to think that in the en- counter with another person we find in him a part of freedom— one could almost say, of grace—upon which we have no power; but that there is also, at the same time, a measure of initiative on our part. As our social language has it, we make advances, we take the first step; we give this freedom or this grace an oppor- tunity of manifesting themselves. There is no doubt that it will be difficult to tell afterwards to which of the two partners the initiative was due, whether in friendship, in love, or in any other social dialectic of union. One thing, however, is certain: there has been, in one way or another, and in various degrees some *co-operation*; there cannot possibly have been only activity on the part of one and only passivity on the part of the other. And, as we cannot conceive of the person of God in a clear way save by analogy with human personality, there is a strong temptation to apply to our relationships with God the spiritual laws which govern the various modes of inter-human com- munion. This temptation is that to which all forms of sympathe- tic magic yield. The natural man will of necessity forget that the theandric relationship is utterly different from the inter- human relationship: we stand before God as creatures before their Creator; we stand with respect to God in a relationship of absolute dependence, which can never be the case in human relationships, even when the social group is built into a strong hierarchy and consists of masters and slaves. Moreover, we have totally alienated the effective power given the creature by the Creator, a power to which our quality as *imago Dei* bears witness; we cannot pride ourselves on it. Therefore, in order to meet God, it is necessary for us, ever since we have left the Garden of Eden, where such a meeting was easy and, if one may say so, natural, to rely completely upon the grace of God who produces in us both the wish and the act. There can be no question of also making allowances for man's part. The most mitigated semi-Pelagianism is still heretical. But how could man become aware of this were it not for the witness of Scripture sealed in us by the Holy Ghost? How could we, without the Revelation of God in Jesus Christ, acquire the certainty that we are incapable of co-operating in this encounter with God, and that the only possibility is that of "being seduced" by God? Our failure to grasp the presence of God at the precise moment when rationally we make certain of His existence remains *equivocal* for the natural man's understanding. He is loath to acknowledge that this failure is complete and definitive. He knows something of God; he can no longer rid himself of the problems of theology, and he clings to the hope of being able to perfect this knowledge and to transform the problematics into dogmatic knowledge. In truth, man cannot judge himself. At least, he cannot bring any definitive judgement to bear upon himself. It is only when he is placed in the presence of God and in Jesus Christ that he will know his real situation, and understand the paradoxical position of man, who demonstrates the existence of God without living upon faith in God. In retrospect, the proofs of the existence of God may have positive significance for the believer; for he knows that the God in question was already the true God, the Father of Jesus Christ, in the sense in which the unknown God of the Athenians was already the God later announced to them by the Apostle Paul. That is why we do not think it useful to resume Pascal's opposition between the God of the scholars and the God of Abraham, Isaac, and Jacob. That God is a necessary being, Heinrich Barth[1] points out, is a valuable truth established by reason and which in no case becomes an error when set against the Johannine statement: God is love. It is merely placed in a new light which confers upon it a meaning. All the Gods of the natural man are false gods, which means that not one of them

---

[1] "Natürliche Theologie", *Kirchenblatt für die reformierte Schweiz*, November 9, 1939, p. 359.

is the living God who saves, whether they are uncouth idols or whether they correspond to more purified ideas. But retrospectively, in the eyes of the Christian, all the false gods cannot be placed on the same plane; some of them, and particularly the God of the philosophers, possess characteristics the truth of which is now about to appear.

Retrospectively also, the Christian grasps the mystery of this strange powerlessness of the proofs of God's existence. He will grasp the fact that it is singularly presumptuous for the fallen creature to want God to become the object of a clear and distinct assertion, and the truth of God to rank with mathematical truth.

What will always distinguish the rationalistic theologies, which in reality are secular metaphysics, from Christian theology is precisely that the latter is dominated by the idea of a hidden God, *Deus absconditus*. Disregarding sin, rational theology imagines between God and man a relationship of adequate knowledge. At times, it does not ignore sin entirely, but it then submits the principle that by faith we find again our nature in its wholeness, so that in faith the clear and distinct vision of God again becomes possible, as if man were already restored. The teaching of rational theology will be true in the scheme of the Kingdom, when the hope of salvation has become actual salvation; rational theology is a theology of glory, and that is why it cannot be the dogmatics of the Church militant. How could faith enable us to know a God who is all freedom and all grace, if until the very moment when He reveals Himself, this God did not remain mysterious and concealed from our grasp, reminding us thereby of the distance which separates us from Him? That is why Pascal is justified in wondering at the "boldness" of those who undertake to prove the existence of God in a clear and distinct manner. "It is not after this manner that Scripture speaks, which has a better knowledge of the things that are of God. It says, on the contrary, that God is a hidden God, and that, since the corruption of nature, He has left men in a darkness from which they can escape only through Jesus Christ, without whom all communion with God is cut off. *Nemo novit Patrem, nisi Filius, et cui voluerit Filius revelare.* This is what Scripture points out to us, when it says in so many places that those who seek God find Him. It is not of that light, 'like the noon-day sun', that this is said. We do not say that those who seek the noon-day sun, or water in the sea, shall find them; and hence the evidence of God must not be of this nature. So it tells us elsewhere: *Vere tu es Deus absconditus.*"[1] And Pascal notes with the same lucidity that in the prophets' testimony, in the Incarnation, as well as in the Eucharist, there remains a veil: a strange secret.[2] It is therefore a peculiar aberration to think that faith can procure us this face to face vision of God. We are still in the order of the promise, and as long as we have not personally and actually experienced the Resurrection, we can lay claim to no other knowledge of God than this knowledge in faith of a hidden God.

What in the last analysis must be indicted in the proofs of the existence of God is neither the sureness of the demonstration nor the notion of God itself, which has reference to an effective experience of the infinite and the eternal; it is, essentially, the intention of him who demonstrates. This intention appears to us as doubly debatable: on the one hand, it wishes to establish an existence and thereby sets God among mere existents, i.e. objects; on the other hand, it claims to supply us with a clear and distinct knowledge of God, thus failing to appreciate the peculiarity of man's theological situation. To philosophy's claims of having founded a rational theology of its own, Christianity opposes two fundamental ideas: the idea of the presence of God which is found, under various names, in the whole Scriptural revelation, and that of the hidden God which governs the life of faith. As a consequence, metaphysical experience cannot serve as a basis for a Christian dogmatics. Even *a posteriori*, Christian dogmatics once constituted can find in metaphysical experience no point of contact (*Anknüpfungspunkt*) for grace. We must keep this confusion well in mind in order to determine the true condition of the Christian philosopher. No one can claim the title of Christian philosopher who has not first of all grasped this fundamental discontinuity between the metaphysical quest for God and the Scriptural revelation of God.

In no way does this mean that Christian theology can make no other judgements on metaphysics than negative ones. That is a temptation to which orthodoxy has yielded all too often. Contemporary dialectical theology has often distinguished

---

[1] *Pensées*, IV, p. 242, Everyman's Ed., translated by W. F. Trotter.
[2] *Lettre à Mlle. de Roannez.*

itself by the haste with which it has thought itself obliged not only
to reject any symbiosis between dogmatics and metaphysics,
but also to pronounce an absolute condemnation upon the
latter.[1] As for us, we believe that the theologian has not completed his task when he has acknowledged the impossibility of
finding a transition between rational and Biblical theology.
He must still endeavour to give *meaning* to rational theology—
and, strictly speaking, meaning can be only positive. Scripture
itself warns us that there exists apart from the grace manifested
by Jesus Christ, outside the scheme of faith, a certain knowledge
of God. The *locus classicus* in Rom. 1.18-20 creates an unavoidable problem of interpretation. Does not this text destroy all
our conclusions? Does it not compel us to recognize that there
may be two ways of knowing God, that it is possible to know
God otherwise than through Jesus Christ? Natural theology,
which has at all times attempted to preserve within the Church
a certain standing on the fringe of Christological theology, has
always leaned upon this text; and secular metaphysics, when
the work of Christians (we are thinking of Descartes) has also
appealed to Rom. 1.20[2] to justify its claims to establish the
existence of God. For if it is true that "the invisible things of
Him from the creation of the world are clearly seen being
perceived through the things that are made, even His everlast-
ing power and divinity", are we not forced to admit that there
exists for reason a direct possibility—the way of self-evidence—
to attain God? Christian dogmatics should therefore acknowledge that there exists besides Him who is the way, the truth,
and the light, a parallel way. But such an admission entails for
Christian theology not only a kind of tolerance but also a
renunciation of itself: for it implies that something in us has
escaped the action of sin, that one faculty has remained whole,
that thanks to this faculty man stands related directly to God
and, thus, that in one point at least salvation is not necessary,
or at least not quite as necessary as for other aspects of human
reality. Such is the danger which normally threatens any so-
called natural theology.

But what does Scripture assert in fact? It asserts (and on this
point there is agreement between such divergent interpretations

---

[1] "There is no greater profanation than a rational assertion about God," writes
Dr. W. A. Visser 't Hooft (*Introduction à Karl Barth*, p. 13).

[2] Descartes, Preface to *Meditations*.

as Brunner's and Barth's)[1] that there exists in created nature an objective possibility of knowing God. God cannot be accused by man of having made Himself unknowable and unrecognizable. Nature does in effect constitute a theatre which speaks of the majesty of God. That is why we are ordered to seek God in nature and to praise Him for His manifestations in nature. A theology as clearly Christological as that of Calvin vigorously emphasizes this point. "Since He has manifested Himself to us through His works, we must seek Him through them; for our minds are not able to grasp His essence. And the world to us is like a mirror, in which we can behold Him, in the way in which it is necessary for us to know Him."[2] It is just because of this revelation of God in nature (which, let us note, remains the revelation of a hidden God) that we should confess Him as the Creator of heaven and earth. Although creation has been drawn into the Fall by man, the invisible perfections of God are still sufficiently manifest to be recognizable by man. Does it follow that they are in fact recognized? Is this objective possibility also a subjective one? In fact, the subjective possibility exists for man only in so far as he does not sin. All this knowledge is subordinated to the "contrary to fact" tense in "*si integer stetisset Adam*".[3] In reality, sin has in a surprising way blinded man to this witness, so clear and obvious in Creation. "Let us then believe", Calvin says further, "that the demonstration of God, by which He declares His glory in His creatures, is sufficiently evident as to the light which is in it, but not sufficiently evident as to our blindness."[4] Such, therefore, is man's situation in the face of the so-called natural revelation: he should know enough in order to recognize God in His majesty and His glory and to worship Him as He desires to be worshipped. But man by his own fault has made himself unable to do so. He is then definitely, as the Apostle says, "inexcusable"; his perversion is such that he can no longer fully recognize that which is nevertheless objectively evident. Thus, this testimony of God in creation and in the history of that creation only serves to remove all our excuses. The day we shall be placed face to face with God, the day we shall confess our

---

[1] Cf. E. Brunner, *Natur und Gnade*, pp. 24-25, and K. Barth, "Nein, Antwort an Emil Brunner", in *Theologische Existenz heute*, No. 14, pp. 42-43.

[2] Calvin, *Catéchisme*, p. 25.   [3] *Christian Institutes*, I, 2, i.

[4] *Commentary* on Romans 1.21.

sinfulness before God, we shall measure the depth of our blindness.

Let us take, along with Scripture, another step. Does blindness consist in man's no longer being able to see, in no longer receiving the testimony that comes from creation? No: it also consists in perverting this testimony and in giving it a meaning other than that which it should have. "Men have changed the glory of the incorruptible God into images of corruptible man, of birds, beasts and reptiles." Such is the meaning of the curse which weighs upon man because of sin; not only does he deprive himself of the knowledge of the true God, but he devotes himself straight away to some false god. Either God is known in all His purity, or else the testimony which He gives about Himself serves as the basis for an idolatry. In a certain sense, there has subsisted something of the knowledge man had of God before the Fall—but the part of this knowledge which subsists in man precisely becomes the direct cause of his idolatry.[1] "We can well conceive", Calvin says, obviously referring not to ordinary pagans, but to philosophers, "that there is a Divinity; and from that, we also conclude that to this divine Majesty, whoever He may be, honour and reverence are due; but at this point our understanding fails before we are able to know who or what God is."[2] Natural or fallen man cannot but know something of God, but he cannot recognize Him so as to make this knowledge helpful towards his salvation. As man knows something of his own sinfulness (he likes to speak of his own misery and incomplete nature), as he knows something about law to the extent that his conscience can accuse him and that he can constitute a civil society where a just order reigns; in the same manner, he knows something of God so that he can conceive the idea of religion, the idea of man's subordination, of the majesty and glory of God; and all these human ideas are by no means profanations of God; in fact, they are exact, and objectively true. But man is unable to extract from the truth he possesses its whole significance. Objectively, this truth is a source of salvation for man. But subjectively man is incapable fully to receive it,[3] that is, to receive it as the source of his salvation.

[1] Cf. Calvin, *Commentary* on John 3.6, on John 1.5, and *Institutes*, I, 6, 2.
[2] *Commentary* on Rom. 1.21.
[3] Calvin; 23, 39, 40; 2, 43, 48; 2, 196, 29 (Corpus Reformatorum). Cf. E. Brunner, *Natur und Gnade*, p. 29.

G

The Christian theologian can therefore neither wish to *build* a system of Christological theology upon this natural knowledge of God, nor absolutely to reject it as null and void. For, on the one hand we cannot hope to complete this natural knowledge of God by the knowledge of God in Jesus Christ. It is because the former knowledge is deviated that it cannot successfully be welded on to Christology: the unity of God's Revelation would thereby be broken. We would be led to juxtaposing the God who manifests Himself in Creation to Him who manifests Himself in Jesus Christ, whereas Scripture attests that it is in Jesus Christ and for Him that God created all things. More subtly, on the other hand, we would be led to dissociating the order of creation from the order of redemption, which would result in peculiar difficulties within Christian dogmatics and ethics. It is in Jesus Christ that Creation must be understood. Only in retrospect shall we be able to grasp that the order of creation, as well as that of preservation, has no meaning but with reference to the order of Redemption. Although the remarks formulated by him are not precisely directed against Brunner's richly varied theology, Barth is right in recalling that we cannot consider in God two kinds of grace, qualitatively and, in a way, temporally distinct: a common grace which could be considered independently, that is apart from the grace which is in Jesus Christ. The former has no meaning but with reference to the latter. But the former would not be grace at all had it not the latter as its object and were it not already enlightened by the latter.[1]

Strictly speaking, God does not act successively and His grace cannot be dissociated into fragments relatively independent from one another. The New Covenant is not simply a complement or an addition to the Old, so that the Old might subsist and keep its meaning and its redemptive value independently from the New. The covenant with Noah and the covenant with Abraham have no meaning unless they are formed with a view to reconciliation in Jesus Christ. That is why it is impossible to avoid the *principle* of the Christological interpretation of the Old Testament, a principle without which there would also be a hiatus between common grace, the special grace granted to Israel and the special grace granted to the Church.

Under these conditions, there can be no question of asking

---

[1] Cf. K. Barth, *Nein*, pp. 20-21.

the deist who believes in a common grace granted by a powerful God, the Creator and preserver of the world, to simply add a complement to his former faith. He too will have to be converted and to change his perspective radically. (Let us insist upon this fact that the Word of God cannot confine itself to reviving that which had been effaced in the heart of man, to making clear that which had been obscure, as certain statements of the Reformers themselves would lead us to think.[1] For the knowledge of God possessed by natural man is neither blurred nor obscured; indeed, it is so clear that very often he will be content with it, and it will even, in many cases, dissipate his religious anxiety. This knowledge ought to be re-oriented. It was self-sufficient knowledge; it submitted God to a kind of rational necessity. Now, instead, it has to submit to the revelation God gives of Himself, at the place and moment which it pleases Him to choose.) We cannot start from any other foundation than that which has been laid in Jesus Christ: in the perspective of redemption, the saving value of the content of the old faith will suddenly appear.

It is no longer possible to arrive at pantheistic idolatry, at deistic idolatry, or at sentimental idealism when one worships God in nature because of His revelation in Jesus Christ. That God sends rain upon the righteous as upon the wicked might simply mean that He is indifferent to good and evil. But because of Jesus Christ we know that this act reveals the patience of His love. And this patience has meaning only because of the Day of the Lord, because of the Kingdom that God has prepared for us since the beginning. Just as in the Gospel, the Incarnation, according to F. Ménégoz's favourite statement,[2] can only be understood by faith in the light of the subsequent event of the Revelation, so the successive revelations of God only assume their full meaning in the final light of Jesus Christ's Gospel which is also the Gospel of the Kingdom. In this sense, all Christian faith is essentially eschatological. It would be possible —and we believe this is the case with many scholastic systems— to write a dogmatics which would contain all the elements of the Christian Revelation in a formal order conforming to Scripture, and which nevertheless would not be a Christian

[1] With reference to the knowledge of the Law of God, see the very ambiguous text by Luther, *W.A.*, 16, 447, p. 26.
[2] Cf. especially the article, "Trinité", in *R.H.Ph.R.*, 1938.

dogmatics, precisely because it would lack between its various elements the *eschatological tension* which alone confers upon them their true meaning and also their saving power. Nothing in the content of the Biblical Revelation is therefore independent of the "last things", that is, of the person of Jesus Christ, in whom we have the earnest of the last things (Resurrection, Judgement, Kingdom). Because of the hardening of our hearts, God had to choose this soteriological order. Sinful man cannot hope to free himself from it. I must therefore first of all accept the knowledge of God as it is proposed to me in Jesus Christ, in order that I may grasp the truth to which nature bears witness and which my reason faintly sees.

The early Church was not mistaken. Retracing the history of the first confessions of faith, Cullmann demonstrates in an especially striking manner that the threefold scheme of the present Apostles' Creed does represent a sort of rationalization of the early confessions, but not the actual order in which they were made in the beginning; the first article of the Christian confession of faith was faith in the Son.[1] Similarly, it is easy to understand that all restoration of faith in the Church has necessarily assumed the form of a struggle against natural theology, or at least of a dimming of the latter, as was the case during the Reformation. It is not that the truths objectively contained in this theology have to be rejected; what is to be feared is that natural theology may constitute itself as an independent discipline and become for the theologian "another" task which he would pursue besides his essential task.[2] What a strange situation is that of natural man who knows God, the true God, and who does not accept the revelation of this true God in Jesus Christ—who can prove the existence of God but does not believe in God—who discovers God in his experience only to transform Him into some immanent value! What a strange situation is that of this man to whom truth—though true—does not bring salvation! The analysis of this paradoxical situation, in which sinful man is really the centre of a tragedy, forcibly leads us again to Pascal's statement: ". . . men are both unworthy and capable of God: unworthy by their corruption, capable by their original nature."

[1] O. Cullmann, *Les premières confessions de foi chrétienne.*

[2] We fully subscribe to this statement by E. Brunner: "The Christian alone, i.e. he who at the same time is grounded in the Revelation of Christ, has the right kind of natural knowledge of God" (*Natur und Gnade*, p. 15).

Chapter IV

UNDERSTANDING REVELATION

ONCE we have avoided the temptation to make of metaphysics a sort of necessary introduction to dogmatics and
to give dogmatics a foundation in the metaphysical experience
of the infinite, reason can still harbour metaphysical pretensions. While bowing to the uncontested primacy of Revelation, and recognizing that there exists a fundamental discontinuity between what reason knows of God and what God
reveals of Himself, the philosopher can still claim that metaphysics necessarily intervenes in order to make possible the
understanding of Revelation. In this new hypothesis, let us
mark well, metaphysics has renounced giving itself its own object, constructing it and determining it. It accepts this object as
a datum. It confines its role to *elucidating the meaning of that datum.*
Just as contemporary epistemology starts from scientific knowledge as a fact and endeavours to discover the meaning of this
fact; just as phenomenology is, generally speaking, an effort to
elucidate the significance—or sometimes merely to make
explicit the meaning—of any existence, so the Christian's
philosophy is, in this hypothesis, an attempt to establish the
meanings implicitly contained in Revelation. Henceforth,
we must remember that this expression, "to elucidate the
meaning of . . .", cannot in itself have an absolute and immediate significance. It is always with reference to certain intentions that a meaning can be discovered. For instance, to discover the meaning of time is to grasp what possibilities, pro-
mises and threats time holds for a mind wishing to fulfil its
spiritual calling. Similarly, the discovery of the meaning of
philosophical knowledge has interest only for a mind eager to
know its own limitations or, on the contrary, the unlimited
character of its power. Thus the search for a meaning cannot be
independent of values. To elucidate the meaning of a reality
means, then, to determine the value of this reality. It will
probably be observed, with reason, that epistemology in no way
pursues the old problem of the value of science and that

phenomenological analysis has been compelled to put into parentheses a number of problems related to value. But this is because an exclusively ethical meaning is attached to these terms of value. When epistemology establishes the phenomenological and legalistic character of contemporary science, it emphasizes the fact that science is located in a certain manner among the degrees of knowledge, with relation to truly adequate and truly satisfactory knowledge. In this sense, whether it says so or not, it finds again a problem of value. And when phenomenology classifies certain forms of existence according to their degree of solidity, it again refers us to value. There is no knowledge of meanings that is not also implicitly the assertion of certain values. It might be maintained that knowledge in all its elementary purity aims at nothing but making the real intelligible to us, and that intelligibility is outside the field of values since it is their first condition.[1] But neither is the intelligible an absolute. It is itself a value, since it is susceptible of degrees and of being deepened, and since it always sustains some relationship with the spiritual quality of our intentions. Thus, to elucidate the meaning of Revelation is to ask the question of the value of Revelation; perhaps not in an absolute manner, as the unbeliever and the doubter ask it; but at least to ask the question of the degree of its intelligibility, to pass a judgement upon the structure of this mystery. The metaphysician will put Revelation to a test in order to ascertain the degree of its intelligibility. Now for the philosopher as such, intelligibility can only mean rationality. The metaphysician who thus conceives his own role sets the problem of the rational structure of the revealed. It should be pointed out clearly that setting this problem does not imply for the philosopher any misinterpretation of the revealed as such—at least, not in the initial moment of his thinking. He does not presume, through his metaphysical endeavour, to be able to dispense with faith. He humbly accepts the act of faith and humility towards the revealed which is required of him at the outset; but, precisely because the revealed is a datum and he believes it to be solid, he purports to treat it scientifically, to establish its meaning, and for this purpose to unveil its rational structure. His attitude is then exactly parallel to that of the

[1] See in this connection, G. Berger, *Recherche sur les conditions de la connaissance*, pp. 37 and 38.

scientist who, having admitted that the physical universe has sufficient solidity to be considered as a real datum, undertakes his work with the firm assurance that this datum will prove intelligible, i.e. that it will be possible to express it in a closely woven and uninterrupted network of well determined relationships.

Nevertheless, we must not forget the difference which separates the orders of truth. Revealed truth is not of an objective, but of an existential type, and it is fully true only in so far as it is personally addressed as a demand to him who hears and studies it. Thus, to examine the rational structure of Revelation and the degree of its intelligibility means to try to establish to what extent its demand is valid; not because one questions its validity, but because one wishes to grasp the "why" of its validity. One then presumes to justify Revelation. With reference to the physical universe, whose essence seems exhausted by its *Dasein*, we remain sufficiently autonomous so that no problem of justification arises spontaneously in the scientist's mind.[1] On the contrary, as soon as a reality—for example, time or duty—in one way or another affects our subjectivity as such, the rational explanation spontaneously becomes an attempt at justification; the scattering out of our consciousness in time, as well as our submitting to duty, only become perfectly clear if their meaning is at the same time a positive value: Plotinus does not explain time because he sees it as an unfortunate accident of being, whereas St. Augustine explains it by showing that it is inherent in the act of creation and therefore justified along with the whole of creation. Thus the metaphysician who accepts Revelation as a datum and hopes to elucidate its meaning necessarily attempts to justify Revelation: he accounts for Revelation to himself, and doubtless thinks that while doing so he is still remaining faithful to the Apostle's exhortation.

These formal remarks were necessary in order to show the direction of our argument. It is not strictly speaking the direction of gnosis, though it presents an indisputable kinship with the latter. But gnosis seeks to elucidate the content of Revelation in order to bring out its consequences or implications which

---

[1] Yet it is true that at certain periods the natural sciences—e.g. in the writings of Cuvier—have claimed to be able to reconstruct the Creator's plan and to this extent implicitly to justify nature in its mode of being.

will promote the thinker's knowledge of God. Because the
hidden God is also the revealed God, gnosis wishes to take
advantage of this revelation in order to wrench from the hidden
God the knowledge of some of His elements. Of course, this
new knowledge is, or at least claims to be, an extension of
Revelation; nevertheless, gnosis leaves the framework of
Revelation, and this is what exposes it almost spontaneously to
Scriptural condemnation. It is as immediately contestable as
the tradition of the Church when, under the pretext of being
only a logical or at least normal development of Revelation,
it claims to be a legitimate complement of the latter. On the
contrary, the rational justification of the contents of the Christian faith purports to stay rigorously within Revelation which
it claims to understand from within: it would confine itself to
the terms of the datum themselves—for the datum is, strictly
speaking, self-sufficient. It is valid through the very fact of
being revealed. It brings about salvation, it is the object of faith.
But it can also become the object of a science. Human thought
has requirements which are only imperfectly satisfied by faith,
it would grasp mystery in its fullness. In order that thought
may be brought captive in obedience to Christ, must it not
understand that Christ is in fact the only possible way of
salvation and that the work of God is the only fully rational,
fully justified act given man to know? From faith, it must be
possible to pass on to comprehension. We must understand that
this is an effective passage, not a mere juxtaposition: one starts
from faith, and with the impetus it gives one attains understanding and grasps that God cannot but be, and that He cannot but
be all love, etc. The intention here is not to scorn the faith
of the humble, but it seems necessary to advance beyond that
faith; and thus the thinker's undertaking, though it turns away
from gnosis, nevertheless bears a certain kinship to gnosticism
since, though perhaps without conceit or contempt for the
humble, it places the gnostic above the mere believer, the state
of knowledge above that of faith. But between the two states
there remains a tie so strong that sometimes it is possible to say,
"*Credo ut intellegam*".

For it is indeed of the philosophical doctrine of St. Anselm[1]

[1] One could find the same sort of orientation, though much less methodically
developed, in St. Augustine's thinking, and especially in those of his works which
remain close to neo-Platonism. When St. Augustine approaches the problem
of the soul (*Soliloquies, De Immortalitate Animae, De Quantitate Animae*), it is in order

that one must think here; it represents, in our view, the purest
type of such attempts to justify rationally the content (or at least
part of the content) of Revelation. Anselm wants to render
to himself a rational account, just as he wishes to make it clear
to the fool who says in his heart, "There is no God", that in
saying so he is indeed a fool. This example is all the more
instructive because the attempt to understand the God of
Scripture through necessary reasons—*rationes necessariae*—
obviously proceeds from faith and has the attraction of a
spiritual adventure lived in faith and controlled by it. Never has
a metaphysics been so rigorously subordinated to faith: "I do
not endeavour, O Lord, to penetrate Thy sublimity, for in no
wise do I compare my understanding with that; but I long to
understand in some degree Thy truth, which my heart believes
and loves. For I do not seek to understand that I may believe,
but I believe in order to understand. For this also I believe—
that unless I believed, I should not understand."[1] Similarly, at
the end of his rational demonstration of the existence of God,
Anselm is eager to make certain that he has not exceeded the
limits of what is permitted, and that he has not confused the
God of the philosophers with the God of the Scriptural Revelation. "There is, then, so truly a being than which nothing
greater can be conceived to exist, that it cannot even be conceived not to exist; and this being thou art, O Lord, our God".[2]

Indeed, Anselm's writings are pervaded by a kind of grateful
admiration because of the marvellous harmony which thus

---

to verify by reason the certainties he already possesses by faith. Since forsaking
Manicheism, he knows that the soul is superior to the body, he knows what its
destiny is, but he also desires the light of reason. His faith does not prevent him
from believing in the virtue of dialectics:

"*Quid sit verum, non credendo solum, sed etiam intelligendo apprehendere vehementer
desidero*" (*Contra Acad.*, III, XLIII).

St. Augustine, as a Christian, also writes: "*Tempore auctoritas, re autem ratio prior
est*" (*De Ordine* II, XXVI).

The *Soliloquies* express Augustine's ardent longing: "To know God, to know the
human soul." What he demands is not to believe—he already believes fully—but to
know (III, 1, 8). He wants to reach the virtue of dialectics, this certainty of which
mathematical truths already give him some idea (III, IV, 10). Faith, hope and
charity seem to him only the conditions of access to knowledge. Beyond faith, there
lurks the dream of an access to wisdom which extends, develops and certifies faith.

[1] St. Anselm, *Proslogium*, translated from Latin by Sidney Norton Deane, B.A.,
Open Court Publishing Company, Chicago, 1903, Ch. I, p. 6; cf. also Ch. II,
p. 7: "And so, Lord, do Thou, who does give understanding to faith, give me, so
far as Thou knowest it to be profitable, to understand that Thou art, as we believe,
and that Thou art that which we believe."

[2] *Ibid.*, Ch. III, p. 8.

manifests itself between reason and Revelation: "I thank
Thee, gracious Lord, I thank Thee; because what I formerly
believed by Thy bounty, I now so understand by Thine illumination, that if I were unwilling to believe that Thou dost
exist, I should not be able not to understand this to be true."[1]
The rational and the revealed are thus identified to the extent
that it would be possible, at least theoretically, to understand
why one does not yet believe. It must be remarked, moreover,
that Anselm had not, at the outset, set down this exact correspondence as a postulate. He ascertains it *a posteriori*. It cannot
be maintained that for him the affirmation of the rational
structure of the revealed (or at least of part of Revelation)
is an affirmation of principle. On the contrary, it is a discovery
of faith: St. Anselm sees in it nothing but a sign of this growth
in faith which the New Testament considers as the normal
path upon which the believing soul engages. There is therefore
in St. Anselm's writings no postulate in principle of the rationality of Revelation: the dialectics is kept in a subordinate
place: "About the object in which one believes one never ought
to dispute as though it might not be; without ceasing to hold
and cherish it, one must seek for the reason according to which
it is. The Christian, if he reaches such understanding, will
rejoice in it; in the contrary case, he will revere that which he
cannot grasp." Thus, the same speculation which in principle
shrinks from no religious subject accepts the fact that in actual
experience certain religious matters are beyond its reach:
understanding is a gift which God imparts to us as it pleases
Him.[2] And this position of principle is illustrated in St. Anselm's
thinking by striking examples: the fact of election cannot be
understood; its rational structure cannot be found out. Why is
there a fool who says in his heart, "There is no God", at the
very moment when the demonstration of God's existence has
just been administered to him? How are we to understand the
absolute contingency of the existence of such a fool? Anselm's
answer is clear: "*nulla ratione comprehendi potest cur . . .*". St.
Anselm's epistemological stand is not without analogy with
that of the modern philosopher and scientist confronted with
the world: science has been undertaken with the hope and the
quasi-certainty that the universe will prove intelligible, that

---

[1] St. Anselm, *Proslogium*, Ch. IV, p. 10.
[2] P. Vigneaux, *La pensée au moyen âge*, p. 33.

contingency will gradually give ground to determinism. In fact, however, there is always resistance, and residues of the un-explained and the contingent. Similarly, there always remains in the revealed a residue which will not yield to any rational structure.

St. Anselm is so conscious of this that he hastens to point out the limitations of his enterprise. Not only are certain subjects outside the grasp of rational justification (*Monologium* and *Proslogium* leave aside the Incarnation but include the Trinity); but it is also clearly stated to what degree of rationality this justification can rise. No doubt, the method which had been imposed upon Anselm by the monks of Bec required him not to persuade by means of Scripture, but to compel by means of reason and to leave no objection unanswered. Doubtless also, though he knows well that the *rationes necessariae* admit of a stronger authority above themselves: the authority of Scripture and of the Church, Anselm maintains that within a discussion these reasons must be self-sufficient, and that, far from being mere likelihoods useful in preparing the ground of the soul for the Gospel, they are truly invincible. Finally, St. Anselm's intention is definitely to make us understand the *summum bonum nullo alio indigens* by means of a *unum argumentum quod nullo alio ad se probandum quam se solo indigeret.*[1] It still remains that Anselm endeavours not to confuse the present time with the time to come, the rational order with the face-to-face vision promised us in the Kingdom. The point is therefore to distinguish among degrees of knowledge and of comprehension, yet there can be no question of dispelling mystery as such. Reason, we would say in modern terms, allows us to approach mystery, not to exhaust it. To quote again from Vigneaux,[2] Anselm's dialectic enterprise only aims at a *aliquatenus intelligere*, and by no means at a *penetrare*: a certain understanding and not a penetration. The *Monologium* has propounded that in order to form the *rationes necessariae* one does not have to grasp how things came to be *thus*, to penetrate the *quomodo ita sit*, to comprehend the object by its inner possibility. One does not reach one's own mode of being, one deals with it by means of some similitude. The Anselmian necessity concerns a hidden essence: *nihil de hac natura potest percipi per suam proprietatem:* "Of this nature, nothing can be perceived by that which constitutes it in its

---

[1] P. Vigneaux, *op. cit.*, p. 33.   [2] *Ibid.*, p. 32.

properties,"[1] this is said about the Trinity. The ultimate reason of the divine designs will therefore not receive justification, but when we assent to this part of inescapable mystery, we can discern a rational structure in the execution of these designs.

This cautiousness of Anselm did not remain merely intentional. It is expressed in the demonstration itself. Anselm does not try to conceal how insufficient the demonstration of God's existence still remains, to the extent that our knowledge of God is always peculiarly antinomical: God can be said to be both seen and not seen by the soul. "Or, is what it [the soul] has seen both light and truth; and still it has not yet seen Thee, because it has seen Thee only in part, but has not seen Thee as Thou art? Lord my God, my creator and renewer, speak to the desire of my soul, what thou art other than it hath seen, that it may clearly see what it desires."[2] The rational knowledge we acquire of God still has to be offered to God, that He may purify it and forgive us for it! And it is quite significant to find that St. Anselm is not content with a positive definition of God as the greatest reality thought can conceive; he has to resort to a definition marking more clearly that God is beyond our reach: "God is a being even greater than can be conceived." In fact, Anselm succeeds without any difficulty in demonstrating the main classical attributes of God: His eternity, His universal presence, His non-spatiality, etc. but these only make up that aspect of God by which He is also the God of the philosophers. When he comes to the triune God[3] the demonstration becomes much more hazardous: he does show that God's nature requires Him to be totally present in the Son as well as in the Holy Ghost, but he in no way demonstrates why it belongs to God's essence to be triune. The necessary reason of the Trinity as such eludes us. In the end, the theologian can only establish, with relation to each of the Persons of the Trinity, the unity and the simplicity of God,[4] which brings us back to rational theology. Reason is asked to recognize that, in fact, the Trinity does not break up the unity and simplicity of God; but reason does not comprehend why it was necessary that God be triune. Similarly, when St. Anselm deals with the Biblical attributes

---

[1] Vigneaux concludes by this sentence which we dare not make completely our own: "The God of medieval speculation remains the mystery of faith."

[2] *Proslogium*, Ch. XIV, p. 21.   [3] *Ibid.*, Ch. XXIII.   [4] *Ibid.*, Ch. XXIII.

of God proper, the demonstration confines itself to proving that these attributes are not contradictory; all the same, this demonstration is very often purely verbal: thus, God may have feeling, though He has no body, for to feel means, in the last analysis, nothing else but to know (Ch. VI); God is omnipotent, though He cannot do everything, for the power to do evil is not real power (Ch. VII); God is both compassionate and passionless, for His impartiality exists only in Himself, and not with regard to men (Ch. VIII).

There is something extremely moving in this unceasing and forever inadequate endeavour of Anselm to grasp the rational structure of God. For at every moment the enterprise of a loyal reason clashes with the absolute of mystery, the mystery of God's grace and freedom. And this mystery expresses itself in acts of God which scandalize reason: for instance, God manifesting His goodness towards the wicked. Faced with this incomprehensible fact, Anselm endeavours to apply his usual dialectic and to resolve the contradictions inherent in mystery. But immediately he must confess that he cannot completely succeed in so doing: "The depth of Thy goodness, O God! The source of Thy compassion appears, and yet is not clearly seen! [*et videtur unde sis misericors et non pervidetur*]. We see whence the river flows, but the spring whence it arises is not seen. For, it is from the abundance of Thy goodness that Thou art good to those who sin against Thee; and in the depth of Thy goodness is hidden the reason for this kindness."[1] "For although Thou dost reward the good with goods and the evil with evils, out of goodness, yet this the concept of justice seems to demand. But, when Thou dost bestow goods on the evil, and it is known that the supremely Good hath willed to do this, we wonder why the supremely Just has been able to will thus. O compassion, from what abundant sweetness and what sweet abundance dost Thou well forth to us!"[2] A rational agreement between God's goodness and His justice remains impossible, but the idea of such an agreement and the desire, if not to discover it, at least to come closer to it, subsist in Anselm's thinking. The attempt

---

[1] Anselm's reasoning is the following: once the infinite goodness of God is postulated, its necessary result is that God is good to the wicked. Reason can perceive this analytic bond. But it is unable to understand why God is good with that particular kind of goodness. It is the source of the gracious will of God which remains unfathomable.

[2] *Proslogium*, Ch. IX, p. 15.

seems hopeless, yet Anselm never gives it up entirely: "For it is hard to understand how Thy compassion is not inconsistent with Thy justice . . . nay, that it is in true harmony with justice."[1] It is according to the same justice that God both punishes the wicked and spares them (Ch. X). But, to arrive at his conclusion: "God justly punishes and justly spares the wicked."[2] In order to arrive at the dialectical victory this conclusion represents, St. Anselm is compelled to give two different meanings to the concept of justice: God is just when He deals with us according to our deserts; He is still just when He does what is in accord with His own goodness, "*quia facis quod decet, te summe bonum*". Finally, the demonstration becomes purely verbal. Anselm agrees to call just all that conforms to the will of God; from then on, all God accomplishes according to His own will is just: "For, it is not just that those whom Thou dost will to punish should be saved, and that those whom Thou dost will to spare should be condemned."[3] No doubt one would easily find antinomic texts of this kind in many other theological systems, and particularly in Calvinism. No doubt, too, we know that the Christian is a man who must hold the two ends of the chain without worrying about the continuity of the links which make up the chain: but the peculiar character of Anselm's position lies in the fact that with him such antinomic formulas proceed not only from the inescapable demands of faith, but also purport to be the normal conclusions of a logical reasoning.

We could have chosen other examples than that of Anselm, for this idea of a rational interpretation of faith, of a dialectical justification of the revealed is not his alone. It is at the roots of every Christian philosophy of the Middle Ages, which Gilson very clearly defines in the following manner: "We mean by this a philosophy which intends to be a rational interpretation of data, but considers as the essential element of these data the religious Faith, the object of which is defined by the Christian revelation." According to Gilson, all the doctors of the Church agree on this point: ". . . that there is a Christian philosophy, that is to say, a philosophy directed towards an object which eludes its grasp, but from which, knowing that it exists, it cannot turn away. Destined to fall short of its object, it will find a foothold, in some manner, upon the prolongation of the ideal

---

[1] *Proslogium*, Ch. IX, p. 16.   [2] *Ibid.*, p. 18.   [3] *Ibid.*, Ch. XI, p. 18.

roads which lead to it."[1] This will to apply reason to Revelation, and as a consequence to discover a rational structure in the revealed, is therefore indeed a constant in medieval thought. The theory of the Middle Ages does involve a rationalistic ambiguity. It revolves around the interpretation of Peter's statement that the faithful must be prepared to account for their hope under every circumstance. Does to "account for" mean to give a rational interpretation, to show the secret rationality, or at least the secret intelligibility of the content of the faith? Gabriel Biel, the last of the scholastics, still asserts that this is the proper role for the theologian. We could therefore have chosen another example than St. Anselm's and devoted our attention to St. Thomas, for instance, or to any other doctor whose attitude would be less reserved than Anselm's. Is there not in the latter's thinking, as we have taken pleasure in emphasizing, a perpetual and pathetic hesitation about the limits of reason's jurisdiction? Are these hesitations not symbolized by the author's ultimate hesitation in chosing a title for his *Proslogium*? Either: *Fides quaerens intellectum* or more frankly: *Exemplum meditandi de ratione fidei*? Would it not be better to refer ourselves to a Richard of St. Victor who would explain to us how the love of God could not have been realized otherwise than through the Trinity? If we have retained the example of Anselm among a thousand others, it is because on account of his hesitations and scruples it is easier to grasp the theological danger threatening the mind when it enters this path. With him, moreover, it is possible to perceive exactly the point at which the formula *fides quaerens intellectum* loses its legitimate use. In his thought the problem is to pursue as far as possible the *understanding of Revelation*. But a sliding from one intention to another occurs almost inevitably, since Anselm is not always addressing believers alone or the monks of Bec alone, but also, in the *Cur Deus Homo*, unbelievers. And therefore he will have to speak to these the only language they understand, that of rational justification. In this appearing of the unbeliever lies the first cause of the sliding of dogmatics towards apologetics, which will absorb it.

To substitute the unbeliever to the believer, to wish to be understood by the unbeliever otherwise than through preaching

[1] E. Gilson, *The Philosophy of St. Thomas Aquinas*, translated by E. Bullough, ed. by G. A. Elrington, B. Herder Book Co., St. Louis and London, 1937.

alone is to risk at every instant falling into the ambiguity of the *logos*: it is to give rise almost inevitably to the confusion between the rational *Logos* of Greek thought and any philosophical thought, and the Johannine *Logos*—the Word made flesh. It is correct to assert that starting with the Creed, i.e., with faith in Jesus Christ come in the flesh, the whole content of Revelation becomes intelligible, and that it then becomes true that the Spirit moves all things, even the depths of God; in the same way, all the prophecies of the Old Testament and the miracles of the New Testament become intelligible, i.e. receive a positive significance because of the Incarnation, the Death, the Resurrection and the Ascension of Jesus Christ. It is perfectly true that reason comprehends, and grasps, a mysterious coherence and indestructible unity, from the instant the act of reason becomes integrated with the act of faith in Jesus Christ. We must not make our criticism bear upon the spiritual progress the reflections described in the *Proslogium* meant for St. Anselm personally. It is the use to which the method of the *Proslogium* can and has been put that we must accuse. Since the content of Revelation becomes intelligible there the unbeliever of good faith will say: "Let us try to seize this content in its intelligibility, which my reason, the rational *Logos*, can test and recognize; and since, according to St. Anselm, a witness of Revelation, this intelligibility implies faith as its necessary condition, we shall be able to trace from this 'doctrine' the act of faith it makes necessary and therefore rational." In reality, Anselm cannot address himself to the unbeliever without giving rise to a most formidable ambiguity; without substituting, for the authority of the living God who gives faith and makes it authentic, the authority of reason; without begetting the myth of a rational structure of Revelation; without making the credibility of Revelation dependent upon this structure.

The unbeliever's attitude may even react upon the witness himself. When, instead of being concerned, as every science should be, with its own objective content, Christian dogmatics allows itself to be influenced first of all by the unbeliever's condition; when, instead of thinking of the only relationship it is allowed to envisage: the Revelation-Church relationship, dogmatics reflects upon the psychological and sociological conditions necessary to make the unbeliever receptive, it is soon seduced by that which at the outset seduced the unbeliever:

the rationality of the revealed. Such a dogmatics, whatever the number of its positive affirmations, betrays its own function. There is no question here of excluding from theology all concern with apologetics; apologetics finds again its legitimate place and function in the cure of souls and spiritual guidance.[1] But a strong distinction has to be made between dogmatics and apologetics, for the Church can only subsist in so far as, at every instant, a dogmatics confronts the contents of its preaching with Revelation as a whole; the implication is that this whole must be known and studied in itself and for its own sake, without any regard for measuring Revelation by any rational criterion, without bothering to "point out . . . the lofty satisfactions reason can find in the luminous sequence of doctrines that our faith has to offer, and in the harmonies which appear between this faith and the condition, the needs and the aspirations of man". The Catholic theologian whom we have just quoted[2] goes as far as presenting the Christian Revelation as "a light able to charm and seduce reason". True, he does so in a chapter dealing with the intellectual aspects of faith, and reminds us time and time again that faith is a gift from God, the working of a mysterious grace; it still remains that the revealed, inasmuch as it is given in fact, is susceptible to reason, amenable to its methods and situated on the same plane as all other truths of any order. "Catholic theology, in the works of its most illustrious masters, and especially St. Thomas Aquinas, who makes use of all the resources of ancient wisdom in analysing with precision and in logically ordering the data of the Christian Revelation, presents a marvellous synthesis of faith and reason. It is the most eloquent commentary upon St. Augustine's exhortation: '*Valde ama intellectum* '."[3] In this work reason plays only an instrumental role, but the very nature of the instrument employed decides the structure of the object under study. If the ancient thinkers succeeded in ordering Revelation by philosophical analysis it is because Revelation lends itself to this and because they saw to it that it should do so. The Christian dogmatician must carry the concern for loyalty to Scripture to the extent of letting the subject of his study impose its own method upon him. The rational justification of

---

[1] We can easily be convinced of this fact by referring to J. D. Benoît's book, *Direction spirituelle et protestantime*. See in particular the Part I, ch. 1.

[2] G. Brunhes, *La foi et sa justification rationnelle*, p. 56.   [3] *Ibid.*, p. 57.

H

faith appears therefore as inspired by a non-scientific, and therefore not receivable, *a priori*.

It will be rightly observed that we are very far from Anselm's attitude. Yet it would be wrong to think that the new attitude which we have just outlined bears no relationship to Anselm's. It is directly derived from his; it represents the extreme limit of reason's endeavour to take possession of and assimilate Revelation.

Now and then, it becomes necessary to elucidate the revealed in rational terms. Now and then it has to be impressed upon the unbeliever that he is a fool—which might appear as a Biblical pursuit, but is not so as long as it is hoped that the unbeliever can grasp this truth in his unbelief and in spite of it: so that his unbelief notwithstanding, the revealed truths might appear to him as *rationes necessariae*, being driven to the verge of faith by the very determinism of reason. Evidently, such a position implies that the Fall was not complete, that reason was spared, since it can compel man's heart to renounce being a fool. The question Anselm asks himself or that he accepts in the terms asked him is indeed: *"Why can there be a fool who denies the existence of God and who denies Christian truth?"* It is necessary to show what an aberration of the mind such an attitude implies; and, by pointing to this aberration, to make it rationally impossible. This raises the question of whether error and hence sin can be known apart from faith and before faith. Scripture bears witness to this truth, found again by Luther, especially in the Epistle to the Romans, that sin is an object of faith which can be only known in faith, and, in the proper sense, confessed. It is therefore in faith alone that the fool will be able to understand, and to admit, by the renewing of his mind, that which constituted his folly.

It might, further, be argued that the figure of the fool is not in the foreground of Anselm's work, that it is only an accessory figure, that it was brought into Anselm's work by the necessities of teaching and could easily be omitted without Anselm's work becoming in any way different from what it is. Let us then again consider the beginning of the *Proslogium*. Is there anything else in Anselm's original intention than this will to render account to himself of the content of his hope, or, according to a more modern expression, to think his faith? And is this not a legitimate enterprise, a sign of this progress in the faith which was such a familiar notion in Apostolic times? Is not this growth in faith a part of the current promise of the New Testament? It is true that we find it first of all in the form of ethical progress, this "abounding more and more" which is defined in 1 Thess. 4.1-8; when the Apostle declares to the Thessalonians (2 Thess. 1.3) that their faith "groweth exceedingly", he means the growth of this faith into charity. However, the progress of faith can also be oriented towards knowledge. A firm and assured faith may have gaps and may need increased instruction (1 Thess. 3.10). Paul insists upon the fact that if certain persons do not share all his opinions and yet are in the faith, they will join with him in the end. God will enlighten them on this point (Phil. 3.15-16). The gift of the Spirit to the believers has the effect of rooting them even more firmly in Christ, and this being rooted in love results in turn in that "ye may be strong to *comprehend* with all saints what is the breadth, and length, and height, and depth, and to *know* the love of Christ, which passeth knowledge" (Eph. 3.18-19). In a general way faith is a growth of man in Christ, so that in Christ man becomes perfect (Col. 1.28). The action of the Lord's spirit is to transform us continually "from glory to glory" into the image of the Lord (2 Cor. 3.18). Now this Lord whom we assume, so to speak, brings us the knowledge of God, which is precisely life eternal. No doubt, and we shall have an opportunity to understand the reason for this, Scripture avoids speaking of this growth as though it were an automatic development from a seed; this growth is not strictly analogous to that of a plant;[1] it presupposes a continuous intervention of the Spirit, which forever produces new changes in us, so that the new man is built up while the old man is destroyed. This growth has not the character of a continuous spiritual ascension with an internal dynamics, obeying a kind of law, as both gnosticism and mysticism would have it. Without the perpetual renewal brought about by the Spirit, the progress would cease; so that we must pray God that He should ever anew give us His Spirit. It remains that the idea of praying to God for new progress in faith and the knowledge of Him faith implies is not alien to the New Testament, and that in this sense there is nothing new or shocking in the Anselmian attempt. The Christian is a man on

---

[1] True, Scripture makes use of this metaphor, but any metaphor remains in a sense equivocal.

the march—"*semper viator*"—he travels on that he might bring about in himself the maturity and the perfect stature that he knows in Jesus Christ.

But where does this pilgrimage of the Christian unfold? This may be the question Anselm did not ask. Yet it is the chief question. This progress occurs in the scheme of faith, in the "*time of faith*"; by this we mean the time which passes between the Christian's baptism and the advent of the Kingdom, the time during which the Church confesses a Lord incarnate but raised to the right hand of God; the time in which the soul can know its own resurrection only through the promise contained in the Lord's Resurrection; the time during which Satan, though fettered in chains, yet remains powerful, and death, though defeated by the Lord, yet continues to prowl around those who belong to Him. In short, the time of eschatological hope: all is accomplished by the Lord, all will be accomplished for us. It is the actual and concrete time into which the New Testament's anthropology places the believer: and doubtlessly this time is not devoid of luminousness and transparency. To the extent that our knowledge is centred upon Jesus Christ and we live in Him, we know; and our knowledge, in comparison to that of the old covenant man, is unimpeded by a "veil" (2 Cor. 3.15-16). But (and hereby believers of the new and of the old covenant both belong, in different ways, to the same order and both have Abraham for father) even in Jesus Christ we do not know face to face; "we behold as in a mirror the glory of the Lord" (2 Cor. 3.18), we walk by faith and not by sight (2 Cor. 5.7). We can know no other light than that of faith. No doubt this kind of knowledge is difficult to define, for one is always tempted to integrate it in a table of the modes of knowledge, that is, to ignore its singularity. To us it appears impossible to characterize faith otherwise than by its object (and that, incidentally, is what the author of the Epistle to the Hebrews does); faith is closely linked with the data of Christology. There is no faith apart from the hope of the Resurrection, the expectation of Christ's return and the trust in the present kingship of Jesus Christ. If we recall such well-known points, it is in order to emphasize the specific character of this time which is ours, and to explain the profound reasons for which Christianity must hold suspect all forms of gnosticism, and all mystical ascensions, even if they possess as high a degree of spirituality as St. Bernard's. In gnosticism as well as in unifying mysticism, the endeavour is precisely to go beyond the phase of faith, to gain a foothold, by one's own strength in a new world; the endeavour is to replace faith by sight. The gravity of such a process must not be overlooked, even if it is true that in practice the Church has experienced difficulties in recognizing heresies as such. In effect, this attempt to surpass faith aims at nothing less than bringing us outside the present Kingdom of Christ of which, by God's will, we must be the subjects. To live by faith and in faith is to accept our place in this earthly kingdom where Christ's kingship is not fully or clearly manifested or recognized. It is to accept being saved only in hope (though this hope is certain and does not deceive), it is to accept possessing only the pledge of the Resurrection (though this is of exceptional value). The Christian knows he has received in Jesus Christ—not only in His teachings, but also in His person—all that is useful for salvation. He knows that it was of benefit to him that Jesus should go to the Father, and that he cannot and is forbidden to follow Jesus there. That is why he must give up any speculation, any gnosis, any *theologia gloriae* by which to establish himself in the order of the seen. What makes so suspect the Newmanian notion of "development" is the fact that, though at the outset it is faithful to the evangelical data, it has a tendency to surpass them and glance beyond that which is necessary for our salvation.

Now, is not this same idea of surpassing implicit in the spiritual attitude taken by Anselm with regard to Revelation? With respect to the Christian in the *Proslogium*, Vigneaux writes: "For this believer, the dialectic of things divine and their understanding takes place between his belief in God and the face to face vision to which he aspires in the beyond. Thought moves between faith and sight—*inter fidem et speciem*; this fundamental situation explains not only Anselm's speculation but also the subsequent scholasticism. Discourse according to necessity has its place between believing and seeing, but belief and sight are both *graces*, gifts from God."[1] Thus comprehension, instead of being kept within faith, instead of being comprehension in faith, becomes a kind of intermediate third term between faith and sight, belonging to a sort of mixed economy which the philosopher institutes fully upon his own

[1] P. Vigneaux, *La pensée au moyen age*, p. 30.

authority and the access to which he reserves to an *élite*. Here
it is a matter of conferring upon man a new power, for he will
not be content with living by faith alone; and, in order that he
may take possession of this power, there has to be restored in
him a figure which does not belong to the present *aeon*. "Anselm's problem, and that of his disciples", Vigneaux adds,
"is to find again some of the knowledge man had before the
Fall, to re-establish man—partially—in the state from which he
has fallen. . . . The function of grace is to give back its form to
the divine image blotted out in man; and in this constitutive
likeness of our nature, there is contained the power to think
God."[1] Thus the believer seeks to anticipate the future vision,
not by faith, which would be legitimate since faith is anticipation, but by reasoning. And this mode of anticipation implies
some confusion as to the action of grace; the action of grace
would result in restoring in us the *imago Dei*, which had been
ever so slightly obscured in us; instead of preparing us for the
day of the Lord, the action of grace would have a retroactive
effect; it would give us again our original nature. Now Scripture never presents the activity of grace under this aspect. It
speaks, not of reform, nor of restoration, but of a new birth.
Jesus Christ is the first-born of a new creation. The astonishing
sobriety of the Bible in describing Eden is not without an
explanation; man must not try to return there.

The passing of time from the Creation to the Parousia is
univocal and this univocity has meaning even in the eyes of
God. This passing is to mere appearance, as it is in many
philosophies. It is bound up with the very will of God. The
Christian's life in faith is indeed as Paul has described it, a race
forward. Moreover, this action of grace remains a secret one, in
the sense that the new creature does not become visible but
remains hidden in God with Christ. No doubt the inner man is
built up and the external man destroyed. But never is the
achievement of this parallel action manifest. The new man
remains for us an object of faith, and belief in the new man is
indistinguishable from belief in Jesus Christ. We must believe in
the action of the Holy Spirit in us, although we cannot ascertain any effect of this action that is not still tainted with ambiguity, mingled with sin, suspect. Man cannot, therefore, in
spite of the action of grace or of the presence of the Spirit,

[1] P. Vigneaux, *La pensée au moyen age*, p. 31 *passim*.

resume even partially—and has this adverb any meaning in
this connection?—his original form; God does not repair His
work; God, in each of His acts, intends to be recognized and
confessed as *Creator*, and this new creation partakes of the realm
of penultimate things: it cannot be for us either an object of
contemplation or an object of possession. That is why the Christian cannot claim to have found again that which sin has
irrevocably destroyed, nor can he presume to have at his disposal this new heart and this new insight which are the constant
objects of his hope. He cannot presume to go beyond the mode
of existence which was acquired for him by Christ, and which
is not located *inter fidem et speciem*, but solely within faith. That
is why, without in any way underestimating the value of the
pious emotion and the will to worship and to glorify God which
animate St. Anselm, we are compelled to hold his enterprise
suspect, all the more so because we cannot dissociate it from
the work of his disciples. Vigneaux has pointed out with perfect
exactness the ultimate tendency of such an enterprise: "The
Anselmian arguments tend towards a logical structure independent from any authority and having universal value: the idea
is not that of a reason appropriate to faith."[1] The work of Christian
dogmatics is, in a sense, a work of reason, but this reason must
remain a reason proper to faith.

We must, however, understand, if we wish to perceive clearly
the nature of a religious philosophy, that the very clearness with
which the work of independent reason surrounds itself constitutes a fearful pole of attraction for the theologian. Is there
really no relationship between this luminousness of rational
knowledge, which is already a kind of vision, and the knowledge
implied by faith? Should not the correction wrought within
man by his faith allow him to capture this independent reason
and make it serve towards extending faith itself? Conceivably,
there is in this a terrible temptation for the understanding, and
one which constantly recurs in the history of the Church. How
can we begin to understand what the Scripture tells us about
seeing, without referring ourselves to the perception of the
rational processes? Will this promised vision not be a perfecting
of that which we already possess in the rational activity? We
shall willingly concede that it is difficult to leave out this relationship and that there can be seen in reason as it works in the

[1] *Ibid.*, p. 42.

exact sciences and in philosophy, a kind of prefiguration of the face to face sight promised by Scripture. But the fact that, for the believer, reason is a prefiguration of the things to come does not mean that the things to come must necessarily be situated upon the exact prolongation of reason. There is in Scripture itself another example in which the figure and that which is figured cannot be conceived of as two moments of the same process: when speaking of the Kingdom, Scripture does so not by borrowing from the Church its distinctive features and describing the Kingdom according to the pattern of the Church; but indeed, as K. L. Schmidt has reminded us,[1] it describes the Kingdom according to the pattern of the State. Thus the State is a figure of the Kingdom to come; the obedience we owe to the State reminds us of that which we owe to the Lord alone. But in no way does this mean that the advent of the Kingdom is a promotion of the State. Similarly, reason prefigures sight, but sight is not a completion of reason, and reason, even when enlightened by faith, is not an outline of the face to face vision. It is perhaps fortunate that the assured perfection shown by reason in the steps where we see it achieve success, which causes reason to appear vastly superior to faith, should keep alive in the heart of the believing man the longing for a knowledge of God more perfect than that which he possesses at present. But it is important for us to know clearly that we cannot on our own bring this longing to an end.

Ultimately, it seems to us that only a sense of the *eschatological limits* can help man to avoid an impasse. The veiled knowledge of faith by no means represents one of the renunciations that philosophical scepticism wishes to impose upon our appetite for knowledge. To accept the condition of man as we have defined it, to accept living in faith and having to show with regard to Revelation no other understanding than that contained in faith, or rather than that of faith, is not to pronounce any restrictive judgement upon human destiny. It is, on the contrary, to give this destiny its true dimensions. To speak of eschatological limits is also a way of speaking of the unlimited and the infinite. The believer sees his life engaged in a tension, in an eschatological expectation. The Christian lives in expectation of the ultimate event which will give to his existence in faith and his

---

[1] K. L. Schmidt, "Royaume, Eglise, Etat et Peuple: relations et contrastes", in *R.H.Ph.R.*, 1938, No. 2, pp. 145 *et seq.*

obedience in faith their whole meaning. And his faith itself
includes this expectation and is nourished by it; Jesus Christ is
not only He who came, but He who is coming to judge the quick
and the dead. Thus faith does not feel hampered by these limitations. These are but the signs of its expectation, hope and life;
the Christian does not suffer from knowing that he cannot
pierce the veil, for he is aware that the veil belongs to the
scheme of Redemption. Not knowing God face to face, he
nevertheless has the privilege of knowing in whom he has
believed; he has the privilege of seeing God in Jesus Christ and
of seeing Him only through Jesus Christ. And he knows that to
this existence in faith there is attached a promise the fulfilment
of which is always presently imminent. (God holds back
nothing of Himself in the moment when He reveals Himself.
In the Platonic philosophy the Idea, the Same cannot be
present in this world without becoming mingled with the Other,
thereby losing its own integrity and becoming distorted. Such
a conception is foreign to the Christian Revelation.) The
Christian knows the incompleteness of his own being, the
incompleteness of his own certainty. He repudiates the apparent
perfection of the finite, that motionless eternity, perceptible
even now, with which the Greeks were satisfied. He no longer
moves in a universe where all has been completed. The Resurrection itself is not an absolute achievement. It too is charged
with promise. It too announces that Christ's victory over death
will be changed into a definitive victory; it announces a new
world. The Christian stands at the threshold of the promised
land and awaits the moment of entering. Thus, certain religious
philosophies appear to him as impious attempts to hasten a
fulfilment which does not depend upon man. It is not possible
for us to determine the instant when eternity will destroy time,
although every instant already heralds and signifies the eternity
that is coming. It is in so far as the theme of eschatology has
vanished from Christian thinking that the latter has been
threatened with invasion by gnoses and speculative systems
belonging to the order of sight or at least, that which is "*inter
fidem et speciem*". Biblical thought admits of no such intermediate
stage; it only knows two terms which are called, now faith and
sight, now the Church and the Kingdom, now time and
eternity. These two terms are not antithetic, they are not alien
to each other, and yet they are not situated upon the same

plane. The latter weighs upon the former, gives it its whole meaning and tension, and will bring about its fulfilment. Faith can only be understood if we see in it the mode of knowledge appropriate to this *aeon*, where the last things are only imminent, in which we must assert at the same time: the Kingdom has come near us, and: the Kingdom is coming; in which we must condense the past and the future into a new time; in which we must simultaneously heed Jesus of Nazareth and the glorious Lord. If human logic is always baffled by faith, to the extent of not knowing where to place it in the table of modes of knowledge, it is because the classification logic gives is timeless, and because, even when it endeavours to make an allowance for becoming, it always leaves out the different qualifications of the periods marked by the great events of Revelation; that is why logic is driven to count faith among the bric-à-brac of human beliefs, thus disregarding the specific certainty of faith.

When the Christian tries to think out his knowledge of God, he is always referring himself more or less explicitly to the table of modes of knowledge with which logic has supplied him. He sees that beliefs, and faith, come in certainty far beneath rational knowledge, and he is then tempted to try to prolong the truth he possesses in the Biblical Revelation by means of reason. His initial error is not to have perceived that it is impossible to enter faith into the table of modes of knowledge. Faith is bound up with a duration which has a tension of its own, and with a history the decisive moments of which cannot be forgotten, even for an instant. Whoever has understood the true nature of faith will understand that it is "unreasonable" to try to surpass faith. If there is such a thing as an understanding of Revelation, it is to be found within faith.

Thus, in all attempts to elucidate, explain or justify the content of Revelation by means of reason, there is a mistake as to the *actual condition of the believer*, as to the time of faith. But could there not also be a mistake as to the very content of Revelation? Is not our perpetual temptation to try to build up a philosophy that would extend Revelation caused by the fact that we rob the Christian Revelation of its essential characteristics?

We take it for granted that Revelation must be grasped by the believer's intellect as a group of given propositions, as a system of ideas and facts, as a *doctrine*. Of course, we know that Revelation has more than an intellectual and doctrinal content, but as soon as we wish to reflect upon our faith we immediately reduce Revelation to being nothing more than a doctrine. We would willingly say that Revelation, inasmuch as it is thought of or thinkable by man—and it must be so—presents itself to us as a body of doctrines to be examined as such. Indeed, the secular historian and philosopher cannot conceive of or grasp the Christian Revelation otherwise than as a doctrine. Within the Church itself, Orthodoxy has always emphasized the importance which ought to be given to *dogma*; and, after some time, it almost always succeeds in convincing liberalism of this necessity. Revelation must be transmitted; it is not enough to announce it and to point to it with a prophetic finger; it must be taught. Doctrines alone can be taught. Now any doctrine must on some ground or other be amenable to reason, even if one must not necessarily pursue an exact demonstration of all its elements. Modern apologetics has often stressed that science itself, a particularly remarkable doctrine, involves postulates, indemonstrables, and first facts. But this whole doctrine must be susceptible of justification, at least on the basis of its postulates; any doctrine must have a *rational structure*. According to modern apologetics, therefore, Christian doctrine, in spite of its indemonstrable presuppositions, should be in no less favourable a position than science; it should be made intelligible and be comprehended as easily as a scientific theory or a philosophical doctrine. For if the Christian Revelation is a doctrine, that is, a body of truths bound into a system, it is hard to see how it could not be subject to the jurisdiction of reason and the logical criteria of truth, or why the Christian should abstain from endeavouring to *understand it after having believed it*. The concern to penetrate that which we have believed by the use of intelligence becomes fully legitimate.

But that is the whole question: is the Christian Revelation a doctrine, and can it be presented as such? Is not the attitude of the secular historian and philosopher, who sum up and systematize the content of the Christian Revelation into a coherent doctrine, absolutely without sense? Or, to ask the question in another way: does the Latin term *doctrina* exactly translate the Greek *dogma*? Is not the Christian dogma ultimately something quite different from a system of truths?

Philological and formal considerations warn us of a difference of meaning between *dogma* and *doctrina*; dogma is not a collection of inert truths, it is the expression of an *order*, a will; it is indistinguishable from the very act of willing; dogma is, in the first place, a decree. Dogma is God's will for us, the divine exigency with relation to a person, the exigency man can acknowledge only by committing himself to serving it. Now Revelation is a dogma, and not a doctrine. In fact, it is impossible to consider it as a doctrine without serious misunderstanding. Revelation cannot be abstractly isolated from the *act of Revelation*. Revelation is the very act of God; it cannot be granted or thought apart from Him. God is entirely present in His act. It is not a mere aspect of Himself, or even an emanation from His person, that God delivers to us. It is known how emphatically John's Gospel attests that in the Son we have the true knowledge of the Father; that the Mediator does effect a mediation, but is not an intermediary, in the sense of an intercalary and subalternate link. "He that hath seen me", says Jesus, "hath seen the Father." The perfect divinity of Jesus Christ, the equality of the Father and the Son in the Trinity shown to us in Phil. 2.6 means indeed that Revelation—the abstraction of the term is regrettable—is a Presence, God's presence for us, therefore a person, and that this Person is divine, and possesses the same divinity as He of whom it speaks to us. This is a capital point which distinguishes the Christian dogmatics from any other theological system; and this point was well brought to light by Barth: God is at the same time He who reveals, He who reveals Himself, and the content of Revelation. These three propositions: God is revealed, God reveals Himself through Himself, God reveals Himself, are identical and express the whole essence of the Christian Revelation. Far from being merely something divine or a discourse upon God, a gnosis about God, Revelation is in fact a self-repetition of God.[1] For lack of sufficiently clear trinitarian thought and through its failure to conceive exactly the relationships between the Father and the Son, the Church has often lapsed into a mythological and imaginative polytheism which has barred it from a true idea of Revelation: Christ falls to the level of messengers and prophets. He no

[1] Karl Barth, *Kirchliche Dogmatik*, I, 1, pp. 311-15 *passim*. The same point of view is expressed in *Credo*: "God does not reveal Himself through any third person. He reveals Himself through Himself."

longer is the only Son, come from the Father, and the glory of
the Father confessed by our faith. On such premises Revelation
does teach us something about God, indeed something essential; for instance, it teaches us the idea of the Fatherhood of
God; but *a priori* nothing forbids us to think that this is but a
landmark in the progressive revelation of God, a phase which
can be superseded. One is led to think that God does not reveal
Himself truly and fully in the Son; one is led to minimize the
Incarnation. It seems to be a constant factor in our Hellenized
philosophical thinking to take it for granted that eternity
cannot fully reside in time, nor the infinite of fullness in a
limited finite; and so the incarnation of the only Son, come
from the Father, ceases to be thinkable for us. *Finitum non est
capax infinito* is not necessarily a Christian axiom; it expresses
the rule in the name of which we refuse to take the Incarnation
quite seriously and to believe that in Jesus Christ we have
indeed hailed the glory of the Father. Now it is precisely to the
recognition of this actual Sonhood and of this perfect divinity
that Jesus attributes the greatest importance, as the joyous
thrill aroused in him by Peter's confession at Caesarea Philippi
attests. If, in our turn, we are not capable of such a confession
(probably on account of the usual norms of our philosophical
thinking), we by-pass the very object of our faith: the Christian
Revelation in its most decisive aspect. If God, the eternal and
infinite God, were not in Christ; if Revelation were not the
very repetition of God, according to Barth's phrase, we would
find it hard to understand the mysterious reason why the
Christian's whole life and destiny gravitate around this moment
of Revelation; why it is in the presence of Jesus Christ that the
question of life and death becomes settled for each of us; why
it is Jesus Christ who comes to judge the quick and the dead.
It must indeed be that God's revelation in Jesus Christ is God
Himself.

Accordingly, if the term Revelation is taken in its exact sense
(i.e. not a doctrine about God, but the living word spoken by
the living God in Jesus Christ); if the act of Revelation is conceived of as identical with God Himself, there can no longer be
any question of justifying and understanding, or rather of
understanding through justifying Revelation. For a *presence* is
neither justified nor understood. It is a being's physical presence, not his spiritual presence which is justified by a series of

assignable contingencies. Why is my friend present by my side on the day of trial: to try and justify this would destroy the purity of his presence. A being's presence—and God's presence foremost—can only be a subject of wonder for us, an object of *ascertaining by faith*. To the friend who says to me: "Fear nothing, I am at your side!" I can only answer: "It is well, I believe you." There can be no question of anything more, not even an empirical finding, or an historical finding, i.e. an empirical one in the second degree. I can only believe that Jesus, the historical Jesus, He of the Evangelists, is the second person of the Trinity, the only Son come from the Father, the absolute self-Revelation of God.

Let us reflect, furthermore, what a justification of this Revelation, of this revealed presence, would be, and what logical conditions it would presuppose. Revelation would have to be measured by and referred to a system of truths existing outside it. For to justify is always to relate to some unquestionable norm. Now Revelation, by the sole fact of its existence, contests the very existence of such a norm. It holds, on the contrary, that all truths, starting with those of the old Testament, have no meaning save with reference to itself. Apart from itself it has no basis that the critic might purport to reach and examine; it is its own basis. It presents itself to man as a supreme court against which there is no appeal. "Without me ye can do nothing." The reality and truth of the Christian Revelation do not rest upon any superior or anterior truth or reality with which it would have to be confronted. The idea of a formal truth that remains external to every concrete step of our intellect, the postulation of logical rules warranting and making possible the movements of our thought are indeed presuppositions of any human epistemology. All epistemologies and all theories of knowledge are compelled to ask themselves the preliminary question: under what conditions is such or such a thought possible or valid? We shall therefore always tend to ask this same question at the moment of making our own the content of Revelation; we shall try at least to place Revelation among the rest of our knowledge and to elucidate it by this knowledge. We shall be all the more tempted to do so because Revelation presents itself as a singular reality and because the singular seems understandable to us only in the light of the general; thus we try to make historical facts clear by the laws of psychology and sociology. But that is precisely the intellectual perspective that Revelation summons us to renounce. As soon as one attempts to set up for Revelation a system of references and measures by which to make it legitimate or even more accessible, one in fact already negates Revelation; one can regard Christ as an historical person, one can accept the most traditional dogmas, and yet one denies the *truth* of Revelation, since this truth consists in its uniqueness and since, far from being willing to submit to man's thinking, Revelation requires, on the contrary, all thought to be brought captive in obedience to Christ. It accepts no criterion outside itself. To look for such criteria outside Revelation is already to place oneself under conditions such that Revelation can no longer be Revelation for us. The truth of Revelation can only be grasped from within when it is accepted as the supreme authority. Faith will be born the moment we accept this supreme humbling not only of reason but of our whole being. Revelation as such cannot be controlled and that is why Jesus refused to grant the sign, the miracle, the external proof asked of Him, which would have taken its place outside Revelation: this proof, moreover, would have been ineffective, and would not have provoked genuine faith, but at the most a gross superstition.

This truth can be expressed in yet different terms: God reveals Himself as *Lord*; the Christian Revelation is that of the lordship of God. To wish to know God is therefore to accept only to move, even in thought, within the limits where this lordship is manifested, i.e. within Revelation. Power is contained within Revelation, precisely in so far as its reality and truth are grounded in themselves, in so far as it need not legitimate and actualize itself otherwise than by the mere fact of taking place, because it has occurred, because it is occurring.[1] One can only know the lordship of God after having acknowledged it as valid for oneself. Here the confession of faith comes before the knowledge of faith. We must recall that the words: God is the Lord, have absolutely no meaning if I do not first of all believe so, i.e. actually yield in my whole person to this Lord's authority. Pascal's doctrine of blunting the

---

[1] Cf. Barth, *Kirchliche Dogmatik*, I, 1, pp. 321-323 *passim*. See also on the same question, Ed. Thurneysen, "Offenbarung in Religionsgeschichte und Bibel", in *Zwischen den Zeiten*, 1928.

faculties[1] may have been interpreted in a purely psychological or psychiatric sense, namely that the fulfilling of certain gestures and certain rites predisposes the soul to accept the feelings and beliefs connected with these gestures and rites. But such is not its true and complete meaning; it means in the first place that there can be no knowledge of God except in subjection to God. It is perhaps not forbidden to think that Satan would know nothing about God had he not at first been subjected to His will. For the Christian, a doctrine which would not proceed from a dogma in the sense indicated above would be utterly devoid of meaning. That is why we are right in considering as insufficient and even inaccurate accounts of the Christian doctrine written by authors for whom God is not the Lord, even though they might bring to bear upon their work all their intelligence and all their scientific probity.

We must therefore reject any comprehension of Revelation which does not respect the specific character of Revelation and which in the end regards the Christian faith as a particular case of a well-known and well-classified general type. Ultimately, we are prohibited from considering the knowledge of God as a particular case of knowledge in general, because the latter always presupposes between the knowing subject and the object known a certain relationship of adequacy which cannot be the condition of the Christian's knowledge of God. No doubt, we must not imagine, as idealism willingly does, that this relationship of adequacy always implies that cognition occurs from homogeneous to homogeneous, by reducing the different to the same; strictly speaking, that is only true in the marginal case of mathematical knowledge; however, any knowledge requires a permanent adjustment of the cognizing subject to the object of his cognition; that is precisely what makes it possible to define for each type of knowledge the normal atti-

---

[1] This refers to Section III, par. 233, of the *Pensées*, where an imaginary dialogue takes place between Pascal and the unbeliever, upon the necessity of wagering for the infinite against nothing. The unbeliever admits the demonstrable wisdom of risking a finite loss where there are "equal risks of gain and loss and the infinite to gain". His reason assents, yet he cannot believe. Pascal advises him to act *as if* he believed: "Even this will naturally make you believe and *deaden your acuteness*." W. F. Trotter's translation does not quite convey the strength of the French *abêtir*: to dull, to blunt, to make stupid. Léon Brunschvicg, renowned Pascal scholar, defines the term thus: ". . . to renounce the beliefs to which 'education' and habit have given the strength of natural necessity, but which are shown by reasoning itself to be impotent and vain. It is to return to childhood in order to reach the higher truths which are inaccessible to the short wisdom of the half-wise", L. Brunschvicg, Hachette Edition, p. 441 (translator's note).

tude to be assumed by the subject towards his object, in the presence of a given, well-determined object. Now, faith is not the mode of knowledge specially adapted to God, as reason is the faculty specially adapted to the knowledge of mathematical objects. For God never becomes for faith a determined and defined object, requiring a certain type of cognitive adaptation in order to be known. Faith attains God in the Bible, in Biblical history, in this or that personal experience. But this Bible, the work of man, this human history and this personal experience are inadequate to the reality of God. So that the object which faith pursues in order to reach the knowledge of God, and which is the bearer of the self-revelation of God, at the same time conceals God and makes it impossible to apprehend Him. Faith does not know God in virtue of any absolutely characteristic signs which connote this object; faith knows God both through revealing signs and in spite of them.[1] Different from other objects we may know, God has no absolutely characteristic signs; He has no specifically divine properties by which we might recognize Him. All his attributes remain equivocal. The work of rational theology, which sets out to establish God's attributes *ne varietur* and in a clear way is therefore vain. I cannot floast of knowing God just because I have recognized one or another of His attributes. The crucial difference between Biblical history and the mythologies is that in the latter every god is connoted by fixed attributes through which men will recognize him with certainty, whereas in the former, God is always beyond His own signs, refusing to be characterized otherwise than by the fact that He is He that is. So that the knowledge of God is not the result of an adaptation of the human mind to a given property of an object; in the last analysis the knowledge of God is accounted for by a miraculous, ever-miraculous initiative on the part of God who triumphs in us over the obstacles erected by our own endeavour at knowledge. God must be grasped in the midst of a reality which denies and contradicts Him; so that it is in vain that the knowing subject is a spiritualized being, he has in vain purified his intelligence and freed himself from the realm of sense; it is not thus that he will know God. In the pagan philosophies, and even in Platonism, the knowledge of God is necessarily bound up with man's effort to turn away from the sensible, to assume

---

[1] Cf. K. Barth, *Kirchliche Dogmatik*, I, 1, pp. 173-174.

I

the inner attitude which befits the knowledge of God, because, in the end, God has a certain nature to which, if we wish to know Him, we must conform. The connection between the problem of knowledge and that of a spiritual discipline has been one of the characteristics of philosophical thought from Plato to Spinoza and as far as Bergson. Indeed, it is the characteristic of natural knowledge; we can define as natural a knowledge which rests upon the cognizing subject's effort to conform to the object to be known. This conception arises from the idea that every object is to some degree a datum; therefore, it has *a nature*. To know objectively is to respect this nature and conform to it. Natural knowledge—and this is where pragmatism possesses a share of truth—always presupposes an adaptation of the subject to the object. But precisely, this adaptation is possible only in so far as the essential nature of the object is, if not known, at least foreseen, before the particular act of knowledge which will reveal it to us completely. Only with the greatest difficulty can the scientist undertake a piece of research if he cannot place the object under study in a certain more or less well-defined group of objects, if he has not the least idea of its nature. Moreover, it is this necessity which gives to the ideas of categories, classes and groups their whole importance in scientific research. Before recognizing the presence of a particular object, we first of all posit the nature of the object, the nature of the group of objects to which it belongs and, finally, nature itself as the indefinite ensemble of all possible objects. Even though we may yet know nothing about the object, we know at least that it belongs to nature and that as such it has certain spatio-temporal properties. This means that, from the start, the object is thought of in a system of determinations, that it is conceived as passive. But it is God's characteristic to have no nature; this is what makes us speak of Him and acknowledge Him as supernatural. It is the ultimate reason why there cannot be any natural knowledge of God. God can be said to be both the object and the subject of our knowledge; for it is He who produces it and gives it form. In faith, we know of God only that He intends for us to know of Him, and never can we extort any fragment of the knowledge of God. It is the same with Revelation as a whole, if it is true that Revelation is the act of God and that the act of God coincides with God Himself.

Accordingly, philosophy is not competent to work *with Revelation as a starting-point*. For this would necessarily mean that it takes Revelation as a datum, as a passive object, and that it treats it according to the nature it believes it has recognized in it. In so doing, it would change Revelation, if not in its form, at least in its content. It would put in the place of Revelation either an historical fact, a psychological or sociological fact, or a group of doctrines. In so far as liberalism and orthodoxy are mere philosophical systems, it is in transformations such as these that they indulge. Anselm himself cannot help reasoning upon the necessity of God, i.e. of a concept substituted to God Himself.

We must therefore conclude that philosophy cannot present itself as a complete comprehension of Revelation. This does not mean that we are to condemn as impossible and illegitimate a philosophical attempt which would consider the Christian revelation as a datum and present itself as a philosophical exegesis of Christianity. But precisely it would be a purely philosophical undertaking and could be achieved even apart from faith, or only resort to faith as an auxiliary form of knowledge, a form of intuition or *Einfühlung*. The believer will be justified in not regarding this as an understanding of Revelation, since Revelation here is no longer the sole norm of intelligibility and since beside and perhaps even above Revelation there are philosophical norms of intelligibility, philosophical criteria of truth, under which the philosopher—and legitimately so as a philosopher—will wish to subsume the content of Revelation. This is indeed an interesting endeavour to understand Revelation, and the theologian will be well advised not to ignore it. But he will be able to state in principle that it is not a *faithful* interpretation, since it is content to take Revelation as an object and since the philosopher has not felt himself related in an exclusive way to Revelation as a whole. The theologian can accept an interpretation of Revelation only to the extent that it finds all its norms in Revelation. In fact, whether we turn to Schleiermacher, or Kant, or Sabatier, we always find a certain regard for the Biblical Revelation in its singularity and uniqueness. But the interpretation thus established finds itself enshrined in a philosophical interpretation of the religious fact.

.   .   .   .   .   .

Must we then conclude that Revelation can only be received and announced in faith, repeated and heard, and that in consequence the Church's sole theological function is *preaching*? One might think so, when seeing the extent to which academic theology has remained in fact, and sometimes even in principle, aloof from the life of the Church. Is not any religious awakening, any pietistic movement, accompanied by a certain distrust of theology in discursive form? Is not pietism often ready to brand any theological construction as pure philosophy? In a sense, it is quite correct to say that Revelation can only be announced, i.e. repeated, through human linguistic and intellectual means. "We are here faced with the capital fact that the recognition of the Christian data is not placed in our hands."[1] But does it follow that the laborious and constant endeavour of all the faithful who have wished to understand their faith is in vain? If no philosophical exegesis can be of use to us in grasping the content of Revelation, does it follow that no effort of thought is necessary here? Cannot the preaching of the Church be done without this reflective effort? Or is it not, on the contrary, at this point that we are obliged, so as to avoid any misconception of the philosopher's part, to define in its true terms the understanding of Revelation? In other words, in the face of philosophies of Revelation which, throughout the history of the Church, may have presented themselves as dogmatics and even as the only possible dogmatics, we feel compelled to define a dogmatic understanding of Revelation. When this is done, we shall at last have acquired the freedom of movement necessary to define the activity permitted to the Christian philosopher.

But let us beware of setting this problem of understanding Revelation in philosophic terms; let us not ask how Revelation can be received by a human mind. For such a pursuit would soon end in our asking ourselves under what conditions—preliminary, of course—the human understanding can accept Revelation. The latter would then be questioned, instead of being taken seriously for granted as the sole norm for our thinking. We would perforce seek to establish a relationship of consistency between our minds and Revelation. As Barth has written, the problem of theological knowledge for the theologian is not: "How is it possible for man to know Revelation?

[1] C. Hauter, unpublished course in dogmatics.

(as if it could actually be disputed that Revelation is known as such! as if we had to expect from an examination of human knowledge the proof of man's ability to know Revelation!) The problem, on the contrary, is: what is man's knowledge of the divine Revelation? (setting down as a principle that it is Revelation itself which, through its own working, creates in man the necessary points of contact (*Anknüpfungspunkte*)."[1] It is perhaps one more error inherited from philosophy to envisage Revelation first of all in itself, then in its relationship to man, as if Revelation were not by its own essence for man, as if God could be or intended to be any other but Emmanuel. Taken as a whole, Revelation is that of the eternal and holy God to finite and sinful man. There is no doubt, and it should even be emphasized as one of the essential features of Biblical Revelation, that it is a miracle that man should be able to conceive of this Revelation, that things "which entered not into the heart of man" can still be understood by this heart of man. This is the very miracle of the Church's existence. For the ecclesiological fact has a meaning for the Christian doctrine of knowledge: it means that God has always created human communities which, whatever the slowness or speed of comprehension of the individuals composing them, have understood not only a part or elements of Revelation, but Revelation as such, and eliminated with rare assurance the heresies, i.e. the partial misunderstandings. It is remarkable that those who elaborated and gave form to the Christian dogmas were not persons of exceptional intelligence. The Fathers of the Council of Nicaea, Hauter points out, were men of very slight theological training; it is astonishing that they should have elaborated a correct dogma. It is striking that the Church has always acted collectively, and that nevertheless it has not fallen into error, but has been able to discard the most sublime innovations conceived by the strongest personalities. It is therefore perfectly vain to try and think a Christian truth, a Revelation, apart from the fact that it is effectively and actually received and understood. In order to give a basis to his natural theology which is in fact a kind of philosophy of Revelation, Brunner insists somewhat heavily upon the fact that there is, in man, an ability to understand and to feel which distinguishes him from animality and predisposes him to receive the revealed message.

[1] K. Barth, *Kirchliche Dogmatik*, I, 1, pp. 27-28.

Such an elementary truth cannot be disputed, but how does this natural faculty in man help us in the least to understand Revelation? On the one hand, this faculty would have enabled us to understand things quite different from Revelation as well, and it has in fact made assimilable and intelligible for man doctrines which are the exact reverse of the Biblical Revelation; on the other hand, this human faculty is at the source of all the errors of interpretation which make up the Christian heresies.

To study Revelation, then, it is necessary to cling to Revelation itself and to avoid trying to indicate under what conditions it is receivable for man. We must renounce considering it apart from the fact that through the assistance of the Holy Spirit acting in our minds, it is understood and received in its integrity. That is precisely what Mohammed does not acknowledge; he thinks he is formulating, as are the Christians, the idea of a Revelation, but he adds that the Christians have not understood it and that some of its points have eluded them. This idea is in utter contradiction to the Biblical notion of Revelation. For the Christian it is inconceivable that certain elements of Revelation should have been lost and that we should only possess a mutilated revelation for which some subtle archaeologist might some day unearth the missing complement. Quite possibly, Revelation has at times been veiled; at certain periods of the Church certain elements may not have been given sufficient value; but in one way or another, either by means of the devotion of the simple or through the reformers God has always allowed the truth to remain intact.

It is a wholly pagan idea which leads us to presuppose a content of Revelation, apart from the reception of this content by certain persons, as if God's Revelation could remain with God without reaching men, as if God had failed to reach them, as if the Incarnation had meant the failure of God! Some believed, many believed. These assertions of the New Testament are essential to the very content of Revelation. Without these hints, Revelation would not be fully itself. God would have told us nothing if He had not also told us that He made us hear Him. That God's Word could remain without effect is Biblically an impossible proposition. When the Prologue of John announces that "the light shineth in darkness, and the darkness apprehended it not", it announces the Crucifixion.

It shows that man could not comprehend the act of Redemption during its historical execution; in no way does it mean that Revelation was to remain an absolute mystery. In fact, the believer is indeed he who does not comprehend the act of God, and who is even scandalized by it, but who acknowledges and understands that he cannot understand, who acknowledges and understands that there could be no salvation for him were it not for this incomprehensible act of God.

Revelation gives birth to faith. In revealing Himself God intends man to repent and to believe. For faith is the comprehension of Revelation. It is as miraculous as Revelation itself. That is also why the theologian will refrain from studying the conditions under which faith is possible and the intellectual and psychological precedents of faith, even when empirical psychology allows him to ascertain the existence of such precedents. For they can never have any common basis with faith itself. If understanding Revelation meant determining the conditions of its possibility; if understanding were meant here in a scientific and analytical sense, the theologian would be he who naturalizes Revelation—which amounts to destroying it *qua* Revelation. For, if we wish to be true to Revelation, we have no right to refer it to a subject of our choice, a being whose receptive power we would predetermine according to our psychological theories and our theory of knowledge. For even though this subject might conform essentially to human reality, he could be of no interest to us; for it is not for such a being that Revelation is intended; it is not by such a being that Revelation is received. When the Word of God is addressed to man it modifies him, it renews his mind, it enables him to understand what the "old man" (the man described by the psychologies and philosophies) could not have understood. We cannot help reasoning as though the cognitive relation which is established in Revelation, were a relation between terms not modified by the very fact of Revelation. In Revelation God— the same God of whom the philosophers speak—becomes Emmanuel, God with me, or more precisely, the Father of our Lord Jesus Christ and our Father; and I become this Father's adopted child; I am myself, in the Revelation which reaches me, benefiting from the grace which is in Jesus Christ. "If any man is in Christ he is a new creature." That is why the cognitive relation of faith eludes the analysis of the philosophers, who could at the most give an external and objective analysis of it, just as philosophical analysis cannot recognize its God in this relationship, though He is indeed the same God, as we have established in the previous chapter. For He who actually is *Ens a se et per se* becomes through the act of self-revelation the Father of Jesus Christ and our Father. When Léon Brunschvicg suspects some impurity in the Christian God and wishes to lead the believer to the true conversion which would make him into a completely spiritual being, he does not know that he is asking of us something contradictory and impossible. He is asking us no less than to leave the bounds of Revelation, the bounds in which Revelation encloses us. We must grasp the epistemological relationship in faith between the subject and the object in its uniqueness; for, on the one hand, the object is at the same time a subject and as such it makes certain claims upon the subject of knowledge; it demands to be grasped as subject and will not accept the objectifying to which the cognizing subject would submit it. On the other hand, the subject and the object cannot be transposed into a *situation* different from that defined in Revelation itself; the subject is the believer and not any believer, but solely he who believes in God the Father, Son and Holy Ghost, one God eternally blest; God is not only the infinite and perfect Being, the Creator of the world as reason grasps Him; He is essentially He whom we know in the Son. Here we have an absolutely unique *epistemological* situation. All other epistemological situations have something in common. Scientific knowledge and even aesthetic knowledge can be described in general terms. It is even possible to see what is alike in both these attitudes, to bring out the identity of the subject in both modes of knowledge and show that the scientist and the artist, different as they are in their respective orientations, are after all the same man. In any case, a common measure can be discovered between these two subjects and all possible subjects in all possible attitudes; but there is no common measure between the believer and the unbeliever,[1] between him who lives and thinks within Revelation and him who merely seeks. There is no common measure between cognitive discovery and Revelation.

---

[1] If such a common measure exists, it can only be found in the fact that the believer actually knows the unbeliever's doubts; that at certain moments of his history he ceases to be a believer.

Let us not forget that the dogmatician coincides with the believer, that dogmatic comprehension is none other than the comprehension of the revealed, the understanding of faith. Accordingly, we can see that the dogmatician will not wish to comprehend in the same manner as the philosopher. In particular, the dogmatician will leave aside all that pertains to the necessity and possibility of his object. In so far as he leaves out any speculation upon the possibility of his object, he is like any scientist concerned with facts. But by discarding any question concerning necessity he immediately differs from the scientist; for the scientist's intention, even if he is an historian, is indeed to show how a fact, be it contingent, or historical, is nevertheless also necessary. Now the dogmatician does not speak of the possibility of Revelation, the Incarnation, or the Resurrection, for if he ventured into this conceptual realm, it might easily be shown to him that such facts are neither necessary nor possible. Only a demonstration of spirit and power can make us accept them. Scheler has often attempted to find again by way of philosophical analysis the Christian ideas of Incarnation and Revelation. Concerning the Incarnation, for instance, Scheler reasons thus: doubtless God could have saved man by any other means. But in any event it was necessary that the Infinite enter in substance into a member of mankind, in order to secure for the latter a state superior to that before the Fall. We do not dispute the apologetic value of such an argument; we do not deny to the minister the right to use it in the cure of souls, and for ourselves, we often find in it a means of assuring our own faith—but not a means of entering it, nor of obtaining it, nor even of understanding what God has done. For such an argument supplies us at the most with *analogical* understanding: as it is necessary that the infinite lift up the finite to itself in order to raise the finite above itself, so it is necessary that God become incarnate in order to call mankind unto Himself. But analogical comprehension is only a makeshift resource, which science hastens to exclude from its methods. Because it was founded upon the principle of analogy, medieval science has fallen in to disuse. More particularly, if an incarnation was needed, it is not thereby proven that it had to occur in Jesus Christ and through the earthly history of Jesus Christ. Let us acknowledge that dogmatics would hardly be a serious science, or that it would tolerate the most foolish assertions, if it were the science of analogical possibilities and necessities.

Moreover, the immediate consequence of such a method would be to build up opposite God a system of references and truths (possibility, necessity) independent from Him. God would be subjected to such a system; and it is well known into what difficulties and what heresies medieval theology fell because it postulated the existence of eternal truths, and refused to admit that creation must be understood as voluntary creation of the eternal truths themselves, *e nihilo*. Though the revealed may be expressed in human terms, we must not believe that human concepts express it adequately; when Jesus speaks of the necessity of His death, He makes use of a concept which is by no means the equivalent of logical necessity, or of moral obligation, or of the spontaneous dynamics of values. This necessity is devoid of meaning if considered in itself, formally, divorced from the soteriological whole of which it is a part. To understand the necessity of Jesus' death (and any theologian as well as any believer must do so in the end) does not mean to make this death intelligible, acceptable to our reason by placing it among a group of rational or empirical causes. But in what then does the activity of the dogmatician's thought consist? What is the dogmatic comprehension of Revelation? That this activity is, at any rate, indispensable appears clearly from an examination of the conditions of existence of the Christian Church. The Church announces (i.e. repeats) the Good Tidings. But it does not do so in the absolute; it does so with a view to the community the preacher addresses. It presumes—and the unbeliever will not fail to think this an exorbitant claim—to pronounce the word of a living God *upon* our time, *upon* our situation, *upon* the condition of each one of us. Let us not say that the Church *adapts* its message to concrete situations; that is a convenient but very false and dangerous manner of expression, for sooner or later it leads to distorting or modernizing Revelation. Let us not say either that the Church *particularizes* its message, for this expression also implies that the truth of the Revelation is purely general, that God does not take man into account in the singularity of his existence and vocation, and that He leaves this concern to the Church, as the lawgiver leaves to subordinates the task of adding to his work according to time and place. On the contrary, let us say that the mission of the Church's preaching is to make everyone realize how the revealed message concerns him personally and actually reaches him in his innermost being as a man; the question is only to shed light by appropriate means upon that which the hardness of our hearts and the slowness of our understandings might make us forget or pass over in silence. The point is to prove that the assertions "God is living" or "the Word of God is for man" are not merely general or approximate statements, but that without changing or adding anything to the Word of God it is actually so every time we study it with attention and respect. The ministry of preaching is not the ministry of teaching in the strict sense of that word, for he who teaches is concerned with lowering his message to his pupil's level, by simplifying and popularizing if need be. On the contrary, the preacher's concern is to make his listener realize that he is facing an absolute, integral and decisive truth. It is of essential importance to prepare the souls for the authentic presence of God in His word. But let us remember immediately that the difficulties we experience in accurately defining the Church's preaching are not merely theoretical; but that every Sunday the Church is tempted to adapt and particularize, to announce an incomplete gospel to such or such a community, and to express with regard to each concrete situation some truths, instead of the whole decisive truth. It is all too easy to divide the truth into successive chapters, as in academic teaching, and to confine oneself to the subject-matter of one's chapter. But a sermon is not about a little question, it is always about the whole of Revelation, as it is contained in both the Old and the New Testaments.

Accordingly, the theologian's intellectual activity can appear at first as a critical activity: he tests and plumbs the actual preaching of the Church, confronting it with Revelation and judging it; whenever necessary he puts it right and warns it. The necessity of the dogmatic activity stems from the perennial danger for the Church of adapting or particularizing a message which in its most intimate structure is already perfectly adapted to man as he really is, and so singular that every man is questioned by it. There can be no question, Barth remarks,[1] of identifying the particular preaching of any Church with the Word of God. So that it is the very characteristic of the

---

[1] *Kirchliche Dogmatik*, I, 1, p. 284.

true Church, the *Ecclesia Militans*, that no dogmatics can be
built which, even if it is entirely positive, is not made of *questions*
causing the mind to oscillate between what the Church announces and what the Bible *requires it to announce*.[1] Thus, Barth
is led to postulate the principle that the characteristic of a
scientific dogmatics rests in the fact that dogmatics questions
itself on the agreement between the Church's preaching and
Revelation contained in the Holy Scripture. Such is the critical
essence of dogmatics, and Barth warns against a dogmatics
which, following the example of Catholic dogmatics, would
essentially be a justification and confirmation of the Church's
preaching. The dogmatician's function is to measure the dis-
crepancy (which we know always exists) between actual preaching and the revealed Word; and understandably (we shall return to this later) these delicate operations presuppose a very
complete scientific and historical knowledge as well as the use
of numerous intellectual or philosophical techniques.

But these operations (and this is a point which, in our view,
Barth has not sufficiently emphasized in his definition of dogmatics) presuppose in the first place an endeavour to conceive
Revelation in a total and systematic manner. The error or
heresy which at every instant threatens preaching rests not so
much in an intentional falsification of the revealed message as
in excessive emphasis upon or weakening of certain elements
of Revelation. The great Christian heresies often arose from
the preaching ministry itself. It is easy to understand how the
preacher, thinking of a particular audience and a particular
spiritual problem may be tempted to lay stress upon certain
features and suppress others. It is important therefore that the
theologian be able to re-establish the lost balance by showing
the exact place of each element within the whole. That is why
we believe the definition of dogmatics as the endeavour to
systematize Revelation, or again to grasp Revelation in its unity,
is legitimate. No doubt, this definition is not free of danger:
any endeavour at systematizing necessarily resorts to a principle
of systematization, and this brings in the danger of subordinating Revelation to a principle (be it formal and purely
logical) which is foreign to it. That is the error which beset

[1] Similarly, P. Althaus (*Grundriss der Dogmatik*) defines theology (p. 7) as the
methodical and self-critical reflection undertaken by the Church in order to
determine its own nature and reality and thus establish the norms of its worship
and action.

many theologians who believed their work to be completed the day they were able to prove that the Biblical message contained no contradiction. It is perfectly normal that Mohammed should manifest this concern in connection with the Koran and that he should give us the absence of contradiction as the criterion of the Koran's truth: the Koran is a human work which can only claim the usual human guarantees. But we think that many a Christian thinker very nearly wasted his time in attempting to establish the perfect logical coherence of Scripture. It is known that in order to answer the neo-Platonist's criticism, and in particular, that of Porphyry, Eusebius of Caesarea, St. John Chrysostom, St. Jerome, and even St. Augustine himself in his *De Consensu Evangelistarum*, endeavoured to establish that the accounts of the Gospels, and therefore the revealed message, manifest a logically satisfactory agreement. It is indeed attractive to win this victory which shelters Christian dogmatics from the most usual and, in the eyes of our understanding, most decisive human criticisms. In reality, this ought not to be the dogmatician's chief concern: his efforts at systematization must start only from a principle contained in and marked as central by Revelation. That is what the Apostles themselves have done. To be convinced of this, it suffices to refer to the first public sermons of the early Church, as well as to its first confessions of faith: the subject never is an exhaustive account of all the great Christian facts, nor of the great Christian truths; it is the centre of perspective starting from which all these facts and all these truths assume their decisive meaning. "Ye crucified [Jesus] whom God raised from the dead" (Acts 4.10). Such is the starting point of all Christian teaching. From the moment when man understands that this Jesus of Nazareth who died on the Cross is the risen and glorified Christ, raised to the right hand of God, or more simply yet, that Jesus is the Lord, the whole Biblical Revelation becomes clear; by this we mean that the whole Revelation orders itself around its centre. Henceforth, it is possible to constitute a scientific dogmatics: that is, to relate all the elements of the Scriptural Revelation to this centre and essence of Christianity. A dogmatics becomes possible, because henceforth we supersede (without despising it) the purely historical point of view which recognizes in the Bible a diversity of sources, inspirations, themes and currents, so that any synthesis will necessarily appear as a compromise in which one Scriptural element or another will have to be sacrificed. Accordingly, without denying the differences of tonality found between John and Paul, or between Paul and James, the dogmatician will realize that these differences have meaning only in relation to a fundamental tone and that they can be really understood only with a view to this fundamental tone.

Referring back a few decades, the reader who may still be bearing in mind the dogmatics of Frommel will say that we are merely reopening the old dispute between deductive and inductive dogmatics; that we are simply taking sides, beyond all the theories of Christian experience, for a deductive dogmatics which sets down a central principle and from it deduces the necessary logical consequences—and through this it is scientific; that the understanding of Revelation consists in introducing into the revealed itself the requirements of rational demonstration; in short, that we are coming back to the dogmatics of Kaftan, who in 1888 proposed, as a dangerous novelty, to prove the truth of Christianity by confining himself to Christianity alone, i.e. without transforming Christianity into a system of objective ideas acceptable by any reasonable being. Here, the attempt would no longer be to show that the truth of Revelation is covered and, so to speak, warranted by those truths before which reason has always bowed, but to prove directly the rationality and universal validity of the Christian faith founded upon Revelation. The principle of this Revelation of God being recognized as rational, it should be possible to deduce clearly and rigorously all the articles of the Christian faith, and to show that each of the dogmatic propositions of the Christian faith represents a necessary moment of it. Thus Christianity should find itself scientifically established or justified.[1]

We believe that our conception differs entirely from Kaftan's. Primarily because we do not seek to establish the first principle of Christianity and even less to establish its rationality. We seek to find the perspective in which to read Holy Scripture, or the significant moment of Revelation, or again, the meaning of the history of Revelation. Jesus Himself attests that such a perspective exists: on the way to Emmaus He explains to the two disciples the meaning and the orientation of the Revelation

[1] Julius Kaftan, *Die Wahrheit der christlichen Religion*, p. 15. See also the last chapter of the book, "*Der Beweiss des Christentums*".

of God in history. "And beginning from Moses and from all the prophets, he interpreted to them *in all the scriptures* the things concerning himself" (Luke 24.27).

Ordinarily, Jesus shows Revelation, is Revelation, and, in a literal sense, produces it. But often also, in the presence of witnesses slow to understand, or whose faith wavers, Jesus explains: "O foolish men, and slow of heart to believe in all that the prophets have spoken! Behooved it not the Christ to suffer these things and to enter into his glory?" (Luke 24.25-6). The dogmatician cannot explain otherwise than Jesus did; he does not start from a principle, he does not reconstruct. Reasoning is excluded from the dogmatician's work, at least as an essential method of construction. This orientation of Revelation is a part of the very act which creates it, it is not a norm outside Revelation, a principle which allows us to judge it. In the second place, the bond of necessity this basic orientation of Revelation allows us to grasp between its parts or between its different moments is in no way comparable to logical necessity,[1] for this necessary bond does not by any means invalidate the radical contingency of Revelation. Christ had to suffer! We are immediately tempted to pass from this Biblical assertion to a sort of spiritual law, that of *Stirb und werde*, to speak of the necessity of suffering and to build up educational systems leading the child to maturity through suffering. But no, that is not the question. This necessity is explained by Scripture alone, because of the prophecy. "This was done that it might be fulfilled which was spoken by the Lord through the prophet," as Matthew constantly repeats. This necessity only appears to

---

[1] We must add, however, that the articulations dogmatics endeavours to discover are in no way in defiance of human logic, a destruction of this logic, or a refusal of the principle of identity. The Word of God is actually a word which must be grasped in its formal content (both logical and grammatical) by man's reason; it does not require, as do the revelations of the pagan religions, a soothsayer in order to be interpreted; the rationality, which is its external characteristic, already suffices to distinguish it from the non-Christian revelations. In order that man may grasp it, he has to have remained man, fully man, and we see that common grace has provided for this by preserving the intellectual ability of mankind (what Brunner calls *Wortmächtigkeit*) in spite of periods of barbarism, and by making possible the progress of enlightenment. Nevertheless, it must be recalled that form is never totally independent of content, and therefore that for him who proceeds to the true understanding of Revelation the principle of identity acquires a suppleness it did not possess in its profane use; similarly the scientist realizes that, in fact, properties which in the layman's eyes were mutually exclusive can belong to the same body—just as the theologian and the believer understand that terms which are contradictory in psychological and moral experience can unite and co-operate in the life according to grace: God's absolute sovereignty and human freedom, grace and responsibility.

him who has accepted to be led by the prophecy towards the
New Testament; it only convinces him who has so been seized
by God that he witnesses truly from within the unfolding of the
redemptive plan through history. In other words, this necessity
is not visible apart from the act by which the Holy Spirit
thrusts us into the history of Redemption. It cannot be defined
otherwise than as the inner necessity of an absolutely contingent
act.

By analogy, we can attempt to view more closely the meaning
of such an expression: by chance, a Christian hears the appeal
of a missionary or an evangelizing cause which is asking for help
towards one of its fields of action. This appeal is not specifically
directed at him. Of course, he has the vocation of a witness; but
he is already exercising this vocation in his own environment
and knows that, there, magnificent possibilities await his action.
And yet, gradually or suddenly the certainty rises in him: you
must of necessity respond to the appeal you have just heard; if
you do not answer, all is lost for you, it is all up with your
spiritual destiny. I know of no necessity more absolute than
that which determines this man, and yet this necessity, which
afterwards he will try to couch in terms as objective as possible,
could not have been disclosed by a religious analysis of his
ethical situation. In its unshakable necessity, his act remains
radically contingent. But even of this analogy it could be said
that it contains, not a real necessity but a moral obligation and
that moral obligation does not entirely elude objective analysis:
the Christian in question could have asked some competent
person's advice and received from him a precise indication and a
confirmation of his calling. On the contrary, the *nexus* which unite
the moments of the Biblical Revelation could not be detected
by any human wisdom. He who is in a position to benefit from
Revelation can alone understand its internal necessity. And
that is when what in the eyes of natural man was indeed sheer
folly, an unco-ordinated sequence of acts without inner meaning
(and we are convinced that to the unbeliever's eyes the Biblical
events present just such a disorderly aspect), becomes divine
wisdom (1 Cor. 1.24). We are not in the presence of a necessity
enabling man to foresee by himself, that is to reconstruct the
scheme of Redemption. In reality, this is indeed man's secret
yearning: for him, to understand is always to do or to do anew.
The concepts of objective necessity and moral obligation are

for him the instruments of this foresight or of this prospective reconstruction of objects, events and even acts.

And that is why, contrary to the thinking of post-Kantian theology, the concepts drawn from ethical experience are unable to express revealed realities fully; to him who gains insight into theology, there truly appears a suspension of the ethical order. Autonomy no longer is the chief value, moral judgement gives way to charity which beareth all things, and moral obligation can neither foresee nor limit the staggering suddenness of vocations ordained by God.

That is also why we are able to penetrate the sense of the history of Redemption only because God has placed us at the close of that history, in the last days when the times are already fulfilled. It will not be the theologian's task to discover in Revelation either a principle or an evolutionary rhythm enabling him to channel the stream of human history and to foresee the sequence of God's interventions in history; Hegel and his dialectical method can be of *no* assistance to the theologian; and the theology of experience has at least done us the service of freeing the minds from the impact of Hegelianism. The necessity of redemptive history only appears when this history is achieved and only reveals itself to him who benefits from its completion.[1]

The theologian must therefore feel constrained to create a new concept of necessity with which neither ethics nor the sciences of nature could supply him. Moreover, this was to be foreseen: Christian truth cannot be reduced to other types of truth, either in its phenomenological structure or in its objective essence; therefore, it is normal that no human science can offer its method to dogmatics. And so it is essential to define the comprehension of Revelation quite apart from all the usual

---

[1] We have chosen at random (for such texts abound) a text by Calvin which seems to appeal to the notion of necessity alone for purposes of dogmatic exposition; the problem is to explain that man could only be saved by the Incarnation. "For since our iniquities having put an obstacle between God and ourselves, had alienated us from the Kingdom of Heaven, and had turned God away from us, no one could be the means of our reconciliation who could not reach God. But who was the creature who could have achieved this? Could it have been one of the children of Adam? But all they, with their first father, would have loathed appearing before His face. . . . Surely, it was a wholly hopeless case, had not God in His majesty condescended to us, as we did not have it in us to rise to Him" (*Institutes*). Here, in appearance, and also in fact if considered from within a Christian mental outlook, is implacable logic. But can we sincerely think that this logic would have any power of persuasion over a mind remaining perfectly Greek or one denying God any kind of anthropomorphic personality?

forms of comprehension. It is because it suggests a possible confusion between the understanding of spiritual things and the understanding of the mystery of God that Anselm's attempt seems to us so dangerous for dogmatics.

Again, the understanding of Revelation, or dogmatic understanding, could be defined as the understanding of mystery *qua* mystery. This formula makes a clear distinction between dogmatic understanding and scientific and philosophical understanding; the latter two are also aware of mystery. But one of them—scientific understanding—attempts to nibble away the share of mystery and to establish clearly under any given circumstances the part which is known and the part which is mystery; and mystery for it is equivalent to the unknown. Now the unknown is always provisional, unless it is identified, as in Spencer's thinking, with the unknowable, which is indistinguishable from the absurd. In fact, we see science shunning more and more certain unknowable problems, reputedly devoid of meaning; among these are the problems of the origin of life and those of the origins of mankind, which are abandoned somewhat disparagingly to philosophical speculation, although for a long time they had been a part of scientific preoccupations. Philosophical understanding, on the other hand, when it is purged of all positivism and true to its calling, does not dissolve mystery, but attempts to show the kind of reality belonging to mystery, to integrate it in its own place in the real, and to show how it should be approached and encompassed. When it is concerned with religion, it shows the necessity of recognizing mystery and of accepting it, as well as the necessity of taking the decisive step towards mystery. It appears that any philosophical quest limits itself to this approach to mystery. Christian dogmatics, on the contrary, setting aside all these prolegomena, takes mystery in itself as its object; by means of critical comparison with other realms of knowledge, it establishes what makes mystery to be irrevocable mystery and probes its extent and depth; it dissolves all attempts to subsume the mystery of God's Revelation under more general concepts which would alter its specificity; then it attempts to understand mystery in itself; which means that, granting mystery in its abrupt and unaccountable brutality, dogmatic understanding shows its internal economy without ever yielding to the temptation of rationalizing its structure. It therefore discards the two questions to which ultimately any scientific or philosophical inquiry can be reduced: the why and the how, and confines itself to emphasizing the strength of the bond which unites the parts or moments of the mystery and to making it manifest in its uniqueness, in its unity and in its totality.[1] The essential difference between the philosophical and scientific forms of comprehension and dogmatic comprehension can easily be grasped in connection with an example[2], that of the mystery of election. Election remains, in the "dogmatic account", a complete mystery; that is, it is impossible to explain the reason why God, for the sake of a few, is willing to leave His hidden existence; we must acknowledge this initiative of God as an absolutely gratuitous act. But, if we do not understand the mystery of this election, the scandal of which is even increased by the fact that it also seems to entail the mystery of dual predestination, (at any rate as a concrete possibility), at least we can comprehend that God would not really be God, the God of Jesus Christ if He did not possess the privilege of freely choosing His elect. If He acted mechanically towards all men, He would be identified with nature. He would not really be the God of love, if man could impose himself on His attention by virtue of his moral dignity. The mystery of election remains insoluble, but by stating its existence clearly the dogmatician establishes the non-natural essence of the Biblical God.

Lastly, it appears to us that dogmatic understanding can also be characterized by an idea essential to any systematization of Christian dogma: that of *dialectics*. Indeed, we shall venture to say that the expression of dialectical theology claimed today by one particular school of thought is actually a tautology: Christian truth—and this is what makes it explode the usual frameworks of logic and denounce their insufficiency—cannot be expressed in a univocal way, or, in other terms, revealed truth cannot be grasped in one single act of human thought, but rather in two acts which oppose each other and between which the mind is then compelled to re-establish, not a synthetic bond, but a *tension*. Let us place ourselves at the very centre of Revelation: before Jesus Christ we are constrained to assert simultaneously (though psychologically these are two successive

[1] P. Althaus expresses this excellently by saying: "Dogmatics is the conceptually accurate critical representation of dogma in its inner relationships and its totality" (*Grundriss der Dogmatik*, t. I. p. 104), translated from the German.

[2] We draw this example from Hauter's unpublished course in dogmatics.

assertions on our part) that Jesus Christ is fully God and that
He is fully man. We are constrained to assert that in Him,
God both reveals and conceals Himself, that Jesus is for us
both a cause of salvation and a cause of stumbling; that in Him
salvation is won, but because Jesus is always He who is coming,
we are saved only in hope; that the hour cometh and is already
come; that in Jesus Christ God alone brings about our salvation
and that, because we are saved by grace we can also work
towards our salvation. The Christian is in the world, but not
of the world. As a sinner, he is held personally responsible for
sin which is original; it is in subjection to the Lord that he
discovers his freedom. Indeed, not one of the fundamental
assertions of Christian theology can be expressed in any other
way than the dialectical. Besides, this fact explains the rise of
heresies and their permanency in the course of history; heresy
is always a denial of this dialectical movement so contrary, not
to all logic, but to our accustomed logic. Heresy is always this
lazy tendency whereby we think one term at the exclusion of the
other, or grant one of the terms of a dialectical proposition a
privilege over the other—whereas the two terms must be
maintained simultaneously, and become false when set down
in the absolute independently from each other: if Christianity
postulated predestination alone, it would be a fatalism—but it
also postulates freedom. If the Kingdom of Heaven were
situated only at the end of time, Christianity would be but an
Utopian millenarianism; but the Kingdom is also at hand, and
already realized among us; if the Christian were merely saved
and justified he would no longer be a man, but he is also, at
the same time, a sinner. Clearly then, the dogmatic idea of
dialectics is very different from the philosophical, and more
particularly from the Hegelian idea. For its problem is not to
oppose a thesis and an antithesis in order to reconcile them in a
higher synthesis or in order to draw from their juxtaposition a
truth encompassing them both. On the contrary, the problem
is to mark the opposition between the terms (which, incidentally, is never a merely logical contradiction) and to emphasize
that they are, nevertheless, absolutely solidary: time is nothing
if it is not radically opposed to eternity, but it would also be
nothing if it were never encountered by eternity. That is why
we say that there is between the two terms a tension by which
they are mutually both opposed and attracted. We might add

that this tension is always eschatological, i.e., that it has reference to the last days. Realities are in this dialectical position
only because of the ultimate fulfilment of all things: because
of the last days. It is because the life of the creature, sinful and
forgiven, unfolds here below, and nevertheless has meaning
only through the coming of the Kingdom, that it manifests a
state of tension. It is for this same reason that the Church is such
an equivocal reality, a reality still totally embedded in the
present and yet already belonging to eschatology; it must therefore live in a state of tension, which is the very sign of its life
and the mark of its action.[1] This state of tension will come to
an end with the advent of the Kingdom itself; it will end with
the reign of faith, and is clearly characteristic of the order of
faith; that is why it must be expressed by the very method of
this special knowledge which constitutes theology, or the
knowledge of faith (*Glaubenserkenntnis*). Accordingly, this use of
the idea of dialectics is strictly reserved for dogmatics alone.
We are faced with a concept which cannot be generalized,
which cannot constitute a logical category, but is not in formal
opposition to any of the logical categories. It would be the
greatest of absurdities to consider theological dialectics as a
mechanical play and to use it as a destructive weapon against
human logic.[2] The notion in question is one which loses all
meaning when severed from the eschatological perspective—it
is not a logical category because it cannot be abstracted from
the historical aeon which is that of the Church; the concept of
dialectics is therefore "*zeitgeschichtlich bestimmt*".

We feel that this attempt, which we have only outlined, to
distinguish between the understanding of Revelation and
all other forms of understanding and especially metaphysical
understanding, is one of the utmost importance. No doubt, the
times have passed when dogmatics ran at every instant the risk
of becoming a metaphysical construction. In our time, dogmatics is almost unanimously defined in its relationship to the
revealed datum that it wishes to make explicit; it no longer
has any constructive pretensions. Because of this, it would seem
sheltered from the temptation of imitating metaphysics or

---

[1] For this latter point, cf. particularly O. Cullmann, *Königsherrschaft Christi und
Kirche im N.T.* (Theol. Studien Heft 10), p. 23: "*Die zeitliche Spannung der
Kirche.*"

[2] The role of this idea has been very well grasped by P. Althaus, *Grundriss der
Dogmatik*, t. I, pp. 107-109.

ontology. But it must not be forgotten that metaphysics, under the impetus of existential philosophy, phenomenology and a new conception of knowledge, has in a parallel way also divested itself of all constructive pretension. It simply aims at describing the form of existence, measuring the dimensions of human experience and elucidating meanings. It too purports to be docile towards the real. Hence an inevitable comparison with dogmatics, of which we have a token in the fact that dogmatics has come to appear in the eyes of many as dependent upon existential philosophy. Hence also the possibility for the philosopher to understand the theologian's work. Hence, lastly, for the theologian, a necessity more urgent than ever to define with meticulous precision the nature of Christian truth, of the revealed datum and of dogmatic understanding.

Chapter V

THE RENEWING OF THE MIND

THE understanding of Revelation in no way belongs to philosophy; it belongs to dogmatics, the methods of which are radically different from those of philosophy. Such is the final finding of our inquiry. No doubt, philosophy can take both dogmatic understanding and its revealed object as themes for its meditations. We do not contest the right of philosophy to do so. There are such things as the philosophical exegesis of religion or the philosophy of religion. All we ask is that these disciplines clearly reveal their names and intentions. This was done by Pradines in a book the title of which is in itself quite significant.[1] But what we cannot admit is a philosophy of religion which presents itself as a true interpretation of Revelation itself; quite specifically, we are thinking of Schleiermacher's *Glaubenslehre*. Does he not write, in his first letter to Dr. Lucke: "This must be printed in large letters: I start from this consciousness of God we all bear in us under the influence of Christ and of the Church; I study its phenomena and gather what they yield to me. My dogmas are but the expression of these." We are not saying that Schleiermacher failed to grasp the essence of Christianity; we are saying that he does not directly study the content of Revelation and that accordingly he ceases to be a dogmatician, though he retains the intention of being one, and, in many ways has a dogmatician's temperament. There can be no dogmatics apart from the direct study of Revelation, and by methods it itself imposes upon us. The doctrine of religious experience, whether it is considered by such different authors as Henri Bois or Frommel, could not lead to the building up of a real dogmatics, precisely because it turned the theologian's attention to states of consciousness and away from the structure of the revealed. When Frommel defines dogmatics as "the systematic and scientific expression of Christian experience, of its conditions, its laws, the knowledge of its objects",[2] we feel that to him also the

[1] *L'esprit de la religion.* [2] *L'expérience chrétienne*, t. II, p. 106.

post-Kantian fear of the thing-in-itself bars the access of true dogmatics.[1]

But if we accept these conclusions, are we not compelled to reject all philosophical activity as outside the theological sphere and even the Christian sphere? Could the condition of the Christian philosopher precisely be to have to practise a secular philosophy only, through loyalty to the Word of God? Furthermore, will the Christian philosopher not find himself forcibly confined to wordly questions only, and to the problems of the self and the world alone? Will access to religious realities be permitted him only from the aspect of phenomenalism? If it is true that he must abstain from any effort to understand the revealed as such, should not his philosophical activity resolutely turn to purely human problems? In other words, the Christian philosopher would be recognizable by his religious avoidance of the problem of God. Such at least is the conclusion to which Gilson would carry Calvinism and Barthian theology, after, it is true, a rather brief contact with these doctrines: the existence of a Christian dogmatics should divest philosophy of all metaphysical pretensions.[2] Gilson remarks upon "the typical attitude of reformed dogmatic theology which, in the name of a religious question first put to philosophy, completely dispossesses man of any aptitude for approaching God by pure reason".[3] By freeing dogmatics from any resort to philosophy in the edifying of its own work and by emphasizing the specific character of the dogmatic understanding, we seem to substantiate Gilson's observation. In that case, we would find ourselves again in a position analogous, in intent if not in fact, to that of Descartes: metaphysical realities belong to theology alone and physical reality is the proper realm of philosophy. Philosophy will be permitted some fleeting incursions on the side of metaphysics only in order to give more solid ground to physics. Perhaps we should then retrieve the positivistic inspiration of Kantianism which wished to condemn

[1] There are, however, in Frommel's work definitions which are more satisfying because they hem in more closely dogma, that is, a will revealed in the very act in which God reveals it: "For Christian dogmatics does not deal with general religious knowledge, i.e. with the relationships between God and man *qua* moral wills in general, Christian dogmatics deals with the moral relationship between God and man as it is constituted in the Gospel" (*ibid.*, pp. 112-113). To make this definition completely satisfying, it would suffice to add that this relationship is instituted by God and that it is in this act that there resides God's Revelation in Jesus Christ.

[2] E. Gilson, *Christianity and Philosophy*, p. 48.   [3] *Ibid.*, p. 50.

philosophy to the limits of a narrow phenomenalism. In the course of our inquiry we already remarked that this partitioning off of the world of celestial realities from a terrestrial world had seemingly satisfied Calvin, who was content with having well defined the object of theology and cared little to know what would become of philosophy. We are not absolutely certain that the theologians of the dialectical school do not also tend in this direction, although no particular text offers absolute confirmation of this impression.

Is it possible not to follow this path? Is there room in the Christian practice of philosophy for philosophy as a truly spiritual function? Surprised that such a question should be asked, Gilson hastens to answer it in the affirmative. It is interesting to hear his reasons. Let us leave aside profane philosophy, that which is founded upon natural insight alone. There is a Christian philosophy concerned with Christian objects, which is not identical with dogmatics. No doubt, Gilson does not ignore the fact that sin has seriously jeopardized our intellectual faculties originally directed towards God; but, on the one hand, all vestiges of the *imago Dei* have not disappeared from man; on the other hand, and chiefly, the Christian is a saved, i.e. restored being. A wholeness is found in him by which his reason eludes the condemnations brought against it by the Reformation. "The danger which besets the Catholic is a semi-Calvinism which leads him to despair of nature; or a semi-Pelagianism which invites him to do without grace. The true Catholic position consists in maintaining that nature was created good, that it has been wounded, but that it can be at least partially healed by grace if God so wishes. This *instauratio*, that is to say this renewal, this restoration of nature to its primitive goodness by grace is on this point the programme of authentic Catholicism." Immediately a certain ambiguity must be noted: does Catholicism consider this restoration of nature, and therefore of reason, as being an acquired and actually realized fact, or is it merely an ideal Catholicism purports to make real? The former appears to be the case, since Gilson continues: "Already prevented from yielding its full fruit even when it stoops to things below it, our wounded reason is indeed still more so, when it attempts to raise itself to God. In order that it may succeed in this, in the measure permitted by its natural perfection, grace must first purify it, dress its wounds

and guide it towards an object of which it is no longer worthy;
but as soon as grace does this, it is indeed the withered reason
itself, which revives under grace, the same reason, but healed,
saved, therefore in another state, which sees and proves. Its
knowledge is therefore truly natural, its philosophy even though
christianized is a true philosophy."[1] Following St. Thomas's
doctrine Gilson believes it possible even now, within the economy
of the present aeon, to define precisely the relationships between
nature and grace, and to present us with the vision of a nature
which has accepted grace. Touched by grace, nature finds again
the fullness of its autonomy as nature. "Grace presupposes
nature, whether to restore or to enrich it. When grace restores
nature, it does not substitute itself for it, but re-establishes it;
when nature, thus re-established by grace, accomplishes its
proper operations, these are indeed natural operations which it
performs. Could a Catholic maintain that what nature cannot
do without grace is no longer done by nature at all?"[2] Thus the
restoration of nature is to be taken in the strictest sense of the
word "restoration": nature turns back, it finds again its state of
before the Fall. It is immaterial whether this restoration is only
partial and does not represent a permanent state; when it
exists, the restoration represents an Eden-like state. Therefore,
inasmuch as our understanding is restored in us by the working
of Grace, the new man is the man of before the Fall. He is the
man who can read in nature "the invisible things of God".
The ontological bond between the Spirit of God and the spirit
of man is re-established. Accordingly, Gilson is able to conclude: "Just as, therefore, there is a natural morality re-
established by grace, there can and ought to be a natural
theology restored by faith. In this sense, since Catholicism holds
for a nature which can be healed, it maintains the possibility of
a philosophy."[3] Thus a Christian who has received the gift of
faith may in perfectly good conscience, and without the
Reformed—and Pascalian—fear of speaking ill of God, devote
himself to an essentially religious philosophy which has God as
its central if not exclusive object, in conformity with St.
Thomas' precept usefully recalled by Gilson: "*Vera tota philosophia ad cognitionem divinorum ordinatur.*"[4] Thus, it would be

---

[1] *Op. cit.*, pp. 21-22.   [2] *Ibid.*, p. 24.   [3] *Ibid.*, p. 24.
[4] III, *Sent.*, dist. 24, art. 3, q. 3 sol I, 3°, quoted by Gilson in a footnote,
p. 131.

possible to speak of a "healed nature", a healed man, a healed reason and philosophy, or again of a "Christian state of philosophy".[1]

It ought to be stressed that this doctrine is not exclusively Gilson's but also the official doctrine of the Church, for, as the author himself reminds us, it is only a commentary upon the Encyclical *Aeterni Patris* which expresses itself in the following terms: "That if natural reason has produced such an abundant harvest before being fertilized by the virtue of Christ, it will certainly bring forth a much richer one, now that the grace of the Saviour has restored and augmented the natural faculties of human thought."[2] These texts raise the real problem with which we are grappling here: in what sense is there a restoration of nature and a renewal of the mind for the man who, through faith, finds himself truly benefitting by grace? Does Christ's work of redemption entail a restoration of our nature in the fullness of its faculties? Is the present aeon, i.e. the time situated between the Resurrection and Ascension, and the Return or Renewal of all things, identical with the time of Eden? What is this renewing of the mind to which the New Testament refers us as to a reality which, even now, has power over our lives?

Let us again emphasize: the Gilsonian and Thomistic doctrine is perfectly coherent; if the Christian's mind is renewed and restored *in re*, it must escape the Apostle Paul's condemnation of the wisdom of the wise. It no longer runs the risk of corrupting the incorruptible glory of God. After centuries of sin, it finds again the possibility of speaking reasonably of God. There would only remain to be settled the difficult question of the relationships between the philosophy created by this renewed understanding, and natural theology. We think they would merge, and Gilson, without stating it explicitly, is not far from sharing our feeling since he accepts for himself the title of theologian.[3] But can we speak of the renewing of the mind with the same assurance and the same limpidity?

Doubtlessly, it is easy to gather all the Biblical texts attesting the reality of the renewal of which we have the intimation in Christ's Resurrection. Faith in Christ makes us partakers in this renewal: "If any man is in Christ, he is a new creature; old things are passed away; behold, they are become new"

---

[1] *Ibid.*, p. 86.   [2] *Ibid.*, p. 92.   [3] *Ibid.*

(2 Cor. 5.17). For this reason, as Causse rightly recalls,[1] entering the community of the early Church meant an actual breaking away from one's past, social environment and former way of life: "There was therefore in the worshipper's life a before and an after."[2] In Jesus Christ the new man made his appearance in the world. "But ye did not so learn Christ; if so be that ye heard him, and were taught in him, even as the truth is in Jesus: that ye put away, as concerning your former manner of life, the old man that waxeth corrupt after the lusts of deceit; and that ye be renewed in the spirit of your mind; and put on the new man, that after God hath been created in righteousness and holiness of truth" (Eph. 4.20-4). The old man was crucified in Christ, the body of sin was destroyed (Rom. 6.6). Now we are walking in newness of life, and the aim of the sacrament of baptism is to seal in us the certainty of our new birth, and the radical difference between "that time" and "now" (Eph. 2.11-13). Rom. 12.2 insists forcefully, as does Eph. 4.23 upon the renewing of our minds which will enable us to grasp the holy will of God (for God is always known in His will). Is it necessary to emphasize that this is not merely Paul's personal viewpoint, but that such was indeed the conception of Christian life of the whole early Church? "To be born anew, to be born of God, to be born of the water and the spirit", such are the most current expressions of Johannine thought (John 1.12 and 13, 3.3 and 7; 1 John 3.9).

The characteristic of the new man is that he has received the Spirit of God, that this Spirit bears witness in his spirit, and that from then on he leads a life in Christ. Cleansed by the blood of Christ (Heb. 9.13 and 14), actually nourished by the body and blood of Christ (John 6), he experiences psychological movements and feelings different from ordinary feelings; there is a joy in Christ (of which we are constantly reminded in the Epistle to the Philippians), and there is also a true sorrow which is not of the world (2 Cor. 7.8-11). There is of course an ethics of the renewed man who, abandoning the lusts of the flesh, |lives according to charity, which has no common measure with natural sympathy. There is a Christian life dominated by *agape* and in which natural *eros* is no longer

---

[1] A. Causse, *Essai sur le conflit du christianisme primitif et de la civilisation.* Leroux, 1920.

[2] *Ibid.*, p. 19.

recognized. There is, lastly, a new way of serving God, since the new man can at last offer acceptable service to God, i.e. present his body in sacrifice to God and see this sacrifice accepted by God.

It is unnecessary to prolong these remarks. They establish with certainty that the coming of Christ and His Resurrection have created a deep gap in the history of man: there is between the old and the new mankind, the first and the second Adam, a difference so great that one can indeed wonder how the subject's personal identity can be preserved from one aeon to the other.[1] Neither would the Resurrection have been the decisive fact it was, and it would not have been the early Church's central and radically new message, if it did not mean man's entering a wholly different body: that which was "sown in corruption is raised in incorruption".

It cannot be alleged that we are here treading the realm of eschatology, and that all this renewal concerns the future alone. The Apostle Paul speaks of it in the past tense, as of an already accomplished reality. The exhortations directing us to put on the new man, to make manifest in all the realms of our concrete life this newness in which our whole being has been clothed—these exhortations would lose all their meaning should they only come into force on the day of the Lord. On the contrary, it is in order to appear pure and blameless on the day of the Lord that we must start upon this new life.[2]

In fact, it has always been admitted that there actually exists a Christian ethics and a Christian reconstruction of man which are not paralysed, but rather activated by the eschatological hope. It is because of this tension towards the last days that we feel impelled to put on the new man. Ought there not to be an intellectual renewal of man parallel to this moral renewal and implicitly contained in it? The theologians have given few descriptions of it; but this is probably due to the fact that gnosticism had made it scandalously explicit for the sake of glorifying spiritual man and had dangerously threatened the unity of the body of Christ. Gilson, aware that we have no gnostic movement to fear in the Church, has no other intention than to describe and promote this renewal of the mind without

[1] That is the most delicate problem in Christian anthropology.
[2] Among the numerous texts emphasizing the presentness of the new life, Gal. 4.19, James 1.18, 1 Peter 1.23 can be quoted.

which the ethical renewal would, furthermore, remain insufficient. For in the end there can be no ethics without discernment of the will of God and of that which is meet, acceptable
and holy. And should not the whole Christian Church rejoice in
the fact that Christians have regained the admirable audacity
of a Clement of Alexandria, and that of the Franciscans, and
that they wish to build a knowledge of God and of the world
susceptible of bearing witness to their own renewal? Is not
Gilson justified in his astonishment at encountering so much
reticence, even in Christian circles, when he speaks of a Christian philosophy?

Yet the problem is less simple than it appears to be and calls
in question the fundamental notions of Christianity, notably
that of salvation, that of justification and reconciliation, that of
Christ's reign and of the Kingdom of God.

The Scripture, having strongly emphasized the reality of the
new man, speaks of him, however, as of a mystery, i.e. not
something difficult to understand but a hidden reality which
can be grasped by faith alone. Something has been accomplished, owing to which we are no longer in our former state.
In a sense, we are raised with Christ (Col. 3.1), but our new
life, that originating in Christ's Resurrection, or again that
born of baptism (Rom. 6.4), does not belong to us already: "it
is hid with Christ in God" (Col. 3.3). Therefore, the new life of
a being made whole by grace is not an anthropological reality.
"It is no longer I that live, but Christ liveth in me." My new
life exists only in Christ, but Christ sitteth at the right hand of
God, He was raised in glory whereas man remains on earth.
Man cannot therefore assert absolutely and without reticence
that he is a new and renewed man, that the vestiges of sin in
him have been eradicated and that he has found again his
former integrity; for this is only true in Christ, and to the exact
extent to which he partakes by faith in Christ's life. That is why
we can only know the new man by looking towards Jesus Christ.
In other words, the new man is quite different from the
Christian type, a historical reality the psychologists and moralists
can fully well describe by opposing this man to the wise man of
ancient times and to the modern citizen. This Christian type
bears the marks of Christianity; something in his behaviour
witnesses to the presence of the invisible God; but as a type of
civilized being he cannot be said to present the image of the

new man. At best he can refer us to this new man, he can be
the finger pointing to the new man. The latter is not an empirical reality. If he were, it would be possible to construct a
theology on the basis of Christian experience alone. As a
Christian philosopher has written: "We have no experience of
the restoration of man".[1] We are therefore not able to speak, as
Gilson does, of this new creature, of this lineage of the second
Adam, as of a reality which has already taken its place in
human history; we are not able to distinguish among the men
we meet those who have not yet put away the old man from
those who have put on the new man. This judgement and this
discrimination belong to God alone. What we are in reality—
that is, in the eyes of God—has not yet been made manifest.
"When Christ, who is our life, shall be manifested, then shall
ye also with him be manifested in glory" (Col. 3.4).

In this sense, it can be maintained that the new man and the
spiritual body which shall be given us upon the day of resurrection
are identical: 1 Cor. 15.22 relates and mingles our resurrection
and transformation in the same instant.[2] The radical transformation of our being to the Creator's image, in which the
new man consists, is linked with the Parousia (Phil. 3.20-1;
cf. 1 Cor. 15.45-9). There is no manifestation of the new man
apart from, or before, the Resurrection. The Resurrection, the
Parousia, that is the hour of the new man. This is why we are
forbidden to speak of the new man otherwise than in an
eschatological perspective. In asserting this, we do not run the risk
of contradicting our previous statements; we are not saying
that the new man is nothing but an eschatological reality, we
are saying that his present reality vanishes if severed from this
eschatological perspective. Gilson may allege that his own
point of view, which remains that of natural theology, does
not concern itself with man in the last days, with the glorious
body given the Christian in Christ. He intends (and this is why
he remains a philosopher) to confine himself to the realm of
nature and to be content with building the Christian philosophy
upon the notion of man restored in his natural integrity, i.e. his
integrity of before the Fall. But, without raising here the
delicate question of whether there is a theology which can be

[1] P. Burgelin, "L'homme pécheur" in the collection of essays, *L'homme chrétien*,
Paris, 1941, p. 34.

[2] This has been ascertained by Fr. Allo, *La première épître aux Corinthiens*, Paris,
Gabalda, 1935, 2nd ed., p. 433.

isolated, at least in the abstract and provisionally, from revealed theology, it must be said clearly that Gilson pursues a reality which, from the point of view of the Bible, is chimerical. God never promised to restore man's disfigured nature; He promised a new creation. He promised to make "all things new". Such a turning back, such a retracing of the series of centuries would, furthermore, contradict the Biblical philosophy of time. Christian time is never a cycle enabling the universe to begin over again, bringing it back to a former state; this cyclical conception of time, a time which begins again and ascends back to its source, is the conception of a *blasé* person for whom there is nothing new under the sun; but the time God gave to the world has a beginning and an end. God does not allow this time to flow back; but He reserves for Himself the right to bring about its fulfilment. He requires the believer to live in hope, turned towards this fulfilment, the end of time: the coming Kingdom, that is both the fulfilment and the meaning of our time, in no way resembles Paradise lost, which is and remains lost.

Nature cannot therefore be healed in the sense of being able to return to its former state of integrity and pristine innocence. The act of the Fall cannot be erased from our destiny. God does not remake His creation. He makes a new creature, Jesus Christ, and that is why the latter is the new Adam and should be considered the first-born of this new creation. Gilson's thinking, as that of the Thomists in general, seems hampered by the idea of nature which, having an eternal essence, cannot disappear; and that is why, realizing that nature had lost its integrity, he would have it regain it. But such a static universe, where all natures indefinitely keep their inalienable essences, where natures are so lasting that sin cannot completely corrupt them, is not the Biblical universe. When we speak of the new man, it can only be that "new man, that after God hath been created in righteousness and true holiness", and whom we are enjoined to "put on" (as he is described in Eph. 4.24). The restoration of man is an idea which can be clarified, not by the story of Eden but by that of the Resurrection, as the Apostle Paul does constantly (especially in Rom. 6). Accordingly, we can only grasp this new man in faith through the act which intimates and heralds the Resurrection—namely, baptism, the sacrament of hope.

But why should we not then remain faithful to Paul's realism and actualism; why not consider the baptized person as the equivalent of the new man? Does not Paul say to us: "Even so reckon ye also yourselves to be dead unto sin, but alive unto God in Christ Jesus"? (Rom. 6.11). Does not Paul speak of our deliverance from sin as of a reality already present and manifest? In order correctly to interpret these texts, it must not be forgotten what a peculiar language the eschatological perspective imposes upon the Apostle Paul. We must remember the time within which we live: between the Resurrection of Christ and the Parousia, i.e. our own resurrection. Through Christ's Resurrection our own has become certain and can be considered as an acquired fact. The reality which we shall become if we remain in the faith can therefore already be presented as actual and present. By accepting Christ's sacrifice, God proclaims us righteous. We who are sinners, and who are to remain sinners to the end of our lives, are proclaimed righteous by God: and this righteousness can be spoken of in the present since it was already manifested by Christ and since what really counts for our destiny is not so much what we are in our empirical reality, but the word which is pronounced upon us.

No doubt, it is this empirical life which is at stake and which must be transformed. That is why the Apostle is not content with recalling the word that makes us righteous and the baptism which makes us like to the crucified and risen One, but bids us to engage upon our new life and to put on the new man. What God has wrought should be spoken of in an eternal present. By God's decree and the act of our baptism we have engaged upon the path of renewal: the concept of *Homo viator* is the only one which truly characterizes the Christian. What is visible and manifest is this involvement in a new life, this march towards the new man. A dogmatician who does not trouble with eschatological considerations, Albert Ritschl,[1] notes with great finesse that justification does not mean that we have become righteous (in the sense of Christ's righteousness), but first of all and essentially that henceforward God no longer considers our former life and our sinfulness as an *obstacle* to our entrance upon the new life, prefigured by our entering the Church. Such are the precious "first-fruits" we own, and that is what gives us the certainty of salvation and of the new man. We can march, we

---

[1] *Die Christliche Lehre von der Rechtfertigung und Versöhnung*, II, 339.

L

can advance. God journeys with us. Thus, *Homo viator* is he who knows with assurance that once the obstacle is removed he is not moving towards catastrophe but towards life eternal.

This condition of man (difficult to subsume under a univocal concept) could again be characterized by saying with Barth that the Christian is neither perfect nor just, but one reconciled with God: for us, in our human perspective, justification means, first, reconciliation. With respect to 1 Cor. 12.1-2, Barth writes: "The Apostle Paul is not addressing perfect, nor saved, but reconciled men who have heard the Word but who, living within time, have not yet broken away from this world but are still awaiting their heavenly city. Such is our situation."[1] Therefore, we do not see the new creation, but very concretely (and not as idealists or utopists) live in this fallen creation in the fallen nature of which we participate; but we see this old creation in the light of the promise realized in Jesus Christ.

The certainty of salvation or, in other words, the experience of the new life, consists essentially in a supernatural assurance, the assurance the Christian possesses by faith, of being *engaged upon* a new path, where he will grow until he reaches the perfect stature of man, the stature of Christ in the last days. And this growth must not be confused with the sequence of empirical or empirically noticeable progress, regular with some, chaotic with others; for, though of course this progress has psychological, social and ethical reality, who is to decide whether it also has absolute reality and whether it is worthy of being included in the personality of the new man? Many spiritual advisers are guilty of presenting it as such to their charges; this error frequently occurs in Catholicism and it conforms with the doctrine of holiness, such as it is expressed in Father Festugière's recent book.[2] It consists in identifying the appearance of the new man with ethical progress. It prepares painful awakenings for scrupulous consciences, for these will be tempted to doubt their salvation when they become aware of the relativity of their ethical progress. Ethical progress is not without meaning for the believer; to him it is a perceptible sign, relative as all signs, of the grace bestowed upon him; it is an encouragement granted him by the Grace of God upon his journey as *homo viator*. It is the mark of a divine pedagogy towards man. It is, with respect to the new man, what Jesus'

---

[1] *Vom christlichen Leben*, p. 13. [2] A. J. Festugière, O.P., *La Sainteté*.

miracles were with respect to the coming of the Kingdom. All too often, Christian thinking has been unduly indignant at sociological analyses showing the relativity of ethical ideas. True or false, ascertaining this in no way ruins the Christian's spiritual life. Indeed, it is necessary that the Christian be warned against identifying the coming of this "holiness" with that of the "new man". Certainly, the saint whom we encounter radiates spiritual light. There are souls of light. They refer us to the new man whom they herald; they are not the new man.

The latter remains an object of faith and not of sight. To assert this is not to underestimate his reality. On the contrary, it is to emphasize the full objectivity of this reality. The character of the Christian faith is precisely to cling to that only which is so objective that it remains completely out of our grasp. The new man grows in me without belonging to me. Philosophical analysis of personality, such as that of Husserl, suggests the existence of a transcendental extra-worldly ego through which the universe is constituted. What it presents to us as a mere possibility and necessity is actually offered to the Christian's faith. Husserlian phenomenology leaves us uncertain as to the content of an extra-worldly "I"; it causes us concern when it tells us of a second, transcendental ego, appointed to contemplate the first, for it does not indicate the reason why it is necessary definitely to halt at this second ego, and why the latter should not in turn be taken as an object of contemplation; at any rate, as far as Husserl's latest thought in this respect is known at present, his phenomenology does not reach a transcendental ego with a content solid or objective enough to impose itself upon us as an absolute reality. As all philosophy, Husserl's phenomenological analysis leaves us in some disquietude.[1]

Here philosophy encounters one of its imprescriptible limits. This ego which it must postulate in order to give meaning to the world and to the self is actually proposed to us in the existence of the glorified Christ.

Scripture has been accused of lacking in clarity when it speaks of our new life; and, after all the theologians, we ourselves have pointed out that the passages concerning this new

[1] Berger, *Le cogito dans la philosophie de Husserl*, pp. 113-177, has very clearly noted the uncertainties of the Husserlian anthropology, which does not succeed in specifying the ultimate nature of the constituting intentionality. This might be, as Berger suggests, "an intention which is prevented by its own meaning from ever being fulfilled" (p. 114).

life sometimes have an eschatological meaning, sometimes an actualistic one, and that Scripture depicts the new man both as an entity to come and an already actualized entity. Let it now be said that to our mind this does not mean that two currents emerge in Scripture, two different or divergent tendencies. We feel that this equivocal language is the only means available for expressing the mystery of the new man, both real and hidden, real but not yet made manifest. Therefore, the language of both the present and the future must be maintained; their separate use will give rise to a heresy. We readily agree that it is difficult to maintain in the teaching of the Church this double language, this perpetual ambiguity; this difficulty was apparently felt from the first days of the Church, as early as in the first non-canonical writings; in the Epistle of Barnabas (16.8)[1] we read the following assertion: "By receiving the forgiveness of our sins and by hoping in the name of the Lord, we become new men and are thoroughly renewed; thus God really lives in us, in our innermost hearts." Here is a text which at first sight has a definitely evangelical flavour. Yet no allusion is made in it to this mystery of the Christian ego, likened to our innermost heart. Paul's statement, "Ye are the temple of the Holy Spirit," is resumed and commented upon, without being oriented by an eschatological vector. We can already feel a certain warping of Biblical thinking.

These few remarks neither exhaust nor settle the question of the new man; they do not claim to do so; rather they call for an exegetical study of the problem as a whole. But they suffice in our view to prove that it is impossible to speak, as does Gilson, of a curable nature allowing the Christian to build up here and now a philosophy which would, without difficulty and beyond dispute, bear the marks of the renewal of the mind; a philosophy which could be called Christian in the very sense in which we do not hesitate to call a dogmatics Christian. In so far as we leave the limits of Revelation and no longer ask Revelation itself to dictate us our method of work and our method of systematization and synthesis, we lose the right to name our work Christian in an absolute way. No doubt, it could be held that in order to regain the right to call our philosophy

---

[1] Quoted by A. Causse, *op. cit.*, p. 20. The sentences following, not quoted by Causse, definitely confirm the exclusively actualistic impression conveyed by this text.

Christian it suffices to show that it does not contradict Christianity. But this idea remains very hazy; in the present aeon, and for beings living in faith and not in sight, there is an infinite variety of opinions which are perfectly reconcilable with Christianity. Tertullian is not a heretic because he held that the soul is material; he is a heretic because he fell into Montanism and believed that the Holy Spirit could speak in the Church apart from any reference to the Scriptural Revelation. In order that this notion of non-contradictory or reconcilable opinions might be a clear one, the revealed truths and the other types of truth would have to constitute a unilinear chain without breaches of continuity. We have shown (Ch. II) that such was not the case. That does not mean extreme limits cannot be established in practice, but within these extreme limits the philosophies reconcilable with Christianity remain very numerous.

.   .   .   .   .

We are therefore thrown back upon the following difficulty: If the new man is not an empirical reality, if he is not the object of an *Erlebnis*, does not the renewal of understanding thanks to which we, who had become slow to understand, have access to the revealed truth, mean anything in the current exercise of our intellectual activity? Is the "old man" alone at work in philosophy? Is philosophy nothing but a homage to the Prince of this world, travestied with the name of God, as extremist orthodoxies have always believed and as Barthianism in its revolutionary initial stages narrowly escaped thinking too.

The notion of *Homo viator* seems to prohibit such radical and desperate pessimism. The fact that the new man is not yet made manifest does not prevent life according to faith from being a movement oriented towards the new man. But how shall we represent the relationship between our present life and the new man's? Immediately, the idea of growth comes to our mind; starting from the present, we grow as does a plant which is developing into a normal type. We ourselves have used this idea, which is suggested by the Biblical texts; and we strongly emphasized that this growth ought not to be confused with the curve of ethical or intellectual progress. The time has come to explain with greater precision how we conceive the nature of this growth, for the term itself evokes the phenomena of vegetative life. Immediately, we tend to interpret the doctrine of the new man in an organic sense: the new man has not yet appeared, for his hour and season have not yet come, but he is virtually present just as the tree is virtually present in the seed, and even more so in the young sprout and in the sapling. Thus the manifestation of the new man would be a kind of organic development, *a progress*. Parallel to this development, we could conceive of a progress of the Christian philosophy; the new man would be but the end of an already initiated process. The whole question is whether it is legitimate to give an organic meaning to this growth, and if we are not being deceived by suggestions of metaphors taken from the vegetative life, thus forcing a parallel between organic and spiritual life. For we cannot forget that even though the new, or inner, man is strengthened while the old, or external, man is destroyed, the perfect achievement of the new man's stature presupposes a decisive crisis, of which organic life offers us no example. Our ultimate transformation will take place in a moment, in the twinkling of an eye (1 Cor. 15.52). This transformation will be radical, since it will make us pass from corruption to incorruption; thus, we cannot refer to it as the completion of an ongoing process, or a crisis of growth. The Lord alone, upon the day of Parousia, and according to the "working" whereby He is able to subject all things unto Himself, can change the body of our humiliation and make it conform to His glorious body (Phil. 3.21). It matters little whether or not in the text of 1 Cor. 15.49 ("and as we have borne the image of the earthly, we shall also bear the image of the heavenly") the future tense is replaced by an imperative; this would still not authorize a commentary such as Father Allo's who, choosing the imperative, writes: "This second reading seems preferable, for its meaning is fuller. Not only does St. Paul foretell us glory, he says we must earn it by *assimilating ourselves gradually to the image of Christ*. Until the blessed day when our own bodies will become like the 'spiritual body' of our Saviour, who was the first to be glorified in His body, as the *first fruits* of mankind."[1] This represents an error about the meaning of the imitation of Christ; for the reason for our final change is not to be found in this imitation. This change is not the result of a gradual assimilation, but of a decisive intervention of the Lord, who will in this way manifest in the eyes of all and primarily in our own eyes His work in us

[1] R. P. Allo, op. cit., pp. 429, 430. Italics by R. Mehl.

and for us. First among men, He was glorified in His body as the first-fruits of mankind; but the chief purpose of this glorification is not, as Father Allo seems to believe, to offer men an archetype for them to realize gradually, as good apprentices; its first and direct aim is to give an object to our faith; we must be able really and concretely to believe in the new man, wait for his manifestation, and because of this faith do our best to obey the orders we receive, remembering that though we may neither achieve nor manifest anything, we are not thereby excused from witnessing to our faith by actions. The new man manifested in Christ is not a goal for us to aim at and reach by gradual gropings and successive approximations. Christ's presence attests that we are, as Pascal has it, "embarked", and that if we remain in the faith, we cannot fall a prey to him who kills the body and soul in Gehenna; that our life is thus taken in charge and led in the right direction, not so much in the way of perfection as in a way from which the mortal risk has been removed, and where in spite of the errors and uncertainties of our thought and life we shall not be separated from the love of God in Christ.

Actually, perfectionism would keep us from viewing the Lord's Parousia, and the final crisis connected with it, seriously enough: it implies that time normally ends in and merges with eternity. We cannot thus dispense with this supreme moment when all works good and evil will be manifested and take on their exact meaning, which at present still eludes us. If we do so, we are grossly mistaken about the ultimate sense of the work of men and nations.

Thus we are once more faced with and able to corroborate the conclusions we had reached previously. The new man is an objective reality grasped by faith, the renewing of the mind is a fact. This newness will only be manifested in the last days. But even now, though hidden, it is at work in us and bears fruit, without our even being able to credit its empirical manifestations with normative or probatory value.

But the benefit from the work the Spirit accomplishes in us is already ours. It is vain to try to make obvious the renewing of the mind; it is not vain to indicate both the demands and the certainties imposed upon us by this renewing. In other words, though the renewal is not a describable psychological and ethical reality, it remains true that our intellectual labour

cannot be carried out autonomously, as if the renewal were
not an acquired fact, a fact acquired for us. Eternity is never
identified with time; but the eschatological relationship between eternity and time results in curving time in a certain
direction. Time feels the coming eternity weighing upon it.
While it remains time and contains no little islands of eternity,
it has lost its own autonomy and no longer has any meaning
in itself; its meaning is beyond itself, in eternity. And such is, in
fact, the character of Old Testament history; it is a history in
the full sense, unfolding itself in natural time, in perfect con-
cordance with the time of the world; the historian cannot treat
it otherwise than any other fragment of history; yet it will only
yield its ultimate meaning and its truth to him who knows its
relationship with eternity. Likewise, there is an eschatological
relationship between the Christian's empirical life and the life
of the new man he has put on. The Christian philosopher's
intellectual and ethical processes are fully intelligible only if
placed in the light of their relationship with the reality, both
present and eschatological, of salvation. No doubt, in order to
account for his attitudes, the historian will be content with
appealing to the Christian influences to which the author was
subjected, to the Christian mental régime in which he grew up;
and such an account is and remains perfectly legitimate, but
also perfectly external. Actually, the very structure of this
philosophy is related to the requirements and assurances of the
new life grasped in faith. Of this new life, the philosophy is
neither the exact representation nor the doctrinal expression.
Yet the deep intention of this philosophy, its themes and
motives, even more than its logical articulations depend upon
its knowledge of the new man. What is even more important
than the components of a philosophy is its *general character*. By
this we mean the intentionalities, in the phenomenological
sense, of this philosophy as a whole; not so much its actual
modalities as its aim. This aim is not indicated merely by the
elements which enter into the philosophy. It is far better
revealed by the balancing of these elements, the permanency of
certain themes, and the more or less dramatic appearance of
the whole. It is this general character which ought to be made
understood, and it can only be fully grasped by realizing the
pressure exerted upon the philosopher's consciousness by his
concern for ultimate realities. A philosophy of time and

eternity will widely differ in its general character according to whether the philosopher had in mind the Greek concept of a motionless eternity, or whether he elaborated his philosophy with reference to Him who is the Eternal, or to the Kingdom of God. The assertions of this philosophy will have a very different weight according to whether its author's purpose was merely to perfect, amend or even to strive against the Greek notion of time, or whether he endeavoured to conceive of time in the eschatological perspective inspired by our faith. The difference between these two philosophies will not be expressed by variations in their rational structures; both ought to be equally amenable to reason. The work of the philosophizing Christian does not consist in introducing among his presuppositions, avowed or implicit, a few Christian propositions to be exempted from rational criticism. But normally rational structures can be very differently oriented. It would not occur to anyone to consider Spinoza's philosophy as being more rational than Descartes' although there is in Descartes' thinking a very real concern for safeguarding God's honour and sovereignty; this concern is expressed in his works by the doctrines of the passivity of the understanding and of the creation of eternal truths. The passivity of the understanding is not a doctrine exclusive to Descartes; it is found in many philosophies and is quite naturally deduced from the realism of ideas; it does not constitute in Cartesianism a strange element difficult to account for through the inner resources of the system. It is not at all necessary to consider it as a patch of Christianity woven into the system. But Descartes' interest in this doctrine he did not invent, the rank he bestows upon it, the intention he makes it bear, these can only be explained by the renewing of the mind in which Descartes as a Christian had a part.

In short, it is no more possible to determine exactly the relationship between the new and the old man than that between the empirical and the transcendental "I". The undertaking itself would be a contradictory one, since establishing a relationship presupposes the discovery of a common measure; but such a discovery would result in the new man slipping to the level of nature, and the transcendental ego to the level of the world. But the fact that a logical bond cannot be established between the old and the new man does not mean that the former is thoroughly independent from the latter; it is also not possible to establish a satisfactory logical relationship between time and eternity, and this very impossibility incited ancient thinkers to drive back time into non-being; yet it remains true that when time possesses any fullness it receives it from eternity and is not therefore independent from eternity. All we can say—but here we are obviously leaving the limits of logical conceptual thought —is that there is, or there may be, a relationship of tension between time and eternity; time is as if extended by the imminence of eternity. It is this kind of relationship we must attempt to establish between the natural and the renewed mind, between the Christian's philosophy and the Good Tidings. It would please us to be able to grasp in a Christian's philosophy the new elements witnessing to the renewal of the inner man; and, like the historian searching for sources, we should like to determine wisely what pertains to the old man and what to the new. This is too simple a view; actually, the Christian's whole philosophy is entirely the work of the old man. But this old man has ceased to live autonomously. He lives under the impact of a judgement and a promise and his philosophy bears the mark of this judgement and this promise.

Let us translate into concrete terms this assertion of principle; philosophy is the work of the former self, which goes on living under the judgement and the promise. Therefore, the Christian's philosophy may not boast of having the new man's insight. Like any philosopher, the Christian philosopher runs the risk of error. He would not run this risk if he had only to deduce from Revelation the philosophical implications it is supposed to contain. At the most, such deducing can be more or less accurate. Of course, the theologian also runs a risk, but it is that of faithfulness. The philosopher runs an additional risk, as the Word of God does not constitute for him a norm to which he can constantly refer. The philosopher's labour is free; the theologian's is constantly controlled by Revelation and must at every moment be confronted with the Word of God. The Christian philosopher's situation as a man called upon to run all the risks comprehension entails can only be understood when compared to that of the honest man who in the Scripture has discovered the meaning of all ethics, but is given no particular direction for his daily action. The problem of action is similar to that of philosophy. In both cases we are required to make use of our natural resources, to appeal to our intelligence and common sense, to reflect and to judge. The Christian knows he will not be deprived of supernatural help, but that this help never is an initial datum to be merely extended or applied; that it will be exactly contemporary with the act of his own commitment. It is because Christ labours in the world since His Ascension that we must labour in turn. Nothing can excuse us from this involvement and this compromising of ourselves whereby we try to build up as Christians our representation of the universe. Just as the honest man in his involvement runs the constant risk of being wrong and of missing the aim he had set for himself, or even of deceiving himself in the hierarchy of ends he has set up, so also the philosopher, who by his reflection endeavours to show that he loves God with all his mind, runs the risk of involving human thought in ways which will make more difficult for it the understanding of Revelation. Certainly the idealistic theory of knowledge, which sees a construction of the mind in every object, has kept many generations from understanding correctly the objectiveness of God. Quite as certainly, Kantian moralism has, in spite of the religiousness of its intentions and the pietistic halo surrounding it, barred a generation still very close to ours from the understanding of grace. Perhaps Gilson makes too light of the risk inherent in Christian philosophy, when following Justin and an old Christian tradition he declares that whenever the philosopher states a given truth, be it even partial, he is exercising a Christian ministry. "All the evil that is done is done against the Word, but since conversely, all the good that is done is done by help of the Word, who is the Christ, all truth is by definition Christian. Whatever has been well said is ours: ὅσα οὖν παρὰ πᾶσιν χαλῶς εἴρηται, ἡμῶν χριστιανῶν ἐστιν. There, already formulated in the second century in definitive terms we have the perpetual charter of Christian humanism. Heraclitus is one of us; Socrates belongs to us, for he knew Christ in part thanks to the effort of a reason which had its source in the Word; ours also the Stoics, and along with the Stoics all those other genuine philosophers in whom already lay the seeds of that truth which revelation discovers to us today in its fulness."[1] This viewpoint is correct only in part; no doubt the Christian—and this is one of the aspects of his philosophy— can find again the meaning of all the philosophies and find the

[1] *The Spirit of Medieval Philosophy*, pp. 27-28.

place of the pagan philosophies with relation to Christian philosophy. Yet for himself personally, the Christian cannot assert that all truths are Christian by definition and that he can fulfil his task as a Christian simply by seeking the truth. For there are truths so fragmentary or so badly oriented that they cannot but involve the mind in ways which will obscure Revelation. We must know that even if we build a philosophy which can resist rational criticism, we run the risk of obtaining a system dogmatics can only condemn. And this is a perennial risk, since no philosophy can ever call itself Christian. We also run this risk when, impelled by the faith of the new man, we draw the plans of a new city or a more concrete ethics. The theocracy of Geneva may have had, in its principle as in its functioning, the intention of giving God the supreme honour; yet it remains, from the point of view of Christian dogmatics, a hazardous thought. We gladly admit that any act is a perilous commitment, in a sort of compromise with a reality we can probably never thoroughly dominate; why not admit that the Christian's philosophical thinking is also a perilous commitment? If we do not admit this, it is because we have become accustomed to consider the exercise of thought as purely theoretical, that is as devoid of any risk completely accepted and run. By reminding us that the Christian's life is indeed a race and a strife, Christianity indicates that we are not called to a life of quiescent contemplation, as the mystical heresies have maintained, nor to a kind of *fruitio mystica*, but to an involvement inseparable from risk. It is by maintaining the meaning of this risk that we can bear witness in the eyes of the non-Christian to the true autonomy of the Christian's philosophy: the non-Christian always fears that the Christian is not perfectly free and that his starting-point or his point of arrival is set in advance. We have sufficiently shown that the conclusions of dogmatics cannot serve as the first principles of philosophy to dispense us from returning to this point; let us only emphasize the fact that the Christian's autonomy of judgement rests upon the doctrine of the new man. The latter has not yet been manifested; but knowing that he will be, and inspired by the hope, which will not be disappointed, that the renewing of mind is a sure promise, the Christian boldly ventures to reflect, just as the soldier who knows that whatever the painful phases of the struggle may be, victory will be won in the end. Boldness of

judgement depends upon some ultimate hope; the possibility
of risk always depends upon this ultimate assurance. One incurs
a risk only when one knows that the loss does not represent an
ultimate value. The analysis of Pascal's wager would show this
easily. Risk does not mean insane temerity. I can only become
involved because I have everything to gain, and because what
I am losing means very little in objective terms. The soldier only
risks his life because in the true scale of values his life means less
than what he acquires by his sacrifice. It may be seen that the
real miser will not risk his money, because for him money has
absolute value. The risk of involvement is always a sign of
freedom with relation to oneself. The Christian philosopher's
judgement receives both its freedom and its audacity from the
ultimate assurances he possesses. These assurances do not make
his philosophy any less serious; philosophy is not a game for
him, any more than existence is a game for the Christian who
nevertheless knows that his salvation does not depend upon
what he will do with this existence. Existence as well as philosophical research remain deeply serious because they are our
opportunity to manifest our understanding of the Good Tidings,
and to give God glory. The exercise of philosophy is a part of
the acceptable offering the Christian owes to God; it consists
in an endeavour to bear witness to our faith in the renewing of
history and to discern, in proportion to this faith, the will of
God in the intellectual order. But if the exercise of philosophy
is serious work, it has not the dramatic or even tragic character
that it sometimes assumes with the non-Christian. The Christian's philosophy can never be a philosophy of despair; or at
least, despair as well as anguish will remain for him not final
ends but values. Despair usually becomes enclosed within itself;
it cannot be inserted in the sequence of values; it interrupts
their hierarchy. The work of the Christian philosopher is to
give it meaning and value, to make it a dialectical moment
related to other dialectical moments. As soon as despair and
anguish are effectively related to other values, they cease to
appear as final events and solutions; relationship prohibits
exclusiveness. Now, as the Christian's proper effort consists in
situating values in the perspective of a forgiven life under grace,
it is essential that he maintain communication between all
values, and destroy all the absolutes which hamper reciprocity
between values as well as reciprocity between persons. That

despair has a meaning is a discovery which makes all philosophies of despair impossible. Neither Pascal nor Kierkegaard
have shown this sufficiently. They were content with despairing
of philosophy, or rather with making philosophy despair of
itself. This is an invaluable result; but it was also necessary to
show that when the philosopher despairs of philosophy, if his
despair is born, not of some philosophical failure but of an
encounter with the Gospel of grace, he can create a pacified
and serene philosophy. Neither Pascal nor Kierkegaard were
willing to undertake this; they had a different message to
bring the Church and the world. But their philosophical
silence should not make us believe in the impossibility of
philosophy.

Thus the Christian can run the risk of philosophizing because
he is completely free, and primarily free with relation to his
own work; he knows that whether this work succeeds or fails
he will always be able to give it meaning. He is exactly in the
position of him who, because he believes in sin, will not tremble
in the face of evil, because he knows that if he remains in the
faith he will experience the grace of forgiveness. He knows that
he can produce the wrong sort of philosophy, i.e. one which,
once constituted, will perhaps imply a false theology; we are
tempted to say that Bergson's philosophy, in so far as it entails
secretly pantheistic views, is the wrong kind of philosophy. But
he also knows that in so far as he remains free with relation to
his philosophy he will not produce a false philosophy, i.e. one
which, presenting itself *en bloc*, would compel us to make a
choice and to decide irrevocably between itself and the Christian theology. It is necessary to call false the kind of massive
philosophy which answers in a final manner all the mind's
questions (Hegelianism and especially Marxism are typical of
this) and forces us to an absolute decision, confining us in a
scheme apart from which there is no salvation. We do not ask
that a philosophy bind us (we are bound elsewhere), but that it
prepare our minds for new paths and values. Positivism in the
Christian's eyes is indeed a false philosophy, because the theory
of knowledge as Auguste Comte formulated it in dogmatic terms
in his law of the three states means, as he himself acknowledged,
an intellectual renunciation. To be a positivist is to resist the
entreaties of our mind itself which spontaneously and especially
upon reflection refuses to limit itself to mere facts, because it

has realized that facts were made, and are mere residues. Positivism is not a doctrine of freedom; not so much because of its negation of freedom, but because of the limits it imposes upon intellectual inquiry. The Christian's unfree will is a source of practical and intellectual freedom. "As everything else," Th. Preiss writes, "philosophy is evidently dependent upon the Christian's freedom: 'All things are yours. . . . Ye are Christ's.' But it is no less obvious that this freedom will only be Christian, and therefore truly free, if it leads the believer to a more and more vivid realization of the fact that it is given and kept in Jesus Christ alone, that it is only a reward, and as it were the reverse side, of this increasingly total captivity of every thought to the obedience of Christ (2 Cor. 10.5)."[1] Gilson expresses rightful astonishment because Christians are sometimes refused the title of authentic philosophers; they are believed to be bound to a pre-established doctrine, and therefore incapable of free inquiry. It may be that the fault is due to the Christians themselves, who were not able to use Christianity otherwise than as a doctrine to be inserted among others and blended with them.[2] It must be acknowledged, however, that it is difficult to make non-believers understand the source of the believer's philosophical freedom; in the last analysis, the believer is philosophically free because for him there exists no philosophical orthodoxy. The very word orthodoxy has no usage in this realm; the point is not to reach a normative philosophy, but to give glory to God by an intelligent exploration of the created world. The generation preceding ours praises Bergson for his doctrine of freedom; at last, thanks to Bergson, freedom again becomes possible in a world of determinism. We understand fully well why Bergsonian philosophy has this ineffable value for non-Christians; but we are surprised to find the same praise coming from Christians. Did they not know already that in Jesus Christ they were free? What Christians must praise Bergson for is having enough freedom of mind to discover, in a period of scientific orthodoxy, that the physical concept of time is a mutilated one, a spatial transposition of real duration. To have opened up the realm of duration, to have given back to existence its true dimension,

[1] *Le témoignage intérieur du Saint-Esprit*, p. 30, n. 1.

[2] P. Sertillanges' great book, *Chrétiens et philosophes*, is a rich repertory of these compromises and syntheses which in effect have imperilled the believers' philosophical freedom in the philosopher's eyes.

that is an achievement of inestimable value; and such is Bergson's great Christian contribution to philosophy; for we know quite well the pagan motives which had prevented the philosophy of time from being constituted ever since Greek antiquity. Thus Bergson's philosophy, with its often pantheistic accents, this exceedingly unorthodox philosophy, has to a very large extent gained the sympathy and approval of Christians. Moreover, the agreement or disagreement of certain Bergsonian conceptions with Christian dogmatics is of little importance to us.

In the last analysis, philosophical freedom is the very sign that we take part in the renewal of the mind, or at least that this renewal is a concrete and living promise; free from all prejudices we are ready to question anew all the concepts without which there can be no real exercise of philosophy.

It is not enough to recognize that faith in the renewing of the mind creates conditions favourable to the exercise of philosophical thought. Philosophy is a labour. The Christian accepts that his work be placed under the joint sign of the judgement and the promise. How will this modify the work? Will there be in the character of the Christian's philosophy any features showing that it also participates in the renewal of the understanding? Does this philosophy which is the work of the old man attest that old things are passed away?

Every philosophy is systematic because it is rational; this means that every philosophy experiences the temptation to be a self-sufficient philosophy. Not content with describing the real, it also wishes to explain it, and explain it thoroughly; and not content with explaining it, it also wishes to justify it. Every philosophy is tempted to try to determine being, to set aside definitively any mystery and to enclose the world in an immutable hierarchy. The ideas of category, order and hierarchy, through which philosophies become systems and lose any capacity to comprehend the real, have never ceased to play an important role in philosophy. By their definitive and necessary character, these ideas become theologies. What is striking in Spinoza's *Ethics*, for instance, is precisely this absolute and definitive character: Spinoza's philosophy is a *theologia gloriae*, valid for the Kingdom. It ignores the reality of the obstacle, or when it encounters one, as at the beginning of the *De Intellectus Emendatione*, it easily succeeds in overcoming it. Nothing opposes the triumph of the rational life. If all philosophy is born of anxiety, it is also true that every philosophical system represents a triumph over and an elimination of anxiety. Philosophy becomes a system precisely in so far as it leads to a certainty. Only the knowledge of sin that faith imparts can keep philosophy from completing and perfecting itself and can maintain alive the problematics of philosophy. Evidently, philosophical analysis will not contradict the assertion of the substantial reality of sin; it may, however, ignore it, or even, paradoxical as this may seem, forget it. Faith alone can drive the philosopher to undertake an analysis which will lead him to discover the reality of the obstacle. All dialectics of obstacle are of primordial interest to the Christian. Those philosophies which are too rigorously systematic do not interest him. Hegel may have passed for a theologian, but the Christian knows that becoming cannot be rationalized; history is nothing if it does not make room for the scandal of sin. It is not so much for having forgotten freedom and chance that the Christian will reproach Hegel, as for having forgotten sin. The Christian will feel more at home with Descartes than with Spinoza, because in the former's thinking the negation of error is less radical, and because Descartes forgets less than Spinoza man's condition as creature (with all the limitations this condition entails) and as sinful creature ("precipitancy and prejudice"). Let us point out that we are not asking philosophy as such to give us the idea of sin or to confess sin or give empirical evidence of it. Sin as such can only be believed and confessed in the Church; but we ask the Christian philosopher who has the knowledge of sin to explore the sectors of human reality unobserved by those who ignore or misinterpret the reality of sin. A correct inventory of the ethical situation of man is possible only if man is known as a sinner. It is a necessary condition for finding the exact equilibrium among the various aspects of man. The description of man which will be given must impose itself; it must find in itself, and not in faith, its own probative strength: it remains to be seen, however, whether the philosopher would have succeeded in this description without the help of faith and the light it sheds on all reality. As the Christian alone can completely and totally assume the human condition, so that those nations which reject Christianity after having professed it rapidly fall below the human level, similarly also the Christian

M

alone really knows human nature. To participate in the renewal of understanding is truly to be capable of a discernment
which is ordinarily refused to natural man.

Calvin judiciously indicated that this absolutizing tendency
of dogmatic philosophy, with its pretensions to make laws for
eternity and to introduce us into the world of being, has its
source in a misinterpretation by the philosophers of the reality
of sin: "And this is why the philosophers became so dazzled,
and surrounded by darkness: it is because they sought a beautiful and whole edifice in a ruin, and well connected relations in
dissipation. . . . Now, Adam's fall being hidden from them, and
the confusion arising from it, it is not surprising that they confused heaven with earth."[1]

To confuse heaven with earth; is this not the error we are
denouncing, the risk of changing into an anticipated theology
of glory what should only be a philosophy of the human condition. There can be no philosophy but of the earth—provided
it is well understood that the idea of God, and transcendency,
are indeed realities of this earth.

And this knowledge of man's radical sinfulness will enable
the philosopher to keep a reserved, truly critical, truly philosophical attitude with regard to his own work. Of course, he will
not avoid systematization; it is a necessity in expression and
teaching. But he will know what attitude to adopt towards his
own systematizations; he will know that his knowledge of man,
the world and God is the knowledge of a sinful man; that any
view of God participates in sin and is therefore to a certain
extent impious and sacrilegious; that any view of man, his
potentialities and his destiny, always depends to a certain degree
upon the measure of confidence we conceitedly harbour towards human nature and ourselves; that any view of the
world concerns a fallen world; that the world in spite of
its laws, perfections and harmonies is in no way external; and
that man need not conform with its order, but that, on the
contrary, the world finds itself associated with the destiny of
man.

It is remarkable that ancient thought elaborated the philosophy of a static and definitive world, the projection of a well-
organized state the stability of which was itself guaranteed by
the local Pantheon; and that this thought sealed man's destiny

[1] *Institutes*, XV, 8.

into rigid frameworks and eliminated from the world any movement which was not cyclic and any becoming which was not
eternal. It is remarkable that any thinking which ignores the
judgement pronounced upon man and the world also seals the
world and man in a motionless perfection and confuses this
motionlessness with eternity itself. It is also remarkable that the
more a philosophy thus tries to discover an immutable order,
the more dogmatic an aspect it assumes; the great thinkers of
Antiquity were not content with contributing original views in a
given domain; they thought it necessary to give a definitive
"sum" of their ideas, including a theory of knowledge, an
ontology, a cosmology, a politics and an aesthetics. No doubt,
the synthetic power of such minds is to be admired, especially
when compared with the analytical impotency of modern
thinkers; it must not be forgotten, however, that this very
systematism entailed a danger which was to sterilize subsequent
philosophical thought. For several centuries afterwards the
philosophers were obliged to confine themselves to acting as
commentators and exegetists of their predecessors' works. Thus
there was elaborated a kind of scholasticism—the very sign of
philosophical decadence. Scepticism alone was able to save
philosophy from this disastrous dogmatism—and at the cost
of what sacrifices!

The above remarks have no other purpose than to make us
understand why the Christian is in a better position than anyone else to undertake a philosophical work free from dogmatism, i.e. open to all appeals and hospitable to all aspects of the
real. A philosophy shows its Christian character by its sense of its
own *limitations*. Thus it testifies that it is the philosophy of a
Christian who places all things under God's judgement. We do
not expect it to burst into declamations about the weakness of
human nature; but we do expect it to be truly humble. It is
quite certain that Christianity is much better vindicated by a
philosophy such as Le Senne's, which is a description of
consciousness, or by those of the phenomenologists or the
existentialists, which are endeavours to elucidate the meaning
of various existential situations. In a general manner, the
Christian's philosophy should be recognizable by his ever-
renewed effort towards concreteness. That is why we believe
that for a Christian the exercise of philosophy is made considerably easier, as well as considerably more fruitful, today,

since the return of philosophy *zu den Sachen selbst*[1] conforms to his deepest wishes. A Malebranche, though Christian, makes Christians feel ill at ease because he appears to dread the contact of the datum itself. The theory of vision in God, which is made necessary by the principle of the radical separation of substances, reduces us to considering creation as a sort of artefact, a mere "occasion"; creation is not really taken seriously. Man cannot know it directly; he knows it only in its archetypes, which are in God. Here we can feel the heavy mortgage which weighs upon a thinking loyal to deductive dogmatism. The example is all the more significant because Malebranche intended to build a philosophy in harmony with the dogmatic truths, a philosophy complementary to the true religion. In spite of all the strains of authentic Christianity which can be found in it, Malebranche's philosophy still does not possess a Christian character. Imprisoned as it is in its own dogmatism, rigorously constructed and deduced, forming an absolutely complete and coherent system—a fact of which Théodore, Malebranche's mouthpiece in the *Dialogues on Metaphysics and Religion*, continually boasts—this philosophy is nevertheless characterized by a denial of the real and the concrete; it is closed upon itself, it confines thought in the definitive. It gives complete satisfaction to the mind. It does not leave room for any disquietude; every time the philosopher faces a serious deadlock, the theologian comes in to pull him out of trouble. Philosophy is directly prolonged by theology; it is itself theological. It is probably because of this that it lacks a Christian general aspect.

Besides its dogmatic character, philosophy also often assumes a speculative and theoretical character. It might even be said that the advent of the philosophical spirit in Western civilization marks the division of knowledge: practical knowledge born of action became separated from reflection and theory. Two groups of values were constituted and began to oppose each other: vital values and intellectual values. This divorce is particularly obvious in the realm of ethics. Renouvier certainly did not invent the opposition between theoretical and practical ethics; but no other philosophy before his had ever given it such consistency.[2] This divorce is all the more serious

---

[1] To things themselves, i.e. to concrete situations (translator's note).
[2] Cf. Jean Lacroix, *Vocation personnelle et tradition nationale*.

because it follows the spontaneous orientation of popular consciousness. No doubt, any thought constitutes a recoil or a retreat into the self which separates it from action; no doubt, also, any thought is a kind of halt. To think is to defer, to procrastinate. But thought cannot be severed from action without losing all its pith and meaning; for action alone places thought in contact with the real. The experience of the real always presupposes action upon the real. Thought which, disengaged from the real and having become pure thought, loses its contact with the real, faces the temptation of constructing its object. But an object is only constructed with the help of the imagination, that is, of passion. As a result, this fabricating activity of thought is, at the same time, myth-building; it is a real aberration of the mind. The Scripture tenders a formal warning against thus separating thought from action and practising such disincarnated thinking in which we as persons are no longer involved in the real. As a matter of fact, it regards this as one of the major manifestations of sin. For it shows us how thinking about God which no longer is the service of God, and theology which no longer is liturgy can beget idolatry (Rom 1.18-23). The only true knowledge of God is the acknowledgement of His lordship (Rev. 2.23; Heb. 8.11). One cannot know without bowing to the object of one's knowledge and conforming to it. No one can claim to know God if he does not know Him in obedience and in submission to the requirements of His Grace.[1] Thus, it is indeed an ideal of knowledge that the Scripture imposes upon us, apart from any theory of the nature of knowledge. According to 1 Cor. 8.4-6, it can be concluded that knowledge does entail a theoretical moment, but that this is never the decisive moment. Philosophy only becomes dogmatic and scholastic in so far as it is unfaithful to its object, that is, in proportion to its theoretical character. It is important, therefore, that philosophical knowledge lose this theoretical and disincarnated character so heavy with consequences. No doubt a reaction can be felt from within philosophy itself; a more serious analysis of judgement reveals in it the necessary and contemporaneous presence of intellect and will. But it is the Scripture itself which makes us realize in a decisive manner the gravity of merely theoretical knowledge; Satan may know God, but does not serve Him. The Christian

[1] Rom. 3.17; Heb. 3.10; Luke 19.42-44; 2 Pet. 2.21; Rom. 2.18; Acts 22.14.

therefore is better prepared than anyone else for this never-ending endeavour which brings thought back to action, reflection to personal involvement; an endeavour made all the more difficult by the fact that we spontaneously tend to dissociate acting from thinking, and to retreat into a pure thought which entails no risks, remains gratuitous and merely affords us an opportunity for aesthetic enjoyment.

. . . . . .

Can we go even further? Are there any Christian ideas or motives capable of exerting a decisive influence upon the unfolding of philosophical thought? Again, let us point out that this cannot mean a mere transposition of Christian ideas upon the philosophical plane. For, on the one hand, we would be secularizing these ideas. Such secularization begins as soon as a Christian idea is abstracted from the Biblical Revelation as a whole; the Incarnation has meaning only when viewed in its relationship to the Resurrection and to the whole work of Redemption. On the other hand, philosophy will lose its freedom and its very quality as philosophy when made to incorporate ideas that it has not itself evolved. Quite possibly, the idea of incarnation is, as Gabriel Marcel wishes, a capital one for philosophy; however, it does not reach this status by becoming an articulation in philosophical dialectics. Its proper role is quite different: it acts upon philosophy, so to speak, from the outside; it prevents the philosopher from engaging in certain directions (its negative role); it brings to his attention fields of investigation of which he would otherwise have been unaware (its positive role). This idea has not been philosophically justified. It is enough if it can be ascertained that it has not inflicted any constraint or limitation upon the philosopher and that it has, on the contrary, widened, or clarified his field of investigation. If such is the case, the philosopher cannot be reproached for his faith. Those who tend to cast suspicion upon the philosophical value of a Christian's philosophy are greatly mistaken; they see in philosophy only a purely intellectual technique, which undoubtedly it ought to be; but a technique needs to be led and given direction. This can only be done by a mind which is oriented in one way rather than in another; thus behind any philosophical technique is concealed some form of spirituality. Now, the sources of philosophical spirituality can be extremely varied. At the source of certain contemporary philosophies, Bergsonianism for instance, might we not find an artistic or musical spirituality, that is, a certain form of sensitivity? Has not Jankelevitch, a philosophical critic, given an interpretation of Bergson's work in purely musical terms?[1] Other philosophies, such as that of Brunschvicg, are dominated by a spirituality which we might call mathematical, since it consists in a certain recognition of the purity of mathematical analysis. If such is the case, why should we not acknowledge the Christian faith as one of the sources of philosophy—not philosophy as a technique (which would situate philosophy upon the prolongation of faith) but philosophy as spirituality? Every philosophy, before it becomes explicit in a doctrine, proceeds from some *a priori*, i.e. from some spiritual exigency. We can only require one thing: namely, that this *a priori* should have enlightening value, and that it should point to evidences capable of being recognized as such by any unprejudiced mind. If this condition is fulfilled, philosophy remains wholly independent. As soon as philosophy is considered as an attempt to describe and elucidate the meaning of the real, the most important point is to bring the real to light or into relief. Christianity, we hold, is a light enabling us to view reality under its most vivid aspect. Possibly, no example is quite as typical in this respect as that of the problem of time.

Evidently, by its origins and purposes, philosophy, as the science of being, was little disposed toward dealing with time, that which passes, which is becoming, a sign of birth and death. The fact is, ancient thought ignored time in so far as it is vanishing duration, the source of the scattering out of consciousness, and a sign of death. Of time, it was only prepared to retain the mobile image of motionless eternity. In order that time might be thought to possess some measure of perfection, it had to be assimilated to a perfect movement: the cyclical motion. As the circle has neither beginning nor end, lacks nothing, and is thus perfect, there was nothing to prevent time being declared perfect and therefore eternal. In Aristotle's thinking especially, precisely in so far as we pass from physics to astronomy, time acquires qualities which make it the perfect common measure of all motion, and thus a perfect and eternal instrument. Time

---

[1] J. Jankelevitch, *Bergson*, in the series *Les grands philosophes*. Note that this work is previous to the publication of the *Two Sources*.

with its becoming, time the locus of risk where living beings gamble their fate, time with all its contingency, unforeseeable-ness and radical novelty, time in which events and actions, i.e. all that is essential in a man's destiny, take place, this time is made away with. No doubt, ancient thought did not always harbour towards time a cold indifference, such as Parmenides'; no doubt, it sometimes granted the past and the present, especi-ally those of the State, a measure of reality; yet time plays almost no part in its philosophy. When time becomes embarrassing, when its real character is seen, it is driven back towards non-being. It was commonly understood that the corruptible and the mortal are not objects for philosophy because they are not objects at all. When Plotinus, concerned with a soterio-logical problem, became compelled to take time seriously, he hastened to view it as a kind of logical and spontaneous deposit of eternity, a sign of the superabundance of being. He could not decide whether the soul which turns to time really suffers a fall or whether it is simply indulging in a kind of excursion without consequence for its destiny. Time is not nothing, but it is utterly devoid of meaning. At the extreme limit of its evolution, Greek thought did not hesitate to suppose the existence of a reality devoid of meaning. That is why Plotinus could not finally make up his mind to admit that the soul really lives in time; in reality, the truly spiritual part of the soul re-mains bound to the eternal and cannot move in time. The latter, therefore, remains utterly alien to us.[1] Plotinus does not suspect any more than his predecessors the bond between time and our spiritual destiny. That time is in the end devoid of any meaning is also attested to by the whole eschatology of ancient thought. The presence of eschatological themes, so numerous in Plato's work, for example, is indeed impressive. Can the future have such value? But very quickly one realizes that this eschatology is mythical, not temporal. Eschatology is not bound to events which are really imminent in time and which come to us as a very concrete promise or threat; eschato-logy is always related to myth, i.e. to a trans-temporal moment thrown back on an unseizable past or a thoroughly unreal future. For ancient thought, eschatology is a manner of con-solation for time, a means of mimicking eternity in time—and not at all a way of discovering the meaning of time and of

---

[1] See on this point Jean Guitton, *Le temps et l'éternité chez Plotin et chez St. Augustin.*

THE RENEWING OF THE MIND

rediscovering the fertile tension between time and eternity. Even in Plato there can doubtless be found an effort to attribute a measure of value to time. Do not the myths of predestination (e.g. the myth of Er in the *Republic*), indicate that time in its cyclical fragments enables the soul to purify itself with a view to a better choice at the end of a thousand years' cycle? But this choice will be absolutely irrevocable for another thousand years. The choice itself is made outside of time, in a sort of suspension of time.

Many additions and changes could doubtless be made in this survey of the philosophy of time in ancient thought. We believe, however, that they would not fundamentally modify it. Let us generalize by saying that ontology and politics are the two real poles of ancient thought and that both of these disciplines prohibit the consideration of time; ontology wishes to ignore it, because time would insert the other into the same, which seems logically impossible; politics meets with the preoccupations of ontology, because the ideal of the State is stability and any movement, any evolution, is considered a sign of corruption.

It is in this spiritual atmosphere that the Christian revolution took place. True, Revelation does not bring with itself any philosophy of time. But it does entail ideas which have pointed up the narrowness and falsity of the Greek conception. First among these ideas is that of *creation*. The Biblical idea of Creation does not seem susceptible of any philosopical use; it contains mostly difficulties; the idea of an *e nihilo* Creation by the Word is a philosophically untranslatable concept. And yet, whoever takes this Creation seriously, whoever takes stock exactly of the state of the creature can no longer try, as Hellenic thought did, to abstract himself from time; for time is a part of creation; it is not, as in Plato, added to the world in order to increase its perfection and make the copy more similar to its model; it is part of the substance of the world. God is in His heaven and we are on earth. The creature cannot rise above his own condition. His condition conforms to the will of God. Time is the very mark of our finiteness as creatures. The Christian, therefore, cannot behave as if time did not exist; he cannot lay claim to the contemplation or possession of eternity. To him, the eternity of the temporal present will be purely symbolic. Thus, the Christian philosopher will first of all be inclined to carry out a very necessary criticism of all systems which establish a natural harmony between eternity and the soul. As we already ascertained, the Revelation fosters a more scrupulous realism in philosophical inquiry. Moreover, whereas ancient thought tried either to drive back time into non-being, or on the contrary to metamorphose it so as to make it utterly unrecognizable, the Christian will no more dispute the reality of time than that of creation; and, on the other hand, he will refuse to admit this spurious assimilating of time to some perfect motion—this spatializing of time whereby ancient thought hoped to confer upon time the fullness of being. Being created, time cannot be thought eternal as in Aristotle or Plotinus; it is necessarily of a passing nature. The Christian, because he very vividly feels the opposition between time and eternity, will orient his thinking towards an analysis of time which respects the nature of time and its intimate contradictions; an analysis willing to point out the paradoxical characteristics of a time which cannot be subsumed under the categories of an ontological or a substantialistic logic. The Greek heritage, reinforced by the geometrical turn of mind of modern man, leads, as Bergson has shown, to schematizing and spatializing time, thus depriving it of all its astonishing contingency, its mystery and the unceasing round of problems to which it gives rise. Not least among the services the Christian spirituality can render is that of freeing the mind for a more accurate analysis of time.

But the Christian faith is not content with bringing us back with invincible urgency to the consideration of man's true condition. It also makes more positive demands. This time faith compels us to look at and live in, this time from which it will not let us escape through any mysticism, is not imposed upon us as an absurd or meaningless reality. Faith does not elucidate the meaning of time; but it bears witness to the existence of time; the very idea of Creation places time in relationship with eternity, and time only exists by an act of the Eternal. If our time has any tension of its own, if it is not the indefinite banality that we sometimes imagine it to be, it is because it is the work of eternity—the work and not, as Plotinus suggests, a by-product; a work that God takes so seriously that He acts in it Himself. It is *in time* that God carries out creation. Time, therefore, has a meaning; it can be the carrier of a positive work, that of God. The sanctification of the seventh day means that even

though time depends upon creation and therefore has limitations, it is nevertheless the locus of a fulfilment and a completion. Our acts will be complete and will have full meaning
to the exact extent that they will be ordered by the creative
act and assure its conservation according to the will of God.
We start, therefore, with the assurance that time is not mere
vanity.

We also have the assurance that time will indeed be a history,
i.e. that it is not the indefinite repetition and the cyclical return
of the same events, but, for the individual as well as collec-
tivities, the unfolding of a destiny. For time marches towards a
termination, creation will have an end. Duration, therefore, is
given us as a possibility of action, decision and commitment.
This possibility will not recur indefinitely, for it is in time
that we meet death. This end might mean annihilation pure
and simple. Here, however, other ideas enjoin us not to stop
at this possibility: coming from eternity yet never identified
with it, time is nevertheless susceptible of being met by eternity,
of being cut through and set straight by the very act of eternity.
For such is the meaning of the Incarnation. In Jesus Christ, the
Word was made flesh and the Kingdom came near us. Doubtless, time is not capable of eternity, it cannot contain it or take
it into itself; time can only be shaken by eternity and set straight
by its action. These rare moments when time has felt the
burning sensation of eternity (the Lord is a consuming fire)
we can never afford to forget. Every moment of our existence
which we relate back to these unique moments takes on a
meaning and gravity which it did not naturally possess. My
whole life has value because of the Incarnation of Christ, who
for me has come into a life similar to mine; my death ceases to
be a physiological accident when seen in the light of the death
on the Cross. Any existence, however miserable, represents a
kind of absolute, if the promise of Resurrection addressed to it
is discerned. The liturgical year constantly compels us to refer
every moment of our existence to those rare instants when
eternity has come close to time and when the spontaneous unfolding of duration has been broken by the intervention of
eternity claiming its rights upon the entire creation.

In short, because of the Scriptural Revelation man regains
possession of time—all his time. Not only does he know that
God rules over time and that God's patience is due to the fact

that time belongs to God; but he also knows that in faith he himself regains the rule over all creation and over time in particular. Our raw experience seems to indicate that the present alone belongs to us, that it alone counts in theory and practice, and that even so it is disappointing because it is constantly vanishing. The past seems to be ours only to make us suffer; sometimes we regret its passing so quickly, sometimes deplore that it is no longer within our reach so that we might modify it. At any rate, it is no longer ours, precisely because it is irrevocable. The future does not belong to us because it is too uncertain; we are afraid lest it do not come, or lest it come too slowly or be a source of too great disappointments. It is not enough determined, whereas the past is too much so. When we try to grasp it, we know well that we only project before us the sum of our desires and that these desires, poignant though they may be, have not sufficient strength to shape the future. It is precisely to this uncertain and unreal future that the Biblical Revelation gives real solidity. The Christian is a man whose future is made. His future is the new man, fully grasped in the risen Christ. Thus the future is accomplished, the future is objective—which does not mean, however, that the future is ready-made: we are only saved in hope. We are still free to be faithful or unfaithful, to commit or refuse ourselves. But a clear future is offered us, not as an ideal, hardly born as yet, for us to fulfil, but as the Kingdom of God which is coming, which is already prepared, so that in a certain sense our present is preceded by our future which dominates and shapes it, since the new man is more real than the old man. That is why we can never again cling to the present alone with passionate exclusiveness. The present loses its prestige on account of the imminence of the Kingdom. Yet there remains the opportunity of an anticipatory experience, that of the eternal present; in its own way, it prefigures eternity, it is the reality which allows us to think of eternity at least in an analogical mode. But most of all —and thence all its value—it is the locus of commitment, an opportunity to be faithful, to begin anew. The realization of forgiveness breaks the absolute solidarity between the present and the past: the present no longer appears as the simple resultant of the past; it can spell freedom. But the past itself loses some of its hardness: no doubt, it cannot be abolished, for it subsists—as does all of time—in the eyes of the Eternal God who judges it; I cannot therefore disavow it or desolidarize myself from it. And yet the promise of grace holds for it also: the past can be transfigured: the Cross and the Resurrection give a new meaning, not only to the future of mankind, but to all its past as well. Though accomplished by man, it can yet change its meaning. Even though the past may be the mere history of our disobedience and of the curse upon us, this disobedience and this curse themselves are, for him who is forgiven and saved, means of grasping his own situation with relation to God.

Such is the experience of integral time towards which the Scriptural Revelation inclines us. The question is, to know whether this experience can be carried all the way, and most of all, whether it can resolve the philosophical problems raised by time. The indications we have given in no way constitute a philosophy of time: they merely supply us with a reason to try to overcome certain antinomies raised by time: Is time objective or subjective? Does it dominate us or belong to us? Is it finite or indefinite?, etc. . . . The raw experience of time leaves us undecided before these problems. The Christian experience of time—that is experience oriented by the demands of the Scriptural Revelation—accounts, we believe, for such antinomies. At any rate, it allows us not to stop at these antinomies and give them meaning. The true object of philosophy is not to resolve all antinomies, but to elucidate the reasons of their existence. As long as the problem of time is thought to consist only in finding out whether time is a substance or the attribute of a substance, whether it is an objective reality or a category of our subjectivity, we are powerless to resolve the real problems of time. The demands of the Christian faith help us to free ourselves of ready-made concepts.

It would be easy to show that the hierarchy of problems itself depends upon one's spiritual sources. Has not the problem of time made its entrance into philosophy essentially with St. Augustine? Ancient thought did not ignore it, but endeavoured to show that it was a secondary problem. Today Lavelle is able to write: "Time is the central problem of philosophy, the one which begets all others and on account of which it can be said that problems exist. It is easily seen that our whole life is a problem to us only inasmuch as it unfolds itself in time: the mystery of life is the mystery of its origin and of its *dénoue-ment*."[1] It is easily seen ... yet all ancient thought failed to see. For it, existence had no tragic character, for it was prearranged with a view to a motionless eternity and to the social framework of the State. One cannot but recognize that it is the irruption of Christianity which, by calling into question our personal existence and viewing death seriously, raised the problem of time before man's consciousness as the central problem of philosophy. Time and eternity are both characterized by belonging to the most general human experience and only manifesting their ultimate meaning in Revelation: eternity is but a particular mode of transcendency as long as it is not the Eternal or the Kindom of God; time is but the condition of our ordinary experience as long as it is not the time of sin, forgiveness and grace. Reality itself runs the risk of being warped when discovered by the mind on a purely secular plane. The Christian philosopher is not one who in his research translates eternity by the Kingdom, and time by the Church and who under the pretext of making a philosophy of time would construct an ecclesiology. He is one who knows that the decisive gravity of the problem of time and eternity comes ultimately from the fact that it refers us to the eternity of the Kingdom and of the Church. It is on account of this particular perspicacity, because of this discerning among doctrines, that we can assert he participates in the renewing of the mind.

It should also be pointed out that when the Christian notices this relationship between eternity and the Kingdom, time and the Church, he should abstain from considering those ideas he is dealing with as secularized substitutes, or as transposed concepts "parallel" to those dealt with by the theologian. It is not true that whoever has a good philosophy of time implicitly possesses a Christian ecclesiology, nor that time is a general concept which includes that of the Church; nor is it correct to hold that existential philosophy potentially contains Christianity. This certain relation which exists between time and the Church, eternity and the Kingdom, existence in Bultmann's or Heidegger's sense and the condition of man sinful and forgiven, can only be perceived by those willing to consent to the

---

[1] "L'expérience psychologique du temps", in *Revue de métaphysique et de morale*, April, 1941, p. 81.

act of faith. With a view to existential philosophy, P. Althaus[1] points out how it does not lead to Christianity, but only to progress in one dimension of experience, where, with the help of faith, we can encounter authentic Christianity.

Our attempt to show to what extent dogmatic ideas can give command to philosophical inquiry would prove vain and pernicious for the Church if the terms could be reversed and if philosophy could be said to present us with a general truth of which dogmatics offers one particular case. As Heinrich Barth[2] points out, the dichotomy between the idea of general and particular which characterizes the opposition between philosophy and theology must not include any attempt to subsume the reality of the particular (i.e. the reality of the unique historical event) under the idea of the general. The truth of that existence which springs from Revelation should not be identified with the general truth of existence dealt with by existential philosophy, and the latter is not, as Heidegger and Bultmann suggest, the general case containing the particular case. What the general and philosophical concept of the existential offers is not the knowledge of God but an analogy of the knowledge of God. That is why philosophy cannot and will not incorporate theology or subject it to itself. It is only in retrospect, starting from Revelation, and not by anticipation, that the philosophical notion of the existential can be of use towards the knowledge of God; it is in no way its instrument.

.   .   .   .   .

Here we can only give a few samples of the Christian philosopher's work—in order to show in what sense his submission to Christian dogmatics, and through it to Jesus Christ, is to be understood. Obviously there is a definite dependence, but indirect and so to say oblique. We can be sure that the character of this dependence rests solely upon the fact that the new man is not yet manifested and that the old man continues to live and act.

The renewal of the mind cannot therefore consist in edifying a *philosophia perennis* which actually would be only the *theologia gloriae* of the "old man" still persistently alive. The regeneration promised us is shown in the activity whereby, availing

---

[1] *Grundriss der Dogmatik.*

[2] "Philosophie, Theologie und Existenzproblem", in *Zwischen den Zeiten*, 1932.

ourselves of the benefits of the promise and taut with the imminency of the ultimate realities, we attempt as part of the exercise of our Christian vocation to create a new philosophy witnessing to our faith. We say: a new philosophy. Too often, Christians have believed it their duty to limit themselves to resuming the works of the pagans and attempting new syntheses or new compromises between them; as if it were enough to reunite these scattered particles in order to show that we partake of regeneration. Far better: we have a truly new adventure to run with the new spiritual forces God has given us. The Christian is not one who, standing at the point of convergence of mankind's various adventures, attempts to profit by their accumulated lessons. He is not dispensed from running his own adventure with the strength given to him by God; he is not withdrawn from the world. Christianity's mistake—which explains the unwillingness of some to admit the existence of a Christian philosophy—was to try to reconcile the existing philosophies. St. Augustine, while still close to neo-Platonism and filled with admiration for Porphyry, believed that an idea could be Christian without its author being converted to Christianity. He even has the *naïveté* to think that had Plato and Porphyry combined together two opinions they held separately about the destiny of souls, *facti essent fortasse christiani*, they would perhaps have become Christian.[1] Does not Gilson write with reference to medieval philosophy: "As conceived here, the spirit of medieval philosophy is the spirit of Christianity, penetrating the Greek tradition, working within it, drawing out of it a certain view of the world, a *Weltanschauung*, specifically Christian"?[2] That is, alas! exactly what happened: faith was not bold enough to create a new intellectual universe and to view seriously, in the order of thought, the demands made upon man's mind by the renewal of the understanding. It may be, moreover, that philosophy is not the only domain where the Christian faith has shown so little assurance: the history of politics would probably reveal the same vicissitudes.

Intellectual courage would have been necessary to break away from the cultural and spiritual traditions of paganism and build the new philosophy upon the new foundations which

---

[1] P. de Labriolle, *La réaction païenne*, p. 295, reference to Sermon 241, pars. 6 and 7 (Patrol., lat. 38, 1,137).

[2] *The Spirit of Medieval Philosophy*, p. viii.

were given it. Had they done this courageously, the Christians would have cut themselves away from the philosophical and cultural tradition of paganism. Yet they should have known that if they made this break they would retrieve afterwards the whole truth contained in paganism, that this would be added unto them. Quite certainly, the pagan religions possess some truths, yet no one can become a Christian without becoming detached from these religions. Similarly, to be a Christian philosopher is to break away from all the philosophers inspired by the various pagan creeds, it is to believe that because God has made all things new it is possible for us also to make new things.

Chapter VI

THE DIALOGUE BETWEEN THE THEOLOGIAN AND THE PHILOSOPHER

A DIALOGUE offers no interest unless it takes place between two partners enjoying equal freedom and dignity. In saying this we have defined the conditions of a fruitful dialogue between the theologian and the Christian philosopher. First, because we have endeavoured to grasp the dogmatic effort in its purity and its contrast with philosophical reflection; further, because we very carefully avoided depriving philosophy —even the Christian's philosophy—of its independence, that is of its rationality. It is too easily imagined that a "Christian philosophy" is one in which rationality is tempered by so-called mystical elements. The Christian's philosophy is simply a philosophy which seeks the guarantee of its legitimacy and ultimately of its rationality in the Christian Revelation; for the Christian is convinced that a reason which does not place itself under the judgement and the promise, and which knows nothing of the renewing of the mind, can only stray outside the boundaries of its normal function: any reason which does not live on grace is passion.[1] The main thing for us is to leave the ground of compromise between dogmatics and philosophy and to define a religious philosophy which is not a dogmatics in disguise. It is all the more difficult to exorcise this compromise since Kantianism has made it into one of the deep elements of our mental régime. But as long as we move upon the ground of compromise, as long as we do away artificially with the opposition between dogmatics and philosophy, no frutiful dialectics can be established between these two disciplines. What we wish to point out here are the various meanings of their coexistence in the teaching of theology.

We already see with some clarity the reasons philosophy may have to lean on or refer to dogmatics. May dogmatics also need

[1] In this sense we fully subscribe to this statement of Gilson: "From St. Augustine to Malebranche and Pascal, through St. Thomas and St. Bonaventure, a Christian philosopher is a thinker who, far from believing he is dispensed from understanding, thinks he finds in the faith he accepts a net profit for his reason," *The Philosophy of St. Thomas Aquinas*, p. 10 (French edition).

the assistance of philosophy? At first this question appears quite astonishing. But it can be easily conceded that the theologian requires a philosophical training and a philosophical turn of mind in working out and systematizing problems. Philosophy brings the idea of a certain order, that is basically the subordination of the accessory to the essential, of the complex to the simple. The discovery of such an order is necessary for the dogmatic understanding of Revelation. Calvin himself states: "Many are seen to torment themselves greatly reading Holy Scripture; they merely turn over the pages, but after ten years they will know no more about it than if they had never read a single line. And why? Because they lack a certain skill and they do little but ramble. And even in the humane arts, some take great pains at them, yet in vain, for they keep neither order nor measure, and merely glean here and there, creating much confusion; thus they will never be able to deduce anything though they have gathered up much knowledge from diverse sources; but there is no tenure."[1] There is a hierarchy of dogmatic questions; the pullulation of sects and heresies is explained in part by the inability of those Calvin calls the "fanciful" to conduct their thoughts in an orderly manner. Doubtless, the object itself demands a certain order; but the intellect is so made that it only grasps this order when it has begun to seek it and when it approaches its study with an intention of order. The same can be said about a distinction essential for the understanding of Revelation: the distinction between a fact and its meaning; between that which is a datum and can only be ascertained and the significance of this datum which can only be grasped in faith. There exists a gross form of orthodoxy built simply upon the ignorance of this distinction. The dogmatician needs a theory of the sign, for it is obvious that the distinction to which we allude only constitutes the first step and that it is also necessary to mark out the relationship between the material fact and its meaning; otherwise the meaning might be little else but a more or less loose, more or less fanciful interpretation of the fact. The theory of the sign involves, we believe, a whole theory on the relation between history and metaphysics. Of course, the Biblical sign helps us to constitute this theory; the theory is nevertheless the work of

[1] Calvin, *C.R.*, XXXV, p. 361 (Meyruis edition); text cited by L. Wencelius, *L'esthétique de Calvin*, p. 318.

philosophy, which the philosopher places at the theologian's
disposal. Dogmatics ought to offer us a systematic collection of
meanings and not of facts, as a certain orthodoxy fond of "the
great Christian facts" would have it. There is doubtless a positive relation between the empty tomb and faith in the Resurrection; yet this material fact of the empty tomb is nothing without
the Resurrection signified by it. It can be rightly maintained that the Revelation itself incites us to distinguish between reality and its meaning and to attach our faith, not to
the materiality of the fact, but to its meaning. On the road to
Emmaus, Jesus explains to the disciples the meaning of the
events they experienced without understanding. But the
theologian must be constantly guarded by an exact theory of
the sign. It matters little that it is precisely Christianity which
attracted the philosopher's attention to the problem of the
sign and of the relationship between the event and its meaning;
it is indeed the philosopher who offers the theologian an
indispensable weapon and method.

It seems obvious, in a more general manner still, that any
theology, being a kind of *figuration of dogma*, needs concepts
borrowed from the various philosophies in order to articulate
its thinking. It can never be sufficiently repeated that in its
essence dogma, i.e. God's order, the act by which God commands, is at first a reality impossible for us to formulate; that
dogma is not doctrine and that in translating a dogma into a
doctrine we unavoidably make use of a preconceived form
which does not depend upon God's act of Revelation.[1] In this
sense, it can be said that all dogmatic elaboration is also
philosophical cognition, in so far as the philosopher's own field
is to conceptualize. Let us refer to the beginning of Calvin's
Catechism for a decisive example: there he attempts to make
explicit the dogma of the Trinity in order to show "that there
is no difficulty in the idea that in one Godhead we may distinctly conceive of three persons; and yet, that God is not
divided ... ". The answer to this problem is given by a distinction
of points of view upon God obtained by means of half-
Christian (or Christianized) and half-Alexandrian terms: "Because in one single divine *essence* we have to consider the Father
as the beginning and the origin, or *first cause*, of all things; His

---

[1] That dogma is not to be confused with the dogmatic proposition (*Lehrsatz*) has
been brought to light particularly by K. Barth, *Kirchliche Dogmatik*, I, 1, pp. 284-288.

THE THEOLOGIAN AND THE PHILOSOPHER

Son, who is His *eternal wisdom*; the Holy Spirit which is *His virtue and His power* shed abroad upon all creatures and which nonetheless still resides in Him."[1] Is it not worth noting that a philosophical gnosis of such distinctly Plotinian character is described at the beginning of the *Catechism*? Now, quite evidently no philosophical terminology or system of concepts is neutral. Every group of concepts implies a scale of values, even a form of spirituality; in short, a human wisdom. We find dogmatics in necessary contact with the philosophical wisdom with which it must at no cost be identified. This necessary contact will reach the point of co-operation: a co-operation no less essential than that which the theologian maintains with grammar and language. There will be a real striving on the theologian's part to transcribe non-philosophical truth into philosophical language. To succeed, he will first have to be acquainted, not only with the meaning, but also with the implications of philosophical language. He must have a clear awareness of the philosophical frame of mind which his language may bring into being. For the problem is not to abstain completely from any philosophical terminology, but to know how to use it. "To bear witness to the Revelation in Christ always means, in practice, to use a language which is the product of philosophical or religious conceptions radically different from this Revelation; for the divine Revelation cannot be formulated in a linguistic vacuum. There is no legitimate objection to using the rich religious and philosophical terminologies of the great non-Christian civilizations, whether Hindu, Buddhist or Confucian. The real problem is not the use of this terminology but the manner in which it is used. Here any fear is erroneous and wrong. It proceeds from an unjustified contempt of natural means. It also ignores the fundamental law of all spiritual life, namely, that if Christians are truly converted they will make all these inadequate terminologies into acceptable instruments, for all the terminologies in the world need to be converted and filled with a new content in order really to express the Biblical Revelation."[2] The Bible as such does not offer to the theologian the concepts which will enable the dogmatic account to have meaning. Here is a striking example:[3]

[1] *Catechism* (French edition, p. 23). Italics by R. Mehl.
[2] H. Kraemer, *The Christian Message in a Non-Christian World*.
[3] This example is drawn from Hauter's unpublished course in dogmatics.

Barth asserts, as does the Scripture, the spatiality of God, often involved by the Old Testament. But what does the Scripture mean by this idea? Evidently, it gives it a twofold meaning; on the one hand, the omnipresence of God which is symbolized by the indefiniteness of space, and on the other hand the distance or alterity of God with relationship to all objects or things, since space appears as a container which cannot be identified with the objects it contains. That the readers of the Old Testament were enabled to grasp this double meaning thanks to the symbol of spatiality, we willingly believe. But to assert the spatiality of God today would be to condemn oneself to being misunderstood. Indeed, it is to risk kindling heresy in the reader's mind. For to him who is aware of the nature of space, of the manner in which we apprehend it and its relationship to the subjectivity of our understanding, the assertion of God's spatiality remains utterly unintelligible. The theologian cannot treat with disdain the meaning philosophical usage and criticism have given to concepts. Let us add that the Christian and the theologian only succeed in this task to the extent that they are clearly aware of the distinctive characteristic of every concept they use. It is doubtless because the Christians of the first centuries were often too ignorant of the exact sense of the pagan philosophical conceptions that they received into the Church with such candour not only pagan philosophers, but also their syncretistic doctrines.

In other words, the theologian, precisely in so far as he is concerned with the purity of theology, must methodically exert criticism over the philosophical terms he is compelled to use. We should like to show with a definite example—that of the idea of nature—what difficulties it may beget in theological discussion if it is not previously subjected to criticism. In the great dispute about free-will between Luther and Erasmus, it is quite obviously the notion of nature itself which stopped Erasmus in his movement towards the Reformation. For him, the idea of nature preserved its Hellenic significance; it is that which suffices to itself, exists substantially and has therefore a precise meaning apart from any qualifications by sin and grace. The idea of nature appears to him as a neutral one; it denotes a reality that neither sin nor grace, which are accidents, can possibly modify. But Luther vehemently protests against this concept of a neutral reality, "for, in the eyes of God, there is no intermediary between sin and justice, no neutral reality which is neither sin nor justice".[1] Now, sin and justice precisely qualify man and all created nature. Man is nothing apart from the fact that he is a pardoned sinner. To conceive nature as neutral is also to consider that man can have a pure will, neither good nor bad, and therefore free to receive in itself either sin or grace, "a will pure and simple which could, with the help of grace, rise towards good or, following sin, stoop to evil".[2] And Luther makes no mistake about the nature of the concept with which his dogmatics is compelled to strive, when he sees in it a pure verbal intention of the sophists, by which he means the philosophers.[3] If man's nature were characterized by free will, as Erasmus would have it, or by necessity, as other philosophers assert, "the new birth, the renewing of our understanding, all the operations of the Spirit and of Faith in us"[4] would be unintelligible and even impossible: a nature which cannot lose its nature cannot be substantially renewed. And if Erasmus does not understand this, as Luther formally accuses him, is it not because he untiringly discourses on the permanent and theoretical possibilities of an abstract man, severed from his true history, on his nature in the Greek sense of the word, on "free will without grace, left to itself"?[5]

But let us go further and establish the counter-proof. Is not Luther himself hampered by the same Greek concept of nature which he had pursued with such theological and philosophical lucidity in Erasmus' thinking? The word nature no longer has any legitimate meaning in Christian dogmatics except that of a passivity begotten by sin. Thus we see human nature countering God's action with untiring resistance. For like a lame horse which continues limping even when mounted by a perfect horseman, sinful man continues to sin even when God acts in him. That is in keeping with his nature. But as soon as this assertion encounters, in Luther's doctrine, the dogma of eternal election, the idea of nature again appears fraught with all its Greek significance and, unknown to Luther, to retrieve all its philosophical vigour. Nature assumes a consistency and an effectiveness such that it can not only set itself against divine Grace, but can oppose it in an absolute manner: wicked, and born wicked by God's impenetrable decree, man is strictly impervious to

[1] On The Unfree Will (French translation, by Denis de Rougemont), p. 296.
[2] Ibid., p. 143.   [3] Ibid., p. 144.   [4] Ibid., p. 174.   [5] Ibid., p. 178.

God's grace, not only because God has hardened his heart, but also in virtue of his own inalienable nature as sinner: ". . . the divine omnipotence drives on and moves the ungodly one so that he cannot keep from sinning, but is forced to will, desire and act according to his wicked nature."[1] It can be felt that the dogma of double predestination is strengthened in Luther's thinking by the fact that he resorts to a philosophical idea foreign to the Christian doctrine: namely, that it is because he has received a wicked nature that, through forced loyalty to his substance, the wicked one cannot but sin. This shows how necessary it is that any dogmatic elaboration should be accompanied by philosophical criticism. It also shows that even independently from its assertions philosophy preserves a theological meaning for the Christian.

It preserves it all the more because any theology requires a certain theory of knowledge to express itself. The theologian's personal work implies recourse to a particular theory of knowledge. It is well known that many nineteenth-century theologians expressly referred to Kant's critical philosophy and spoke of faith in Kantian terms. In fact, it is difficult for a theologian not to use the theory of knowledge of his time; but it is important that he should not profess it implicitly but should have a philosophical knowledge of it, not consider it as a matter of course and above all not integrate it surreptitiously into his theology. The Reformation itself may have given the impression of considering as inevitable and necessary the scholastic doctrine of knowledge. All too often, also, idealism has invaded theology, in the end depriving the knowledge of God of all objectivity. One of the most nefarious consequences of idealism and of an exclusively psychological outlook is that of having forced the religious phenomenon back into the sphere of pure subjectivity, even of sentimentality. It was difficult to recognize the objective transcendency of the religious object as long as the principle was laid down that the cognitive act goes from the homogeneous to the homogeneous and thus that we can know only the psychological; in order to understand that religious knowledge is truly and fully knowledge, it had to be grasped that transcendency is contained in any act of knowledge; that the most humble cognition transmits to us "the other"—a reality which resists and does not depend upon us;

[1] *On The Unfree Will*, p. 204.

that in other words the act of cognition is receptive rather than constructive.

Thus, theories of knowledge are not indifferent to Christianity. The theologian cannot possibly assert an equal scepticism towards all. Of course, he must remember that not one of them is a perfectly adequate tool. But he must also remember that John used the idea of *Logos*, this summit of monistic thought, to express the Incarnation, the doctrine which is a scandal to all monistic religious thinking; and that Paul used legalistic language to speak of grace. Nevertheless, certain philosophies facilitate theological reflection while others hamper it. Some time ago Cullmann[1] showed what incidences the problem of knowledge may have upon Biblical exegesis. Evidently, as long as one stops at an historical exegesis, there are hardly any philosophical problems. At a certain point, however, it becomes necessary to pass on to a theological exegesis, a *Sachexegese*. Now, in order to practise this exegesis, one has to resort to a phenomenological interpretation of knowledge. "In order to understand a religious assertion, it is an error of method on the historian's part to want to remain in the historical realm as a matter of principle and to avoid expressly the question of whether the idea considered true by the Apostle is also true in an absolute sense. In refusing to ask this question, he renounces grasping the essence of the Pauline idea. Bultmann has well shown that the so-called neutrality of certain modern exegetists proceeds from an inadmissible *a priori*: the historian is supposed to be capable of *immediately* grasping the truth expressed by the text, provided he knows exactly under what circumstances and influences this text was written, and what its author's character is. These representatives of modern criticism will further concede that the interpreter of a religious text must have a certain sympathetic understanding for religious phenomena in general; but they will not judge it necessary nor *even legitimate* for him to reach the understanding of his object by way of religious *knowledge*. On the contrary, the critic is expected to dispose in advance of that which is the very substance of the text." Thus there exists among the defenders of a purely historical criticism a sort of disregard or contempt of the objective reality the author wished to express. This bias is

---

[1] "Les problèmes posés par la méthode exégétique de l'école de Karl Barth", in *R.H.Ph.R.*, 1928, No. 1, pp. 70-83.

clearly explained by reference to a theory of knowledge which radically separates knowledge from religion. In religion and its doctrines one should only look for states of mind which one will attempt to explain psychologically, historically and sociologically. It is understood in advance that a religious idea has no essence and therefore no meaning; in other words that the Bible does not possess any content. It is exactly as if we claimed to understand a theory of physics because we had gained insight into the mechanism of its author's psychological life; or as if we claimed to understand Einstein's theory of relativity by relating it to its author's Semitic origin. That is why Cullmann is justified in opposing a phenomenological theory to this theory of knowledge: "A religious doctrine is not merely a state of mind expressed by intellectual categories, it is an objective truth to the same extent as other scientific truths, though it can be grasped only by the act of religious meditation which faith presupposes. . . . In religious meditation upon the text the exegetist must arrive at the discovery of the objective essence of the Biblical doctrine in his own consciousness. It is not enough to know the author's faith; one must also have the same faith in order to reach the same knowledge he does." Without going as far as this conclusion, which may only point to an extreme and rare case, it can be said that exegesis is only possible when the exegetist has recognized as objectively valid the meaning aimed at by the author. It is not by mere chance, in our view, that the return to theological exegesis corresponded historically with the phenomenological endeavour.

This does not mean that the theologian must wait until the philosopher supplies him with a propitious theory of knowledge. It is the Christian philosopher's duty to have sufficient knowledge of the revealed truth so that, guided by this mode of knowledge, of the validity of which he is personally aware, he may elaborate a theory of knowledge which will enable him to account for it. Lachelier's statement remains profoundly true: "It is philosophy's offer to *understand* all, even religion."[1] The religious knowledge of the Revelation is a truth proposed to the philosopher's intellect by the life of the Church. One of the objects of religious philosophy is to make explicit the nature of the relationship between subject and object in the knowledge of the God of the Biblical Revelation. Here, its work is exactly

[1] *Œuvres*, II, p. 205.

parallel to that of the philosophy of science. The latter draws from the present state of scientific knowledge the resulting consequences for the significance of the main rational ideas: the concepts of cause, necessity, space, time; or again, starting from scientific research itself, it endeavours to specify the subject-object relationship in the act of knowledge. In reading the works of contemporary epistemologists, one receives the distinct impression that all the old idealism is in the process of crumbling. Science, similar in this to Revelation, constitutes itself without any regard for philosophy; accepted by philosophy as a fact, it teems with philosophical substance. What must be asked of philosophy, and will reveal it as Christian, is that it should respect Revelation and the God-man relationship proposed in it as facts, not seeking to replace them by a general idea about the nature of religion, nor adopting a normative attitude towards the facts it studies. Then, quite certainly, the Christian Revelation can shed new light upon problems philosophy studies in other domains: for instance, the relationship between subject and object in knowledge, for though the knowledge of other persons offers a sample of cognition in which the object to be known can, at times, assume the characteristics of a subject, only the knowledge of God as it is proposed in the Christian Revelation offers us a type of knowledge where the object possesses a subjectivity infinitely more marked than the cognizing subject's, and where the initiative of knowledge belongs to the object itself. This relationship is truly unique; yet it helps us understand more general and commonplace relationships. Cognitive relationships of a common type, such as we maintain with objects within our possession, with our fellows and even with ourselves ultimately are but degraded forms of real knowledge, the disinterested knowledge of love witnessed to by the Biblical Revelation. In order to understand the general and commonplace it is necessary to illuminate it by the unique, the singular. It is necessary to reverse the perspectives of customary logics which attempt to explain the singular by the general, and, with Kierkegaard, to follow the reverse order: the commonplace relationship between one anonymous man and his fellow-man does not teach me anything about the problem of knowing others; the person to person relationship, the living dialectics between one "I" and another "I", though singular, is exceedingly instructive. But it will not acquire its full value for us unless the "I" to be known is the Person *par excellence*.

In a parallel manner, dogmatics presents philosophical reflection with ideas whose use on the philosophical level will prove fruitful. This concern for the permanent, the eternal, the essence, which neither relativisms nor scepticisms were able to overcome, is one of the constant factors in philosophical research. Hence, doubtless, the considerable part played by the idea of substance in philosophy; hence also the philosophical conception of a universe at rest, from which all movement and all contingency are to be gradually eliminated. This effort lacks neither greatness nor value. It points to a yearning for the Kingdom that the theologian can understand, though he knows it is only yearning—that is, impotency. But it also introduces into philosophical inquiry a certain rigidity which bars the access to delicate problems. The philosophy of substance is barred from the understanding of time, history, personality, interpersonal relations and all true dialectics. This rigidity must be corrected. Here the theologian renders another service to the philosopher: it happens on occasion that the philosopher improperly burdens the theologian with his substantialistic ontology; but it also happens that the theologian attracts the philosopher's attention to the interest of more dynamic ideas: the ideas of events, decision, involvement, refusal and invocation,[1] which are normally applicable to the relationships between the Christian and his God. Schleiermacher and Barth have the joint merit of having restored the use of these ideas by refusing the object of faith any *Gegenstandlichkeit* and by freeing theology from the vestiges of substantialism. But these same ideas are susceptible to a kind of philosophical transcription, or rather, of secularization. They make it possible, in our view, better to measure the dimensions of man's destiny.

We do not hesitate to say that the Christian truth is thus capable of contacts on the plane of philosophical truth. These contacts are always partial. The theologian must not consider it his own task to bring them to light. On the contrary, he must fear lest the use of the term "event", for instance, by the philosopher tend to make the latter lose sight of the uniqueness of that Event with which the theologian is concerned. Between

[1] See Gabriel Marcel's *Du refus a l'invocation*.

the event in an existentialist sense and the Event of the Incarnation, there can only be an analogical relationship. This must always be remembered. But the analogy remains valuable for exploring human existence. Philosophy as such cannot receive revealed truth as a whole, yet it can receive certain of its aspects, or rather, it can translate certain aspects of the Revelation into analogical truths. Let not the reader accuse us of sacrilege. It is the same with the problem of Christian civilization. The Christian civilization of the Western nations has only a rather loose bond with the Revelation: in the complex of ideas and feelings of which it is made no specifically Christian notion is to be found. The identity of terms is very often deceptive. The justice of which civilization speaks has nothing in common with the Justice of God; human brotherhood is not the Communion of Saints. In passing through the plane of civilization all Christian notions have undergone a kind of refraction and distortion, which sometimes makes them unrecognizable. None the less, it remains true that the Christian civilization was born of the life of the Christian Church, and that it is impossible to decipher it without the Christian Revelation; that it represents for political and social life an ideal the ultimate meaning of which is only revealed by Scripture. It is not the Church's end to make a Christian civilization, but it has, in fact, created it. This civilization arises spontaneously from its witness, and if it did not arise, the value of the witness itself would have to be questioned. This accounts for the fact that the Church is both fully free with respect to civilization and able, under certain circumstances, to refuse to let its cause be identified with that of civilization; and that, at the same time, it feels absolutely responsible for the destiny of civilization.

That is also why the Church must feel responsible for certain forms of philosophy which are necessary consequences of a Christian mental outlook; at present, obviously, two philosophies must be considered as the signs of the Church's presence in the realm of rational thought: existentialism and personalism. No sign can be considered as being absolutely perennial. It is possible that at some other period Christian dogmatics will transmit to the realm of philosophical reflection other ideas than those of existence, event, involvement, vocation and personality. Christianity is not condemned to have no other philosophical satellites than personalism and existentialism.

Let us acknowledge that these philosophical forms are bound up with the spiritual dangers characteristic of our time, that they are necessary reactions against abstract intellectualism and individualism, and against the false universalism bequeathed us by idealism. But it is difficult to see how a philosophy which always aims at being *Philosophia perennis* could have freed itself from this idealism if Christian thinking had not offered it concepts which, though abstracted from the Revelation as a whole, have still preserved a sufficient intellectual vigour to effectuate radical changes of orientation in philosophy. No doubt, they possess such dynamism only in so far as those using them are capable of connecting them with the total Revelation and of grasping their abstract and secularized character; but they come to terms with philosophy only in this abstract and secularized form. We should even be glad of it, lest we should see reconstituted a philosophy which would be a mixture of philosophy and dogma.

.   .   .   .   .

Thus the dialogue between the theologian and the philosopher continues, lively, difficult and always fruitful. In the preceding chapter we have already drawn attention to the first action to which the theologian submits philosophy by making it profit from the eschatological tension in which the intellect takes part. We did not return to this question. Yet it is evident that therein lies the primary reason for the dialogue some of whose aspects we have just envisaged. We believe that the philosopher will really agree to enter into relation with theology, to respect it in its purity and to co-operate with it only if he has understood beforehand what he receives from it; the philosopher must in the first place clearly see that the whole problematics of philosophy is bound up with the promise of the renewing of the mind, so that he can face, together with theology, not an eclectic compromise or a *modus vivendi*, detestable signs of the confusion of the minds, but a common subjection to the same order and the same promise. Let us not provoke any encounter between the theologian and the philosopher, if the philosopher is not yet aware that the promise of renewal stands for him also, and for his work.

This is to say that the essential condition for a Christian exercise of philosophy is that dogmatics be fully itself and that it refuse to camouflage itself as philosophy in order to make contact easier for the philosopher. We could conclude with Barth's statement: "Notoriously, theology can only become interesting for philosophy from the very moment when it no longer wishes to be interesting. . . . It must *prove* its existence, possibility and necessity by the fact that it exists."[1]

[1] *Offenbarung, Kirche, Theologie* (*Theol. Existenz heute*, No. 9), Munich, 1934, pp. 35-36 (quotation translated from the German).

THE DIFFICULT CONDITION OF THE CHRISTIAN PHILOSOPHER

IN ending this study, it appears that we can better grasp why the discussion about Christian philosophy is both so irritating and so sterile. Historians and philosophers feel that Christianity which has so profoundly renewed ethics cannot but have affected philosophy as a whole; yet they fail to define the main characteristics of a Christian philosophy; they cannot discover any doctrine directly drawn from Christianity and they do not detect in Christianity itself any aspect susceptible of elaboration or exploitation by philosophy. Far from creating a new philosophical current, Christianity is the constant beneficiary of philosophy, thanks to which it succeeds in expressing the contents of its beliefs in intelligible propositions: such is, customarily, their conclusion. What we are tempted to call Christian philosophy is in reality nothing but the eternal philosophy diverted from its natural ends by a religious movement anxious to transmit itself through teaching and to attract scholars and intellectuals.

As long as it is considered acceptable to set the problem of a Christian philosophy in traditional terms, as it is attempted merely to make evident the existence of a sort of compromise, a disgraceful eclecticism between a religious movement and pre-existent philosophies, it will be difficult to reach conclusions less disappointing than these. We must renounce considering the Christian philosopher as a man who seeks to establish harmony between his faith and the demands of his reason. For such an enterprise remains foreign to the profound inner life of faith; at best, it would constitute an epiphenomenon of this life. It would proceed from the idea that faith, new as it may be, must become reconciled as best it can with the intellectual universe in which it is called upon to live and bear witness. If faith were but a dynamism coming to terms with other mental forms, it would not be for the Christian the absolute and supreme decision that it actually is. The Christian philosopher's problem is not: how can I become resigned to a philosophy which, ultimately, is foreign and means nothing to me; but rather: how can I renew philosophical reflection itself, not only in its themes but also in its basic intentions? As Maurice Blondel wrote with a clarity not always wholly confirmed by his works: ". . . the point is to resume the whole problem of philosophy, as a function of the very idea of the unique and supreme destiny which perforce is ours, that we receive from Christianity and its *rationabile obsequium*; whereas the customary procedure had been to accommodate pre-existing, preconceived systems such as Platonism and Aristotelianism with the teaching of the gospel considered as a foreign body, superimposed upon these systems, but unfit to penetrate and leaven the whole mass of philosophy."[1] Only by refusing the idea of a *philosophia perennis*, and a philosophical tradition in which to simply integrate himself and play his part as if it were a point of honour that Christianity be represented in the field of philosophy, will the Christian show how seriously he takes the renewing of the mind. It is in this refusal of the eternal philosophy and of the problems themselves as couched in their traditional terms that the true presence of Christianity will be made manifest. All Christian philosophy seems to us to reside in the Christian's decision to bear witness, in the philosophical field, to the reality of the renewing of the mind; this is what makes it impossible to discern for historians and philosophers. Thus, the nature of Christian philosophy will be grasped, not by examining doctrines and systems, but by visualizing the Christian philosopher's spiritual condition. Let us not call Christian a philosophy using Christian data or even suggestions —such a philosophy can remain profoundly pagan; but let us call Christian the philosophy—whatever its assertions—of a man who knows that the Kingdom is at hand, that all things will be made new, and who is preparing himself through philosophical reflection for the coming of that Kingdom—in short, the philosophy of a man whose thought feels the eschatological tension. It is worth emphasizing (though it is obviously a commonplace remark) that the signs of Christianity which are to be sought in philosophy are not different from those which we seek in ethics, politics or art. We are not indebted to Christianity for any new ethical conception, but we are

---

[1] *Le problème de la philosophie catholique*, p. 39.

indebted to it for having found the significance of all ethics. Similarly, thanks to Christianity we understand the relationship between philosophical activity and the ultimate realities of the Kingdom. The specific character of a Christian philosophy can be grasped only by viewing the Christian philosopher's spiritual condition, his existential situation.

This condition is a difficult condition; this situation contains a paradox.

In order to characterize them, we would say that the Christian philosopher is one who "knows the time" in which he lives (Rom. 13.11): he does not live in the midst of a progressive evolution nor in the fullness of being. He lives in the time of the Church, which is a very peculiar time. All is fulfilled; there are no more problems; there is no more metaphysical anguish. All is fulfilled but all remains hidden; the Kingdom, the face to face knowledge, the glory, these are eschatological dimensions. In the expectation of that which is to come, all is still to be done and philosophy remains a task to fulfil, an adventure to try. Whereas the non-Christian philosopher settles himself in the midst of being, so that it has been possible to define metaphysics as the science of being itself; or else, humble again, he confines himself within a becoming which will never emerge into being, the Christian philosopher moves in a time where being is given while becoming is not yet abolished; where becoming is taken with full seriousness, although in it there already appears the shadow of being, whicn is the very negation of becoming. All the originality of the Christian's philosophy stems from the fact that he acts and thinks in a mental universe which possesses both these dimensions: that of eternity and that of time, that of achievement and that of struggle, of victory and conflict, of value and obstacle. The Christian philosopher's universe is never univocal and that is why his philosophy is never an option between the contradictory terms in which *philosophia perennis* purports to enclose us. The Christian does not have to choose between Plato and Bergson; he is grateful to Plato for having emphasized the subject's participation in being, and to Bergson for having inserted the subject into becoming and motion. For the experience of a man who is fully a man, such as Christianity reveals him to us, is the experience of this living dialectic between time and eternity, sin and salvation, death and life.

At the outset of this study, we said that we would accept as valid only a philosophy which had its foundation in Jesus Christ. A strange assertion, if one remembers how severely we excluded from philosophy all that could be an imitation of dogmatic thinking and how rigorously we maintained rationality and intelligibility as the supreme amibitions of philosophy. No, Christian philosophy treats neither of Jesus Christ nor of the ideas of Jesus Christ and the disciples. But it places man in a universe whose dimensions are given us by Jesus Christ.

BIBLIOGRAPHY

ALL Biblical quotations in the present translation are drawn from the Revised Version in the American Edition.

The following bibliography lists the editions used by Professor Mehl in the preparation of this volume, except in cases where the translator consulted English translations of books quoted in the text, or where references were made to books best known by their English titles.

ALLO (R. P. E. B.), *La première épître aux Corinthiens*, Paris, Gabalda, 2nd edition, 1935.

ALTHAUS (Paul), *Grundriss der Dogmatik*, Erlangen, 1936.

ANSELM OF CANTERBURY (Saint), *The Proslogium*, translated from the Latin by Sidney Norton Deane, B.A., Open Court Publishing Company, Chicago, 1903. *The Monologium*, same translation.

ARON (Raymond), *Introduction à la philosophie de l'histoire*, Paris, Gallimard, 1939.

AUGUSTINE (Saint), *Confessions* and *Soliloquies;* "De Quantitate Animae", "De Ordine", "Contra Academicos".

BACHELARD (Gaston), *Le nouvel esprit scientifique*, Paris, Alcan, 1934.

BARTH (Heinrich), "Der Christ in der Philosophischen Fakultat", *In Extremis*, 1935, No. 7-8.

—— "Natürliche Theologie", *Kirchenblatt für die reformierte Schweiz*, Nov. 9, 1939.

—— "Philosophie, Theologie und Existenzproblem", *Zwischen den Zeiten*, 1932.

BARTH (Karl), *Die Kirchliche Dogmatik*, I, 1, Zurich-Zollikon, 4th edition, 1944.

—— *Word of Man, Word of God.*

—— *Credo.*

—— *Nein. Antwort an Emil Brunner.* Theologische Existenz heute. Heft 14, Munich, 1934.

—— *Vom christlichen Leben*, Munich, 1928.

—— *Offenbarung, Kirche, Theologie.* Theologische Existenz heute. Heft 9, 1934.

—— Le Réforme, une supreme décision, *Foi et vie*, 1933.

BENOIT (Jean-Daniel), *Direction spirituelle et protestantisme*, Paris, Alcan, 1940.

BERDIAEV (Nicolas), *Five meditations upon Existence.*

BERGER (Gaston), *Recherche sur les conditions de la connaissance*, Paris, Presses Universitaires de France, 1941.

—— *Le Cogito dans la philosophie de Husserl*, Paris, Aubier, 1936.

BLONDEL (Maurice), *Le problème de la philosophie catholique*, Paris, Bloud et Gay, 1932.

BOIS (Henri), *La valeur de l'expérience religieuse*, Paris, Nourey, 1908.

BREHIER (Emile), "Y a-t-il une philosophie chrétienne?", *Revue de métaphysique et de morale*, April-June 1931.

BRUNHES (G.), *La foi et sa justification rationnelle*, Bibliothèque catholique des sciences religieuses, Paris, 1928.

BRUNNER (Emil), *Natur und Gnade*, Tübingen, 1935.

BRUNSCHVICG (Léon), "L'expérience religieuse de Pascal", *Revue de théologie et de philosophie*, Lausanne, 1924.

—— *Le progrès de la conscience dans la philosophie occidentale*, Paris, Alcan, 2 volumes, 1927.

—— *La religion et la raison*, Paris, Alcan, 1939.

BUBER (Martin), *I and Thou.*

BURGELIN (Pierre), L'homme pécheur, in *L'homme chrétien*, Paris, Je Sers, 1941.

CALVIN (Jean), *Christian Institutes.*

—— *Commentaries.*

—— *Catechism.*

CAUSSE (Antonin), *Essai sur le conflit du Christianisme primitif et de la civilisation*, Paris, Leroux, 1920.

CLEMENT OF ALEXANDRIA, *Stromateis.*

CULLMANN (Oscar), "Les problèmes posés par la méthode exégétique de l'école de Karl Barth", in *Revue d'histoire et de philosophie religieuses*, 1928, No. 1.

—— *Königsherrschaft Christi und Kirche im Neuen Testament*, Theologische Studien, Heft 10, Zurich-Zollikon, 1941.

—— *Les premières confessions de foi chrétienne*, Paris, Presses Universitaires de France, 1943.

DESCARTES (René), *Discourse on Method.*

—— *Meditations on First Philosophy.*

—— *Correspondence.*

DEVIVAISE (Charles), "La philosophie religieuse de Jules Lachelier", *Revue des sciences philosophiques et théologiques*, tome XXVII, 1939.

ELLUL (Jacques), *Le fondement théologique du droit*, Cahiers théologiques de l'Actualité protestante, No. 15-16, Neuchâtel and Paris, Delachaux et Niestlé, 1946.

FROMMEL (Gaston), *L'Expérience chrétienne*, 5 volumes, Neuchâtel, Attinger, 1916.

GILSON (Etienne), *The Philosophy of St. Thomas Aquinas*, translated by E. Bullough, Ed. by G. A. Elrington, B. Herder Book Co, St. Louis and London, 1937.

—— *The Spirit of Medieval Philosophy*, Gifford Lectures, 1931-1932, translated by A. H. C. Downes, New York, Charles Scribner's Sons, 1940.

—— *Christianity and Philosophy*, translated by Ralph Mac-Donald, C.S.B., Sheed and Ward, London, 1939.

GOBLOT (Edmond), *Traité de logique*, Paris, A. Colin, 2nd edition, 1920.

GUITTON (Jean), *Le temps et l'éternité chez Plotin et saint Augustin*, Paris, Boivin, 1933.

HAUTER (Charles), "La présence divine comme problème de la dogmatique protestante", *Revue d'histoire et de philosophie religieuses*, 1936, Nos. 3-5. *Unpublished course in Dogmatics* given at the University of Strasbourg.

HERING (Jean), *Phénoménologie et philosophie religieuse*, Paris, Alcan, 1925.

—— *Le Royaume de Dieu et sa venue*, Paris, Alcan, 1937.

HERMANN (Wilhelm), *Der Verkehr des Christen mit Gott*, Stuttgart, 1892.

HUSSERL (Edmund), *Meditations on Descartes*.

JANKELEVITCH (Vladimir), *Bergson*, "Les grands philosophes" series, Paris, Alcan, 1931.

KAFTAN (Julius), *Die Wahrheit der christlichen Religion*, Basel, 1888.

KIERKEGAARD (Søren), *The concept of Dread*.

KRAEMER (Henrik), *The Christian Message in a Non-Christian World*. Passage translated into French and published in *Foi et Vie*, 1939, No. 1.

LABRIOLLE (Pierre de), "Culture classique et Christianisme", *Revue de théologie et de philosophie*, Lausanne, 1917, No. 23.

—— *La réaction païenne*, Paris, L'Artisan du Livre, 1942.

LACHELIER (Jules), *Œuvres*, 3 volumes, Paris, Alcan, 1933.

LACROIX (Jean), *Vocation personnelle et tradition nationale*, Cahiers de la Nouvelle Journée, No. 10, Paris, Bloud et Gay, 1942.

LAGNEAU (Jules), *De l'existence de Dieu*, Paris, Alcan, 1925.
LAVELLE (Louis), "L'expérience psychologique du temps", *Revue de métaphysique et de morale*, April 1941.
LEENHARDT (F. J.), *La foi évangélique*, Geneva and Valencia, without date.
LEENHARDT (Henry), "Connaissance religieuse et foi", Montpellier, *Etudes théologiques et religieuses*, 1941.
LE SENNE (René), *Obstacle et valeur*, Paris, Aubier, 1932.
LUTHER (Martin), *On the Unfree Will*.
—— *Works* (Luthers Werke, Weimar).
MALEBRANCHE (Nicolas), *Dialogues on Metaphysics and Religion. Traité de la nature et de la grâce.*
MARCEL (Gabriel), *From Refusal to Invocation.*
MÉNÉGOZ (Fernand), "Trinité", *Revue d'histoire et de philosophie religieuses*, 1938. Nos. 5-6.
PASCAL (Blaise), *Pensées*, translated by W. F. Trotter, Everyman's, Dent, London and New York, 1948 edition, based upon Brunschvicg's edition.
PRADINES (Maurice), *L'Esprit de la Religion*, Paris, Aubier, 1941.
PREISS (Théodore), *Le témoignage intérieur du Saint-Esprit*, Cahiers théologiques l'Actualité protestante, No. 13, Neuchâtel and Paris, Delachaux et Niestlé, 1946.
REYMOND (Arnold), "Philosophie et théologie dialectique", *Revue de théologie et de philosophie*, Lausanne, 1935.
RITSCHL (Albert), *Die christliche Lehre von der Rechtfertigung und Versöhnung*, Bonn, 1900.
RIVAUD (Albert), *Les grands courants de la pensée antique*, Paris, A. Colin, 3rd edition, 1938.
SCHAEDER (Erich), *Religion und Vernunft*, 1917.
SCHELER (Max), *Der Formalismus in der Ethik*, Leipzig, 2nd edition, 1921.
—— *Krieg und Aufbau*, Leipzig, 1916.
—— *Lesens de la souffrance*, transl. by Pierre Klossowski, Paris, Aubier.
SERTILLANGES (R.P.), *Le christianisme et les philosophes*, Paris, Aubier.
SCHLEIERMACHER, *First letter to Dr. Lücke*, Paris De Boccard.
SCHMIDT (Karl-Ludwig), "Royaume, Eglise, Etat et peuple: relations et contrastes", *Revue d'histoire et de philosophie religieuses*, 1938, No. 2.

Spinoza, *Ethics.*

—— *Works.*

Thomas (Saint), *Summa Theologica.*

Thurneysen (Eduard), "Offenbarung in Religionsgeschichte und Bibel" *Zwischen den Zeiten,* 1928.

Vigneaux (Paul), *La pensée au Moyen Age,* Paris, A. Colin, 1938.

Visser t' Hooft (W. A.), *Introduction à Karl Barth,* Paris, Je Sers.

—— "Droit naturel ou Droit divin", *Correspondance,* January-February, 1943.

Wencelius (Léon), *L'Esthétique de Calvin,* Paris, Belles-Lettres, 1937.

INDEX

Aeterni Patris Encyclical, 155
Alexandrian Christianity, 56
Allo, (R. P. E. B.), 159, 166, 167
Althaus (Paul), 140, 147, 149, 191
Ambrose (Saint), 10, 35
Animism, 48
Anselm, (Saint, of Canterbury), 22,
    90, 104-112, 114-119, 131, 146
Anthropomorphism, 41
Aristotelian philosophy, 33
Aristotelianism, 209
Aristotle, 10, 22, 24, 183, 186
Aron (Raymond), 45
Atheism, 84
Augustine (Saint, of Hippo), 10, 22,
    68, 69, 82, 103, 104, 105, 113, 141,
    184, 189, 192, 194
Autonomy of philosophy, 14-15

Bachelard (Gaston), 44
Barnabas (Epistle of), 164
Barth (Heinrich), 14, 92, 191
Barth (Karl), 11, 53, 63, 69, 91, 96,
    98, 124, 125, 127, 129, 132, 139, 140,
    152, 162, 196, 198, 201, 204, 207
Barthianism, 165
Basil, 10
Benoît (Jean-Daniel), 113
Berdyaev (Nicholas), 54, 82
Berger (Gaston), 62, 63, 102, 163
Bergson (Henri), 130, 174, 175-176,
    183, 186, 210
Bergsonianism, 183
Bernard (Saint), 117
Biblical theology, 95
Biel (Gabriel), 111
Blondel (Maurice), 209
Bois (Henri), 61, 151
Bonaventure (Saint), 22, 194
Bossuet, 41
Bréhier (Emile), 25
Brunhes (G.), 113
Brunner (Emil), 90, 96, 97, 98, 100,
    133, 143
Brunschvicg (Léon), 10, 18, 21, 27, 38,
    41, 43, 128, 136, 183
Buber (Martin), 88
Buddhist civilization, 197
Bultmann, 190, 191, 201
Burgelin (Pierre), 159

Calvin (John), 38-41, 54, 57, 96, 97,
    145, 153, 176, 195, 196
Calvinism, 41, 110, 152

Cartesian idealism, 62; Cartesian philosophy, 68
Cartesianism, 53, 56, 80, 169
Catholicism, 153-154
Causse (Antonin), 156, 164
Christological theology, 95, 96, 98
Church Fathers, 33
Clement of Alexandria, 10, 11, 35, 158
Cogitatum, 60, 63
Cogito, 16, 17, 60, 61, 62, 63, 73, 74
Comte, Auguste, 174
Confucian civilization, 197
Copernicus, 41
Couchoud, 52
Cullmann (Oscar), 14, 100, 149, 201,
    202
Cuvier, 103

Descartes (René), 12, 13, 40, 41, 57,
    73-78, 90, 95, 152, 169, 177; cf. also
    Cartesian, Cartesianism.
Determinism, 175
Devivaise (Charles), 89
Dialectical theology, 94-95, 147, 148,
    149, 153
Doctors of the Church, 34

Eclectic compromise, 206
Eclecticism, 50, 208
Ecumenical movement, 41
Einstein (Albert), 202
Ellul (Jacques), 50
Empiricism, 64
Epicure, 84
Erasmus, 198-199
Eusebius of Caesarea, 141
Existential philosophy, 150, 179
Existentialism, 205

Faye (E. de), 11
Festugière (A. J., O. P.), 162
Formgeschichte, 25
Franciscans, 158
Frommel (Gaston), 142, 151, 152

Geneva (Theocracy of), 172
Gilson (Etienne), 9, 12, 22-25, 28, 35,
    36, 110, 111, 152-155, 157-158, 159-
    160, 164, 171, 175, 192, 194
Gilsonian postulates, 56
Gnosticism, gnosis, 11, 115, 116, 117,
    121, 124, 157
Goblot (Edmond), 22
Gregory (Saint, of Nazianzus), 10
Guitton (Jean), 68, 184